WHITE DREAMS, BLACK AFRICA

Imaginary scene on the Niger showing the mythical Kong mountains.

WHITE DREAMS, BLACK AFRICA

The Antislavery Expedition
to the River Niger 1841–1842

Howard Temperley

YALE UNIVERSITY PRESS
NEW HAVEN AND LONDON 1991

Set in Baskerville by Excel Typesetters Co., Hong Kong
Printed and bound in Great Britain by St Edmundsbury Press

Library of Congress Cataloguing-in-Publication Data

Temperley, Howard.
    White dreams, black Africa: the antislavery expedition to
the River Niger 1841–1842/Howard Temperley.
        p.   cm.
    Includes bibliographical references and index.
    ISBN 0–300–05021–6
    1. Slavery—Africa, West—History—19th century.   2. Slave-trade—
Africa, West—History—19th century.   3. Slavery—Great Britain—
Anti-slavery movements—History—19th century.   I. Title.
HT1332.T46   1991
326′.09662′08034—dc20   91–10073
                                                              CIP

In memory of Rachel Temperley

Contents

List of Illustrations

ACKNOWLEDGEMENTS

I am grateful to the National Portrait Gallery for permission to use the illustrations on pages 24, 34, 41 and 56 and to the National Maritime Museum for those on pages 26, 67 and 70. The illustration for the cover and on page 100 comes from William Allen's *Picturesque Views on the Niger*; for the frontispiece from Laird and Oldfield's *Narrative*; on page 3 from the *Illustrated London News*; on page 8 from Hare's *The Gurneys of Earlham*; on page 73 from John Duncan's 'Some Account of the Last Niger Expedition' and on pages 51 and 101 from M'William's *Medical History*. The remaining illustrations all come from Allen and Thomson's *Narrative* and are based on sketches made by William Allen. Further particulars about the books and articles from which these illustrations come are given in the Bibliography.

HT

'So then, Oh God, this mighty work is fairly launched. The Nation is to put forth its strength to save annually hundreds of thousands from slaughter and bondage; a whole Continent plunged in the depths of dark superstition is to be opened for Missionary Labours; a quarter of the Globe visited and blessed with our discoveries – arts, commerce, agriculture – and above all that which is the great Civilizer, the great Improver of mankind, Christianity. Oh God, oh pray heavenly God, leave us not to ourselves in this mighty task.'

(Thomas Fowell Buxton, 30 December 1838)

Beware and take care of the Bight of Benin
Where few come out though many go in.

(Traditional British sea shanty)

Preface

I first learned of the Niger expedition some quarter of a century ago while working on a history of the British antislavery movement. It intrigued me because it was intended to be the grand climax, the crowning glory, of that movement. Its supporters, who included Prince Albert and members of the Cabinet, regarded it as the beginning of a new national crusade to redeem Africa. Hitherto, they argued, emancipationists had attacked only the outposts; now they would strike at the citadel itself and carry Christianity, civilization and legitimate commerce into the very heart of the continent. It failed, of course. But the conception was remarkable, not least for its sheer grandeur.

I was also surprised that the British Government was persuaded to go along with the scheme. It was not the first exploratory mission to go to the Niger, nor even the first to receive official support, but it was by far the most ambitious to date. Three specially designed steamers, fitted with air filtration systems, carrying some one hundred and fifty Europeans set out from Devonport in the spring of 1841. A fourth vessel and a hundred and fifty additional personnel, mostly Africans, joined the flotilla at Sierra Leone. In short it was a very impressive affair indeed – almost, one might say, the Victorian equivalent of a moon shot. What special circumstances, I wondered, could have led Lord Melbourne, a Prime Minister not noted for his public altruism or support for projects requiring large-scale spending, to agree to such an improbable venture?

The expedition intrigued me, too, because it was so well documented. The participants were well aware that they were on a historic mission. No less than eleven of them kept journals. They included a botanist, a clerk, a retired soldier, a merchant captain, two doctors, two missionaries and three naval officers. Their accounts were all subsequently published, except for that of the merchant captain, which contained allegations thought to be libellous. Here, then, was a remarkably detailed body of material, complete enough to enable one to observe the same events from several different points of view. What the scientists made of things could be, and usually was, very different from what, say, the naval officers or missionaries made of them.

Like many historians I have always envied novelists their freedom simply to invent. But here, in one or other of the participants' journals, was most of what one would need to know, at least as regards what happened to the expedition once it got to Africa, to construct a tolerably complete account. Not quite everything, to be sure. These explorers were writing for their contemporaries, not for us. They provided admirable descriptions of the Africans they met but failed to tell us what they themselves looked like or even what they wore. All the same, viewed from the British side, the record was remarkably complete, right down to the state of the weather – temperature, humidity, strength and direction of wind – at any given moment. If meteorological effects were required, there they were!

The one obvious omission was any account of how these events appeared to the Africans involved. What they made of this extraordinary flotilla that came steaming up their river can only be surmised. As with all descriptions of encounters with pre-literate peoples the record is one-sided. Reading between the lines, however, it is clear that the Africans found their visitors every bit as puzzling as the British found them. There is no reason to suppose that African responses to the sudden intrusion of visitors from another continent were any less shrewd, various or diverting than those recorded by the visitors themselves. Viewed objectively, the Victorian attitude towards human nakedness, particularly in tropical Africa where clothes were largely an encumbrance, makes little sense, whereas the Ibo's suspicion on discovering that the doctors on the expedition were collecting African skulls makes very good sense indeed. Charles Dickens's hilarious account, based on the verbatim reports compiled during the expedition, of Her Majesty's Commissioners' interviews with the Obi and the Attah (see Epilogue) aptly catches the bizarre nature of such encounters. Unflattering though his portrayal of Africans is, it was plain to him that it was they rather than the Europeans who had the firmer grasp of the realities of the situation.

Nevertheless, looking at these events largely through Western eyes, as we necessarily must, what we are left with still adds up to a marvellous tale. A great antislavery expedition goes to Africa and establishes – a slave plantation! At least that was one version, but there were others. As in all good stories the interpretation of events depends largely on the viewpoint of the observer. Whether, in the longer view, the expedition was the abject failure it appeared at the time is something that can still be debated. Very little of this, however, could be got into my antislavery book. That, I also discovered, was a problem others had encountered. In fact, apart from the odd article or chapter here and there, there had been no proper treatment of the episode since the participants published their own accounts in the 1840s.

Any intention I had of remedying this situation was put aside on account of more pressing obligations. However, returning to the topic after a lapse of some two decades I was surprised to find that what had been true then was still true. In the meantime excellent books had appeared, among them Daniel R. Headrick's *Tools of Empire*, which dealt with steamers and quinine in a way that answered many of the questions that had earlier puzzled me, but there was still no adequate account of this particular expedition.

Something else that I discovered was that *had* I attempted to write such an account at the time the idea first occurred to me it would have been woefully inadequate. This was because, without the superb collection of Buxton Papers presented to Rhodes House, Oxford, by the Buxton family in 1975, it would have been quite impossible to understand the mind-set of Thomas Fowell Buxton and those around him who were responsible for launching the expedition. The evangelical conscience was a powerful engine that seldom rested and its workings have perhaps never been better exemplified than in this remarkable collection of letters, reports and confessional writings. That they were well-intentioned people is now plain to see. Their dedication, spirituality and sense of mission shine out from every page they wrote. Yet what seemed to them Christian duty often impressed others as stubbornness, arrogance and a simple refusal to face facts. There are even moments when Buxton sounds remarkably like the future Field Marshall Sir Douglas Haig. High-minded and ethnocentric, eager to do good yet obsessed with the state of their own souls, forever seeking to read into events evidence of God's intent, these reformers were driven by an innocent, naïve and often overwhelming conviction in the righteousness of their cause that propelled them into fantasies which, to their genuine astonishment, were later punctured by reality.

The British Government, which put up £79 143 to finance the expedition, an enormous sum by the standards of those days, was, of course, moved by somewhat different considerations, among them a desire to placate political colleagues at home and secure strategic and economic advantages abroad. Yet even here, moral concerns of the kind that moved Buxton and the members of his circle were not entirely absent. Fundamental to the thinking of both groups was a consciousness of Britain's expanding power and with it that characteristically Victorian dream of creating a new world order based on Christianity, civilization and trade. It was Britain's destiny to carry all three to the dark places of the earth, creating a circle of prosperity and enlightenment which would ultimately girdle the entire globe. 'Forward, forward let us range,' wrote Tennyson in 'Locksley Hall'. 'Let the great world spin for ever down the ringing grooves of change.' Yet power implied obligations. Along with the steam-ships, railways and jingling guineas which Tennyson saw as heralding this new age of expansion went a belief in moral responsibility towards those whom the British deemed less fortunate than themselves, not all of whom, needless to say, shared this vision or were prepared to accept the interference in their affairs which it implied. The line between benevolence and imperialism is not always easy to draw, least of all when it involves cultures so different as those of nineteenth-century Britain and West Africa.

When I came to writing this account I soon became aware that providing a footnote for every item of information taken from the Buxton Papers would mean carrying normal scholarly conventions to unwieldy lengths. My assumption has therefore been that anyone wishing to find out more would do so by consulting Patricia Pugh's admirable *Calendar of the Papers of Sir Thomas Fowell Buxton* (1980). The same applies to material taken from William Allen and T.R.H. Thomson's standard two-volume *Narrative of the Expedition to the River Niger . . .* (1848), which, being largely chronological, makes finding out what happened to the explorers on any particular day relatively simple. Other sources, however, such as the voluminous Admiralty and Colonial Office files on the expedition, are cited in the usual way.

One of the delights of writing this book has been learning about things far removed from my normal area of professional expertise. This applies particularly to African history, about which I previously knew almost nothing, but also to epidemiology, medicine, pharmacy, chemistry, meteorology, even nineteenth-century chivalric revivals. A corollary of this is that a good many plainly puzzled people have been put to no small trouble answering what must have seemed to them rather arcane questions. For their patience and good nature as well as their professional advice I would like to thank Professor J.F. Ade Ajayi, Professor Michael Brock, Dr R.D. Cannon, Dr Alun Davies, Professor Seymour Drescher, Professor J.D. Fage, Mr Peter Goldfinger, Professor Paul M. Hair, Mr Edward Jobling, Dr Brian Laurence, Dr Brendon McCann, Mrs Verily Anderson Paget, Dr Geoffrey Searle, Mr Geoffrey Stanger, Mrs Ann Thwaite and Mrs Norma Virgoe. I am also indebted to Lady de Freitas for allowing me the use of her flat during the time I was working in the Public Record Office; to the National Portrait Gallery and the National Maritime Museum for allowing me to print illustrations from their collections; to the curators of the British Library Ethnographic Department for arranging a private viewing of the artifacts collected during the expedition, and to Rose McMahon of the Wisbech and Fenland Museum for showing me the William Stanger materials now in her care. In particular I am beholden to Mrs Jeanetta Pollok of the University of East Anglia for the uncomplaining way she undertook the typing and retyping of the manuscript in its many different versions.

Howard Temperley
Norwich, February 1991

CHAPTER ONE
So Holy a Cause

'You will be glad to hear,' Thomas Fowell Buxton reported to his wife, 'that our meeting went off to perfection. Only think of our having got Prince Albert, Peel and a whole file of Bishops!'[1]

The inauguration of the African Civilization Society, held in London's Exeter Hall on 1 June 1840, had indeed been a remarkable occasion. Since it had first opened its doors seven years before, Exeter Hall in the Strand had become the acknowledged temple of British philanthropy, the meeting place where social and religious institutions of many different persuasions gathered to discuss and proclaim their plans for the betterment of mankind. But, as the newspapers all agreed, this was by far the most socially distinguished gathering ever to have graced its Graeco-Corinthian halls. As early as seven o'clock that morning crowds had begun gathering in the surrounding streets so that well before the arrival of the platform guests the four thousand seats in the great amphitheatre were filled. The aristocracy were there in force along with their women-folk resplendent in bonnets and crinolines. So too were the representatives of the Established Church and of the nonconforming sects. Mingling with the crowd were several dozen MPs. Mr Gladstone was there, as were Sir George Grey and Lord Nugent. Arriving later than the others, Daniel O'Connell was greeted with a cheer by the radicals in the assembly. Many had plainly come simply to enjoy the spectacle. A number of diplomats had also turned out, among them Monsieur Guizot, the French Ambassador.

It was certainly a notable sight as onto the platform there filed the élite of Victorian society, led by the Duke of Norfolk, Viscount Sandon and Sir Robert Peel, leader of Her Majesty's Opposition. Flanking them on either side were the representatives of the nation's principal religious and benevolent organizations, the Church Missionary Society, the British and Foreign Bible Society, the Baptist Missionary Society and other bodies, both Low and High Church. But for the presence of so large a contingent of the pious and benevolent, among them a good many

Quakers, readily distinguishable in the frock-coated throng by their broad-brimmed hats and knee breeches, it might well have been mistaken for a state occasion rather than a public gathering for the launching of a new philanthropic body.

In one respect, indeed, it *was* a state occasion to the extent that it represented the first appearance on the public stage of the young Prince Consort. Since his marriage to Queen Victoria the previous February there had been much speculation about what role he would play in British public life. His decision to take the chair on this occasion was important, all the more so because it represented a significant departure from recognized practice so far as the policy of the royal household was concerned. Previous monarchs and their consorts had scrupulously avoided identifying themselves with public issues in this way. That such an innovation carried with it political implications had been recognized by the Government even though slavery, strictly speaking, was no longer a matter of political controversy. Its last defenders, the West Indian planters, had been defeated. Few now doubted that it had been wrong. After years of struggle and obloquy abolitionism had finally become respectable. The Prince's decision to embrace the cause, therefore, had been taken in the knowledge that it was one to which the British nation was already fully committed. All the same, the mere fact of his appearing on the public platform had led to a flurry of letters between the Prime Minister and his colleagues. They had finally agreed that while it was in order for the Prince to appear in his own right he should avoid touching on political questions and, in particular, take care not to implicate the Queen. A letter to this effect had been sent to the organizers of the meeting. The Prince, for his part, was understandably nervous and, according to the Queen, had spent the early morning reciting his speech to her from memory.[2]

In the event he appeared perfectly composed. He was ushered onto the platform, the assembly rose, the organ played the national anthem, a cheer went up and the Prince bowed modestly in acknowledgement. His opening address, delivered in a slight foreign accent, was repeatedly interrupted by enthusiastic cheering. He had agreed to become President of the society because it stood for humanity and justice. The slave trade was a great evil. He only regretted that despite 'the benevolent and persevering exertions of England to abolish the atrocious traffic (renewed and prolonged cheering), at once the desolation of Africa and the blackest stain on civilized Europe (renewed cheers), they have not yet led to a satisfactory conclusion'. Nevertheless, both he and the Queen (more cheers) believed that Britain must continue and indeed strengthen her efforts. He trusted that if she did so 'Providence will prosper our exertion in so holy a cause.' It was a short speech but, as the correspondent of the

Anti-Slavery meeting at Exeter Hall.

Morning Advertiser reported, one that 'won him the golden opinions of as vast and respectable an assemblage as ever met together to further a great movement of Christian philanthropy in England'.

It was left to Buxton, the impresario of the occasion, to spell out the full horror of the evils which it was Britain's intention to eradicate. He was a tall, bespectacled man, somewhat scholarly in appearance but with a commanding presence. The British people, he informed his audience, stood on a proud pinnacle. They had withdrawn from the slave trade in 1808 and banished slavery from their own dominions in 1834. Their civilization was the finest in the world. No other people had done so much, or made so many sacrifices, in the cause of humanity. Yet in spite of all their efforts the slave trade, carried on now in the ships of foreign powers, remained undiminished. If anything, it had actually grown since Wilberforce's day. Thirty years of diplomatic and naval effort had left the British people feeling 'disappointed, defeated and baffled'. So what was

3

to be done? It was time for a new and mighty effort. Unless that were undertaken Africa would remain what Europeans had made it, 'one universal slaughter house'. Every day of the year, every hour of the day, thousands perished or were carried off. Wherever one looked it was the same: 'Multitudes, thousands are destroyed in the nightly combustions; thousands more fall by day traversing those burning sands, and the slave ship, it is impossible to describe it except in the words of scripture – the pestilence that stalketh the waters.'

What, then, was proposed? Their object was to bring peace to Africa, 'to transform the face of the country and spread abroad flocks, and herds, and harvest, and plenteousness'. And how was this to be achieved? By mobilizing Africa's own resources against the trade. The trouble with what had been done so far was that it had been aimed at the branches, the traders and the slave-importing nations. What was now intended was to strike at the roots. To do this would require penetrating into the heart of the continent, to where the trade began. It would mean persuading Africans themselves, instead of preying on one another, to develop the agricultural and commercial resources with which Africa was so amply endowed. It would also mean introducing missionaries, schoolmasters, agriculturalists and merchants; above all it required Christianity. The first prerequisite, however, was to mobilize once again the people of England who for fifteen years had campaigned against colonial slavery and brought about its abolition. 'We want,' he concluded, 'the hearts of this assembly . . . we want the hearts and influence of the people of England – nay, for this is not confined within the seas, we want all Christendom to stand forward on this subject.'

Other speakers followed. The Bishop of Winchester pledged the support of the Church of England. Archdeacon Wilberforce spoke of his late father's achievements. Stephen Lushington outlined in detail the problems of naval interception and the shortcomings of the treaty system by means of which Britain had sought to induce other countries to follow her example by outlawing the trade. Sir Robert Peel drew the audience's attention to the sense of common purpose which had characterized the meeting and congratulated His Royal Highness on having made so worthy a cause the occasion of his first entry into British public life. The proceedings ended with formal approval being given to a list of 70 vice-presidents, among them 3 archbishops, 5 dukes, 6 marquises, 14 earls and 16 bishops. No private body had ever enjoyed the support of such a glittering array of the great and the good. Finally, to oversee the day-to-day running of the new organization, a smaller executive committee, chaired by Buxton himself, was elected.[3]

The only discordant note was sounded at the very end. Responding to repeated calls from some of the radicals present, Daniel O'Connell, the leader of the Irish party in the Commons, rose to his feet only to have his words drowned by an impromptu organ voluntary. Who ordered the organist to play was never disclosed, although given the Government's warning about political controversy it could well have been one of the members of the organizing committee. O'Connell was understandably furious, later claiming that he had merely intended to add his voice to those of the other speakers in supporting the proposals before the assembly. But, apart from this minor intrusion of domestic politics, it was generally agreed that the most striking feature of the meeting was the sense of unanimity and purpose already alluded to by Peel. It was, according to the correspondent of the *Morning Chronicle*, a very *English* occasion and one of which his countrymen should feel proud. The *Watchman* struck a similarly patriotic note. On mundane, everyday matters it was natural for men to disagree, but on important moral questions such as the ending of the slave trade the British people stood united. Britain would stretch out her hand and Africa would be free. 'The glorious first of June,' it concluded, was 'a great day for Africa'.

For Buxton it was a triumphant moment, the culmination of three years of brilliant political manœuvring. He had, it is true, long been regarded as the leading spokesman of the antislavery cause. As Wilberforce's chosen successor he had carried the bill abolishing slavery in Britain's own colonies through Parliament. But the vision of redeeming Africa, which he had so vividly presented to the audience in Exeter Hall as a national obligation, the grand climax and crowning glory of all Britain's efforts on behalf of the Negro, was an entirely new departure, a radical extension of the sphere of Britain's moral responsibility, for which he alone was accountable. So too was the initiative which had led to the enlisting of Prince Albert as sponsor of the enterprise. It seemed almost too good to be true.

Within days he had been offered, and had accepted, a baronetcy. Agreeable news also came from the City where his brother-in-law, the Lombard Street banker Samuel Gurney, had called on twelve commercial houses and collected a donation of £100 from each. 'I was mightily pleased with your letter,' wrote Buxton, 'bagging £1200 in your first twelve shots was not bad sport.' Gurney was also able to report that Joshua Bates, a partner in Baring Brothers and widely regarded as the City's leading expert on commercial matters, was convinced of the practicality of the proposals for opening up Africa to legitimate trade. Most important of all was the final confirmation, long awaited, of the Government's willingness to put up £61 000 as its initial contribution towards an expedition to ascend the Niger. 'How a gracious Providence,' wrote Buxton's son-in-law relaying this news, 'does seem to countenance the great cause thus far!'

That he had much to thank Providence for was something that Buxton did not for a moment doubt. Looking back over his fifty-four years he was persuaded that fortune had smiled on him more than most and far more than he deserved. Statesman, humanitarian, wealthy brewer, squire, patriarch and now a baronet, life had showered its gifts upon him. Yet, in spite of all, he remained inwardly troubled. Providence had rewarded him far beyond his just desserts. So impressed was he, both by the singular blessings that had been granted him and his own unworthiness to receive them, that he had lately felt impelled to commit his reflections to paper.[4]

His childhood, as he recalled it, had been peculiarly happy. It had also nurtured in him the attitudes and principles upon which he based his subsequent life. 'Born in a Christian and free Country, with a vigorous constitution, of a respectable father [and] opulent family, my mother a woman of a large and generous mind', he grew up in an environment remarkably free of religious and class prejudice. His father, an East Anglian squire and one-time Sheriff of Essex, had died while he was young, leaving him the senior male in the family. It was a comfortable world of well-staffed country houses, of coaches and grooms and elegant dinner parties. In the autumn there was partridge shooting and in the winter hunting, in both of which as a youth he took robust delight. It was at this time that he made the acquaintance of the Gurneys of Earlham, near Norwich, a Quaker family of wool merchants and bankers into which he was later to marry and whose broad liberal views first turned his mind towards social questions. The Gurneys lived in grand style. Earlham Hall, with its tree-lined approaches and surrounding parkland stretching down to the river Yare, was a light-hearted place, overflowing with guests, where something amusing was always going on and family jollity combined with serious intellectual discussion. Three of the eleven Gurney children went on to careers scarcely less notable than his own – Elizabeth Fry as a prison reformer, Joseph John as a leading member of the Society of Friends, and Samuel as a banker and philanthropist. The readiness with which they welcomed him into their charmed circle he regarded as among his principal blessings. 'Tho' I had been baptized,' he noted, 'I was in some sort a Quaker – or half of one.'

The intellectual stimulation provided by this lively and talented family had also, he believed, contributed to his subsequent academic success. In the expectation that he would inherit from a distant Irish relative it was decided that he should attend Trinity College, Dublin, rather than one of the English universities. Arriving there at the age of 19 he proceeded to carry away all the major academic prizes. Yet this was not, he hastened to record, on account of any particular aptitude for scholarship. Other students were much more gifted than himself. But what he lacked in talent, he made up for in perseverance. 'I was, and have always been, conscious . . . that I must work hard to win, but that by working hard I could win.' It was to this belief that he attributed all the successes that had marked his career at college and since. Essentially it was a 'conviction that I could do nothing without labour – but that I could do anything, or almost anything which others did, by dint of vigorous application – this, coupled with a resolved mind, a kind of plodding determination over which difficulties had little influence'. Industry, application, the will not to give up, these were the talents Providence had committed to his trust.

Whether he had made good use of them he much doubted. Looking back over his twenty years in Parliament what impressed him most was his own 'entire unworthiness'. The work was God's work. That God had selected him as the instrument for such noble achievements was another of the many blessings that the Almighty had showered on him. In the event the expected Irish fortune failed to materialize with the result that he went to work for his maternal uncle, a partner in the well-established brewing firm of Truman Hanbury and Co. in Brick Lane, Spitalfields. He had meanwhile married Hannah, the fourth of the Gurney sisters. The union proved particularly happy and produced five fine children. As the brewery expanded he found his energies increasingly directed towards raising funds for the relief of poverty, promoting the work of the Bible Society and other such causes. In company with Hannah's elder sister, Elizabeth Fry, he visited Newgate and assisted in the formation of the Society for the Reformation of Prison Discipline. A contemporary print, *Mrs Fry at Newgate*, shows them both, he tall and bespectacled, she stout and benevolent, surrounded by a throng of bedraggled women prisoners.[5] Elected to Parliament in 1818 as a Whig member for Weymouth he so distinguished himself as a spokesman on humanitarian issues that in 1824 Wilberforce formally requested him to become his successor and principal spokesman in the campaign which, ten years later, resulted in the ending of slavery throughout Britain's dominions.

And yet, glorious achievement though it undoubtedly was, it did little to quieten Buxton's spiritual unease. Although his achievements were God's, his failures he regarded as very much his own. 'Why,' he demanded, 'do I not live up to that standard which my reason and my Bible recommend? To things of little consequence and trifling value I give profound attention.' What was it, he wondered, that made him feel so spiritually unfulfilled? It was not ignorance, nor any disbelief in the scriptures. And plainly it had nothing to do with domestic or public distractions. He was rich, his family was flourishing, the freedmen of the West Indies had behaved far better than he or anyone else could have anticipated. It was all so extraordinary as to be disquieting. These were

7

Thomas Fowell Buxton *c.* 1833.

not entirely new thoughts. Some years earlier he had felt constrained to note down the number of times he had narrowly escaped death. Coaches had overturned, guns had gone off or failed to go off, a boat had been swamped in high seas, a horse had dragged him by the stirrup. 'Do I believe that they are really accidents? I have reason to know . . . that a sparrow falleth not to the ground except by the decree of God. How then, believing this, can I work out a conviction that . . . strange deliverances are the creatures of chance.' Surely more was expected of him.

How much weight should be given to such reflections it is hard to say. Soul-searching was very much a nineteenth-century passion, as Gladstone's diaries, among many others, bear testimony.[6] Often it gave rise to reflections much gloomier than those recorded by Buxton. Among Quakers, in particular, an annual spiritual stock-taking was a recognized

8

convention. To what extent it influenced the actual behaviour of those concerned depended very much on the individual. When, however, the religious conscience was linked to personal talent and a zeal for social reform, as in the case of both Buxton and Gladstone it so plainly was, it became a powerful motivating force.

Its workings had been clearly exemplified by Buxton's behaviour following his rejection by the Weymouth electors in the general election of 1837. His doctors had already warned him that his health would hardly stand up to more than two or three more parliamentary sessions. In spite of his magnificent physique and dedication to outdoor sports he had suffered for many years from mysterious bouts of illness. Months of intense activity would be followed by weeks during which he was incapable of any work at all. His doctors put it down to overwork and nervous stress. He had lately also been having trouble with his eyes and found difficulty in writing. More alarmingly, he had experienced fits of giddiness and shortness of breath suggesting cardio-vascular problems. For his own part he was delighted to be relieved of his parliamentary duties. There was, he noted, less hurry and distraction than formerly: also more leisure for exercise and country pursuits. He looked forward, he said, to 'a long life of idleness and inutility'. In September 1837 he visited Scotland and tried his hand at deer stalking on the Duke of Argyll's estate. It was, he informed his sons, an exciting experience although he had to report that he found his constitution scarcely up to it. What he appreciated most of all was time to reflect, and as he did so he found his attention turning increasingly towards the problems of the slave trade and Africa.

Such ideas had begun to germinate in his mind even before the Weymouth election. According to his daughter Priscilla, it was one night at Earlham in June 1837 that the idea, out of which the Niger expedition grew, first occurred to him. His eldest son similarly recalled his father walking into his bedroom early one morning, sitting on the edge of the bed, and announcing that he had lain awake all night reflecting on the slave trade and that he believed he had finally hit on the true remedy.[7]

At first Buxton read in a desultory way but by November he was hard at work. There was, he soon discovered, much that was new to him. As a former associate of Wilberforce's and a committee member of the now defunct African Institution he was, of course, familiar enough with the historical background. But for the past fourteen years his energies had been almost exclusively taken up with the issue of West Indian slavery. Meanwhile the suppression of the international slave trade had become essentially an administrative matter, or more precisely a diplomatic and naval one. There was no doubt that successive governments had wrestled energetically with the problem. In 1837 there were sixteen naval vessels stationed off the West African coast for the specific purpose of intercepting slavers. This was difficult and often dangerous work. Over the preceding twenty years bilateral treaties providing for the search and seizure of suspected vessels had been concluded with most of the major maritime powers; their provisions had been progressively extended to allow for the detention of ships equipped for the traffic as well as of those with slaves actually on board; admiralty and joint-commission courts had been established to deal with the various cases that arose; liberated Negroes had been settled in Sierra Leone and elsewhere; and year after year weighty reports had been presented to Parliament describing the results of these efforts.[8]

Digesting all this information proved a formidable task. His method, as he explained to his brother-in-law Joseph John Gurney, then on a Quaker mission to the United States, was to assemble all the books and parliamentary papers bearing on the subject and 'begin from the very beginning, partly in person, still more by deputy'. As with all his previous undertakings this was very much a family enterprise. Not the least remarkable of his achievements had been to assemble at his home, Northrepps Hall, near Cromer, and largely out of his own family and that of the Gurneys, what was, in effect, a highly professional research team. Its two permanent members were his unmarried sister, Sarah Maria, and his wife's cousin Anna Gurney, who lived together in nearby Northrepps Cottage. Anna, in particular, was a woman of formidable learning, the author of the first ever published English translation of the *Anglo-Saxon Chronicles*. She was fluent in many languages and, in spite of being confined to a wheelchair, widely travelled. It was Buxton's practice while in Parliament to send them batches of documents for 'winnowing' or requests for drafts of speeches. 'The Cottage Ladies', as he referred to them, were sufficiently attuned to his way of thinking to provide material he could use virtually without alteration. 'My dear Ladies,' he wrote typically of a meeting of the Aborigines Protection Society, 'Your speech, as delivered at Exeter Hall yesterday, was very good. I took an hour and ten minutes, by the watch, and never spoke more at my ease, or more to my satisfaction.' Sarah and Anna had long since been persuaded that Buxton was a great man whose achievements ought to be recorded for posterity. When not working under specific instructions they busied themselves filing and transcribing copies of his incoming and outgoing mail and collecting newspaper clippings describing his meetings and the progress of his various causes.[9]

Also present at Northrepps that winter in 1837–8 was Buxton's elder daughter Priscilla Johnston, now in her early thirties, together with her husband Andrew. Andrew, who habitually referred to his father-in-law as 'the Chief', had been Buxton's parliamentary lieutenant but had also lost his seat in the 1837 election. Priscilla, however, was Buxton's principal confidante. Because his wife Hannah was in poor health, being afflicted with a recurrent eye ailment, Priscilla had assumed what was in many respects a wifely role, encouraging him in his efforts and consoling him over his disappointments. Since his own eyesight was also weak and he suffered from frequent bouts of insomnia it was his practice to dictate letters and sections of his books to whomever happened to be around at whatever hour of day or night. Sometimes it was his secretary, Luke Wiseman, but as often as not it was some member of the family circle, Anna, Sarah Maria, Priscilla, his son's tutor John Richard or the children's governess Christiana, whom he pressed into service.

It was in these surroundings, then, that he began his 'tour' through the slave trade literature. 'I traversed the whole subject,' he told Gurney, 'and such a scene of diabolism, and such an excess of misery as I have had to survey never, I am persuaded, before fell to the lot of an unhappy investigator.' What he found more than confirmed his worst suspicions. To Buxton, as to most of his contemporaries, Africa appeared a dark satanic place which the march of human progress had passed by. What it had been like before the advent of Europeans no one quite knew since reports were so scanty. It was plausible to suppose, however, that life there had been happier and more harmonious than it had latterly become. Early accounts gave support to this view. Travellers such as Sir John Hawkins had left reports of flourishing villages, lands well cultivated and peaceable relations between neighbouring tribes. Everyone agreed that Africa was an exotic place, a land of tropical luxuriance, of perpetual summer, where crops grew all the year round and wild fruits and vegetables were found in great profusion. Gold and gems and spices were found there; also ivory and aromatic woods. Birds were brightly coloured and strangely plumaged, quite unlike their dowdy European cousins. Nurtured by the thermogenic sun, trees and ferns and flowers grew to wondrous size, as also did the animals. Many assumed that this fecundity was one of the causes of Africa's relative backwardness. Why labour, build cities, elaborate systems of government, cultivate the arts, when nature was so beneficent and sustenance so readily available? Unlike the inhabitants of harsher northern climes, Africans had never had to labour in order to feed and clothe themselves, still less develop that energy and sense of enterprise which characterized Europeans and, in particular, the British. Viewed in this light they were the victims rather than the beneficiaries of their own good fortune.[10]

But whatever the original causes of Africa's backwardness the effects of European contact had been wholly deleterious. Those who went there were the dregs of European society. Instead of bringing religion, arts and science the traders brought guns and liquor, in return for which they exacted an ever-increasing toll on Africa's own population. The result was to spread bloodshed and war, first among the coastal tribes, but ultimately throughout the whole continent. Where once there were prettily laid out villages there were now overgrown ruins. Whole regions had been systematically depopulated. In place of the former peasant cultivators there had arisen a horde of petty chiefs and warlords whose cruelty beggared the imagination. Recent travellers' accounts were re-plete with descriptions of African horrors – captives tortured for amuse-ment, mass human sacrifices, fetish trees festooned with dismembered bodies, headless torsos left to the buzzards and many other gruesome details calculated to shock European sensibilities.

Not all accounts, to be sure, were of this variety. Even the most sanguinary contained evidence that there was more to Africa than a gloomy catalogue of barbarities. There were Africans who were not ferocious savages. Many were friendly and courteous. Tribes differed markedly in appearance and social customs. Those communities in touch with the Islamic world contained men who were literate, some even able to discourse knowledgeably on matters of theological doctrine. Further inland, it was rumoured, lay lost civilizations, even cities of great wealth. But for the British public at large, few of whom had so much as set eyes on an African, it was the brutal image that prevailed. Africa in the abstract was, quite simply, an abode of disorder, anarchy, poverty, misery and wretchedness.

Paradoxically it was abolitionists, missionaries and others who, wished well by its inhabitants, had done more than anyone to foster this belief. In the case of the abolitionists it was partly a matter of political tactics. When attacking British slaveholding it had proved expedient to present slavery as the antithesis of British freedom, and on occasion to exaggerate the scale of its cruelties. Now that Africa was being brought into the operative sphere of Britain's moral responsibility it was natural to pursue a similar strategy. In the case of the missionaries it was important to view Africans as unregenerate. This did not mean that they regarded Africans as naturally inferior. On the contrary, their whole argument rested on the assumption that Africans *were* redeemable, in fact were in all their essential attributes very much like themselves. Europe too had once been barbarous. The practices of their own druidical ancestors did not bear too close examination. Africans were simply behaving much as they themselves or any people would behave in such circumstances. The notion that all blacks were inferior to all whites was a later, post-Darwinian phenomenon associated with the belief that racial differences resembled differences between zoological species. This was a view with which early nineteenth-century humanitarians were unacquainted and which they would, in any case, have rejected as being contrary to scripture, which taught that all men were descended from a common pair of ancestors. God had not merely created Adam and Eve physically but endowed them with the attributes of civilized beings. After the Fall and their expulsion from the Garden of Eden, their and mankind's tribulations had begun, in the course of which some had fared better than others. Those who had drifted furthest from the Holy Land, cut off from the rest of mankind by great oceans and impassable deserts, had reverted entirely to barbarism. Yet they could still be saved. What West Africa suffered from was social, not racial, degeneracy. Most blacks, it was true, were poor and uneducated but those who were not – black abolitionist lecturers who visited Britain from the United States, for instance – were readily welcomed into British middle-class circles. Some, like Frederick Douglass, were lionized. The great hope for the black race in the West Indies, but more still in Africa where the climate was so harmful to whites, was to train up cadres of such men to assume positions of leadership. 'If you ask me,' Buxton wrote to Daniel Wilson, Bishop of Calcutta, 'what of all things I should like, I answer: to see somewhere on the coast of Africa, in a healthy situation, a great Black College, for the education on the purest and most Evangelical principles, of native missionaries and schoolmasters.' His own work with the Lady Mico Charity, an endowment originally intended for the redemption of British sailors enslaved in North Africa but now devoted to educating freedmen in the West Indies, was intended to create just such élites. Some of their members, he hoped, could be prevailed upon to assist him in his African project.[11]

Initially, however, it was whites who would have to take the initiative, and to do this they would need general support. It was necessary, therefore, to show not only that Africans were unregenerate and in need of spiritual guidance, but that Europeans had contributed to their degradation by carrying away millions of slaves, thereby spreading civil war and anarchy. To have complicated the issue by suggesting that, in spite of this, Africans might have their own ways of governing their affairs and that these might be peculiarly suited to their needs as village dwellers and peasant cultivators, would have been to weaken the argument. Beginning with the manifest wickedness of the slave trade and moving on to the desolation of Africa and thence to the need for immediate and forceful intervention was a natural progression. As Buxton told his audience in Exeter Hall, wherever one went in Africa it was 'all the same'. The fact that Africa was not all the same, and could be shown even on the basis of existing knowledge to be culturally highly diverse, did not matter. The object was not to describe Africa but to redeem it. The details could be left until later.

The corollary of the humanitarians' denigration of Africa was their emphasis on Britain's own peculiar blessings. This did not mean that they were unaware of the poverty and misery in their own society even though it sometimes suited their critics to claim that this was the case. More than most they were conscious of the need to relieve the distress of Britain's own poor and, like Buxton himself, were engaged in a multitude of good causes ranging from temperance to revision of the criminal code. Some were more radical in their beliefs, calling for a widening of the suffrage and other political changes. None regarded suffering as the exclusive prerogative of men with black skins.[12] Nevertheless, it was hard to escape the conviction that, of all nations, Britain had been especially fortunate. No other nation was so rich or so free; she was experiencing a rate of economic growth never before achieved; her technical inventiveness was the wonder of the world; her imperial possessions spanned the globe. Without too much stretch of the imagination it was possible to see the blessings of Providence, which Buxton ascribed to himself, as having been granted in generous measure to the nation at large. To those of an evangelical and reflective frame of mind it was plain that such felicities were not intended simply for the material gratification of Britain's own population. That was the path of temptation which would inevitably lead to corruption, as it had in the case of other great empires in the past. Virtue was not simply its own reward; it also implied obligations to others which, if they were not honoured, would eventually destroy virtue itself. The salvation of their own souls, therefore, depended on their willingness to spread these benefits throughout the world at large. No other nation had been so successful in reconciling the advantages of freedom with the need for order. It was but a short step from this vision of Britain as a model for others to emulate to supposing that what others required was British tutelage. The power of this belief in the superiority of Britain's own institutions had been manifested in the struggle, first against the slave trade, then against slavery itself.[13] Could such generous impulses now be allowed to wither? Salvation was not to be attained in a state of idleness. Surely, both as a Christian duty and as a measure necessary for their own moral well-being, the British should now dedicate themselves to the task of bringing the light of their civilization to the dark places of the world, but especially to that least favoured portion of all, the unregenerate inhabitants of Africa.

The problem was, as Buxton became increasingly convinced as he pursued his researches, that so far as the slave trade was concerned their methods had so far been wholly misapplied. He had expected to find that, in spite of all that Britain had done, the trade remained on an unacceptable level. What he now believed he had found was that nothing whatever had been achieved. Year by year more Africans were being butchered in their villages, marched to the coast, carried close-packed across the Atlantic and there systematically and deliberately worked to death. 'Will you believe it,' he informed Gurney, 'the Slave Trade is now double what it was when Wilberforce first began, and its horrors not only aggravated by the increase of the total, but in each particular case are much greater than they were in 1788?' Into its enormous maw were pressed a thousand victims a day and still it remained unsatiated. Worst of all was the discovery that Britain's measures had not only failed to diminish the traffic but had made the sufferings of those caught up in it worse than they otherwise would have been. As many had warned at the time, the effect of Britain's withdrawal had been to create a vacuum which others had hastened to fill. Her subsequent attempts to suppress the trade by means of naval treaties had merely exacerbated the problem by turning a legitimate traffic into a clandestine one. What ultimately determined its scale was the willingness of Africans to supply slaves and of Europeans and Americans to purchase them. So long as that remained true there was little Britain could do. Naval intervention would never, of its own, suffice while countries such as Spain and the United States continued to deny her the right to search their ships. In levying a toll on the traffic by intercepting some vessels and releasing their captives she was simply adding to the total volume of misery since others would inevitably be enslaved to take their place. It was the law of the market-place, of supply and demand, that prevailed. Britain's navy might drive up the price of slaves, but only marginally, never to the point at which purchasing them would become uneconomical. Nor was there any real hope that the receiving nations could be persuaded to forgo the con-tinuing supply of labour upon which their economies now depended. It was all very well for ministers to argue that the trade could be got rid of by means of treaties. Thirty years of experience had proved only too convincingly that this was not so. The only hope was going to the fountainhead and cutting off the source of supply. Unless that were done it would be better to do nothing at all.

Armed with these findings Buxton set about lobbying ministers. Most were old acquaintances. They, for their part, were happy to receive him, the more so because there were pressing matters on which they needed his advice. Chief among these was their need to respond to the pressure which had lately been building up outside Parliament for further inter-vention in the affairs of the West Indies. In theory slavery there had ended in 1834. In practice, however, the freedmen had been required, for a transitional period, to go on working for their masters very much as before. A minority of these so-called apprentices, those not engaged in field work, were scheduled to receive their full liberty on 1 August 1838, the remainder two years later. Plainly it was a tricky situation, made all the more so by recent revelations about the way in which the system was being abused. Whipping had been forbidden but had been replaced by treadmills many of which, being poorly constructed, inflicted fearful lacerations on the bodies of those undergoing punishment. From all over the colonies came stories of planters determined to exact as much labour as possible from their charges before freedom came.

Like other abolitionists, Buxton had never wanted apprenticeship and had agreed to it only as a necessary concession to the planter interest. This was also the view of the Cabinet. But having entered into a formal agreement they could hardly break it without first collecting evidence that the planters had not kept their side of the bargain. That would take time. With apprenticeship destined to end so soon it hardly seemed worthwhile. In the meantime, however, they were faced with a mounting clamour, led by their former colleague Lord Brougham, for the immediate scrapping of the whole system.[14]

Buxton appreciated their quandary. His private belief was that the popular campaign was a mistake and that his abolitionist colleagues would have been better advised to wait until 1840 and then make sure that the freedom granted to the ex-slaves was as fully safeguarded as the law could make it.[15] Compared with the continuing horrors of the slave trade the question of whether apprenticeship should end in 1838 or 1840 seemed inconsequential. But now that public opinion had been aroused he inclined to the view that the Government should give way or at least make some concession. To have suggested otherwise would have placed him in an embarrassing position with the humanitarian party whose support he hoped to mobilize on behalf of his own schemes. More immediate, however, was the need to enlist the support of the members of the Cabinet who, in their embattled position, saw him as a sensible moderate, perhaps even a useful ally.[16]

Ministers therefore greeted him warmly. Lord Glenelg, the Colonial Secretary, was a friend of more than thirty years' standing. His father, Charles Grant, had been an associate of Wilberforce's and an energetic member of the Clapham sect, that evangelical group, many of whom lived on or near Clapham Common, which had spearheaded the attack on the slave trade and been responsible for establishing Sierra Leone as a refuge for slaves freed by British cruisers. Glenelg and Buxton had started their parliamentary careers together. Calling on him on 28 March Buxton found him utterly miserable at the predicament the Government had got itself into. As a second-generation Claphamite, defending the planters against their critics went very much against the grain. Yet what else could he do? Legislation had been enacted, contractual obligations entered into. Glenelg also referred to the problem of Lord Brougham whom the Prime Minister, Lord Melbourne, had excluded from the

Cabinet. Brougham's pride and arrogance made him an insufferable colleague. Many thought him mad. But, mad or not, he was a formidable adversary. The fact that this banished Lucifer had taken up the cause of the apprentices made it difficult for the Government to act. Melbourne could not allow Brougham a triumph. It was a great pity that Buxton was no longer in Parliament to handle the matter for them. Glenelg hoped he would not embarrass the Government even more by speaking out against it. So concerned was he with his own problems that he had no time for anyone else's. 'He appeared, poor man,' Buxton reported, 'as much perplexed as I ever saw anybody. He was much to be pitied. I offered two or three times to go away, but he detained me and seemed relieved by our conversation.'[17] Other ministers proved more receptive, in particular Lord Palmerston, the Foreign Secretary, and Spring Rice, Chancellor of the Exchequer. Both listened attentively as he outlined his views. Palmerston urged him to pursue his researches further and set out his conclusions in writing; Spring Rice, for his part, undertook to bring the matter to the attention of the Cabinet.

For Buxton it was a relief to find that his rejection by the Weymouth electors had in no way diminished his standing at Westminster. More interviews followed. In late March 1838 a proposal for the ending of apprenticeship, in support of which his name was much invoked, was defeated by a vote of 269 to 205. Although relieved, at least for the time being, of this embarrassment, ministers proved as welcoming as ever. Glenelg assured Buxton that despite their public stand they were privately urging the planters to give way. Buxton's own ideas were arousing much interest. What all the ministers pointed out, however, was that if he wanted the Government to act he would first need to submit a set of written proposals.

Advice as to the best method of proceeding came from Palmerston and Lord Howick, Secretary at War. While Parliament remained in session, they pointed out, ministers were far too busy to read anything. He should therefore set about producing a written submission, printed in pamphlet form but intended for their use exclusively, in time for the parliamentary recess in July. Ministers could then read it over the vacation and decide what to do when they reconvened in the autumn. Even then, given the Government's past reluctance to take the initiative on antislavery matters, it was unlikely that much would happen unless it was provoked into action by public opinion. Having presented his pamphlet, Buxton should immediately begin work on a second version for general publication at the end of the year. In this he should emphasize, as forcefully as possible, the extent, character and full horror of the slave trade. He should also, in a calm, reasoned manner, set out the steps proposed for dealing with it.

Acting on this advice Buxton promptly set to work. 'I am,' he informed the Cottage Ladies, 'more hard run than I used to be even *in* Parliament.' Plainly he was enjoying himself immensely. He began on the pamphlet but soon found, even with the help of Andrew who had now moved to London, that his time was too taken up with interviews and committees to make much progress. A trunk of books and official reports was sent to Anna and Sarah by the Norwich coach. Once they had sorted out the slave trade material he wanted them to turn their attention to commercial statistics. As spring gave way to summer his letters became more insistent. 'I know your answer will be that this is beyond your ability,' he wrote to Anna. 'You can do it; and do it you shall.' The whole family, it was reported, were labouring around the clock.

Meanwhile, in London, he had enlisted the aid of James MacQueen, a noted African expert and the author of several books on the subject of African development; also the Reverend John Scoble, a former peripatetic lecturer employed by the Agency Anti-Slavery Society. He consulted Macgregor Laird, a Liverpool shipbuilder, and Captain John Beecroft, a West African trader and formerly acting governor of Fernando Po, both of whom had personal experience of Niger navigation. Much time was spent visiting city merchants and collecting samples of African produce. These, too, he despatched to Norfolk for examination. The Kola nuts, he explained to the puzzled Cottage Ladies, could either be roasted and eaten like chestnuts or, should other means fail, used for lighting. 'I am,' he wrote, 'now lighting one up on the tip of my knife, and it burns most brightly!'

Mindful of Palmerston's warning that Government support might well, in the last resort, depend on popular pressure, he was anxious to remove any suspicion that his inaction over the apprenticeship issue implied disapproval of the campaign that had been mounted. It was too early yet to reveal his own schemes. However, he attended committees and spoke at public meetings. The apprenticeship issue was given an unexpected twist when, on 22 May, in a thinly attended House, the Government was defeated by a vote of 96 to 93. Buxton was in the public gallery with a group of Quakers who gave such a shout of triumph that they were summarily turned out into the street by the Sergeant at Arms. The housekeeper, seeing them return home, described them as 'coming tumbling into the room, shaking hands with each other . . . sitting down, bursting out, laughing, etc. etc., so delighted they were'. The Government responded by refusing to vote the necessary enabling legislation. Matters thus dragged on until July when it was learned that the planters, heeding the ministers' advice, had agreed to end apprenticeship of their own accord.

By this time Buxton's two teams of researchers had finished their work on his pamphlet. Throughout July and the early part of August he laboured with MacQueen and Scoble putting together the final copy and rushing sections to the printers as they were completed. For reasons of security he had decided to limit the printing to sixty copies. On 14 August he reported to Priscilla that these were now in his hands and looked, in their externals at least, very magnificent. *Letter to Lord Melbourne* was certainly much more than a normal pamphlet. Running to 215 pages and some 50 000 words it was, in fact, a good-sized book. Having asked for written proposals, ministers were getting more than they had bargained for.[18]

To ensure that they were aware of their obligation to read and consider his work, Buxton took it upon himself to deliver copies personally. As always, ministers received him graciously. Melbourne, in typically urbane fashion, assured him that the Government was much in his debt for going to such trouble on its behalf. He also professed to share Buxton's view that the policies pursued so far were a great mistake. 'In short,' Buxton concluded, 'if old experience had not taught me to put no trust in princes I should have considered him a proselyte.' Palmerston, who was largely responsible for instituting those very policies, appeared, not surprisingly, less impressed. 'I did not quite know what to make of him,' Buxton reported. 'Mighty civil – tells me he thinks he will get the Portuguese treaty through. Talked very rationally about commerce and yet seemed to think the world was to be moved by Protocols.' Other ministers proved more supportive. Spring Rice congratulated him on having gone about his lobbying in exactly the right way. All undertook to read his book carefully and see that his proposals received full consideration from Cabinet.[19]

For his own part, Buxton was delighted at the way it had all gone. 'I got home to dinner . . . remarkably well satisfied with the day's work. The book is fairly launched and I can only wish it God speed.' He was now, he reported to Priscilla, a gentleman of leisure and looked forward to being as much occupied with rabbits and partridges as he had lately been with the Niger and Fernando Po. Whatever happened next was up to the Government.[20]

CHAPTER TWO
The Politics of Benevolence

Ministers had much else on their minds in the autumn of 1838: unrest in Ireland, rebellion in Canada, Russian expansionism, war in Afghanistan and above all the precariousness of their own position in Parliament. Compared with these pressing issues a proposal to mount an expedition to ascend the Niger might appear a small matter. Nevertheless, it was one that required their attention. Certainly the case for reassessing their slave trade policies, if Buxton's findings were to be believed, was compelling.

If nothing else, *Letter to Lord Melbourne* represented a powerful indictment of everything that had been done so far. According to Buxton's estimates, upwards of 150 000 slaves a year were being taken from Africa by the Atlantic trade and a further 50 000 by the Islamic trans-Saharan and East African trades. Of the former, approximately 80 000 were destined for Brazil, 60 000 for Cuba and the remainder for Puerto Rico, Texas (at that time an independent state) and Buenos Aires. The resulting figure of 200 000, however, represented only a fraction of the total loss to Africa, for in the process of seizure, march to the coast and detention awaiting transportation more died than survived. Similar rates of mortality occurred in the trans-Saharan and East Coast traffic. Allowing for these it seemed probable that the final total was not much short of 500 000. In comparison with this figure, the number intercepted and freed by the Royal Navy for subsequent resettlement in Sierra Leone, amounting to some 8000 a year, was puny. Of Britain's good intentions there was no doubt. Yet in order to produce this insignificant effect she had, in the course of the previous thirty years, spent some twenty million pounds in the form of bribes to foreign powers and payments for the maintenance of her African squadron. This was an enormous sum, falling not much short of one year's annual government expenditure on the entire army, navy and civil establishment.

What in Buxton's view made such a waste of resources particularly galling was the fact that if even a small proportion of the sum had been spent differently it would have brought enormous benefits not only to Africa but to the people of Great Britain. Potentially Africa was a rich continent, well able to provide Britain with virtually all that she needed in the way of palm oil, cotton, sugar, dye woods, timber, ground nuts, ivory and other tropical products. Africans were skilled in weaving and domestic handicrafts. They were also potential consumers of Britain's manufactures. This was a market Britain should not ignore. The problem was that the slave trade, breeding as it did tribal conflict, drove out other forms of commerce. Britain's policies to date had been diffuse and undirected. Her warships had ranged far and wide, arresting a slaver here, imposing a temporary blockade there. What was now required was for her to concentrate her efforts on establishing areas where agriculture and trade could develop safe from the scourge of the slavers. Only by creating such enclaves could Africa be delivered from the misfortunes which had engulfed her.

The steps by which this new strategy was to be developed were outlined briefly in the two concluding chapters of the pamphlet. The first essential was to acquire an off-shore base of operations. Fernando Po in the Gulf of Guinea, where Britain already had a small naval establishment, was an ideal site with a good harbour refreshed by cool sea breezes. It should be immediately purchased from Spain. From there it would be possible for cruisers to police the coast and negotiate treaties with the chiefs. More important was the fact that it was less than a day's sail from the mouth of the Niger, a highway easily navigated by paddle steamers, leading directly into the heart of the continent. It had already been established that the interior tribes were eager for legitimate trade. There was reason to suppose that they would also prove useful allies against the marauding coastal warlords. The steamers should as far as possible be manned by African crews supervised by white officers. In this way forts and trading posts could be established along the river. The principal internal settlement would need to be some three hundred miles from the coast, probably at the confluence of the Niger and the Benue, a 'great internal citadel' destined in the fullness of time to become 'the New Orleans of Africa'. From there merchants and missionaries could penetrate into the deepest recesses of the Kong Mountains and beyond to Timbuktu. But this was looking far ahead. What was needed in the first instance was a steam vessel of light draft, commanded by a resourceful officer, to ascend the river. He would introduce himself to the African chiefs, explain Britain's benevolent intentions, survey the country and, where appropriate, acquire territorial rights to locations that he believed suitable for settlement. Two steamers would obviously be better. But at the very least there should be one steamer detailed to ascend the river before the end of 1839.

There were, he conceded, objections to this plan. One was possible loss of life. It was perfectly true that 'so long as the country remains uncleared

and uncultivated, and settlements are made on low and swampy situa-
tions, so long will the country continue to be exceedingly unhealthy.' But
the settlements proposed would be in the interior, well away from the
coastal marshes, and in areas at least as healthy as many others over
which Britain already held sway. The men, moreover, would be selected
for their physical fitness and thus be quite unlike the drunken ruffians
who normally visited the coast and succumbed to the African climate.
Ways of preserving health in hot climates were much better understood
than formerly. 'Activity, cleanliness, sobriety, living on fresh instead of
salted animal food, and the wearing of flannels next the skin . . . render
life within the tropics not subject to very much greater hazard than in this
country.' There was certainly 'nothing under this head that should deter
this country from such a magnificent undertaking'.

There was also the problem of expense. But in this respect it had to be
remembered that Britain was already spending enormous sums to no
avail. 'Better surely, by one great effort, to accomplish our object, than to
linger on, spending, perhaps, something less, but perpetually baffled and
disappointed.' When assessing the costs, ministers should bear in mind
the very real benefits that would accrue to Britain once trading links had
been established. At present Britain relied entirely on the United States
for her cotton. 'Any sudden civil convulsion in America would bring
ruination in Lancashire where vast numbers would find themselves
without employment.' The Africans themselves grew and wove cotton,
although not in any great quantity and not, as yet, for export. Yet the
gently rising plains stretching from the Delta to the Kong Mountains
were ideally suited to its cultivation. If properly developed they could
supply all of Lancashire's needs. The Delta itself was well adapted to the
growing of rice and sugar. 'It does appear to me,' he observed, 'a strange
kind of economy to carry away the population from their native fields,
which need nothing but those hands for their cultivation, in order to
plant them, in diminished numbers, at a prodigious expense, in another
hemisphere, and on lands not more productive.'

So, purely on the grounds of Britain's own economic self-interest, the
course he was proposing was well worth pursuing. However, it was not
for that reason that he was putting it forward but on the grounds of
humanity, justice and his obligations as a Christian. There he stood as
upon a rock. The Cabinet might well decide to reject his proposals but if
it did so it should at the same time admit the illogicality of its present
policies and withdraw from the struggle altogether. It was 'better to do
nothing than to go on year after year, at great cost, adding to the disasters
and inflaming the wounds of Africa'.

Although ministers had encouraged Buxton, their initial responses,
when presented with these proposals, were sceptical. What most aroused
their suspicions was the sheer grandiosity of Buxton's vision. Like some

modern Prospero he seemed to believe that Christianity, commerce and steam power could work miracles, only in this case he did not command the powers of magic and the area in question was not an island but an unexplored continent of whose vastness he seemed to have no conception. Even reduced to its absolute essentials his scheme would involve formidable problems of organization. Treaties were the responsibility of the Foreign Office, naval deployment of the Admiralty, settlements of the Colonial Office, commerce of the Board of Trade. If, as Buxton wanted, an expedition were to ascend the Niger, Treasury approval would also be required, perhaps even the authorization of Parliament. In each case assent would have to be obtained at the very highest level. The key figure, therefore, was the Prime Minister.

Melbourne was not a man given to moral excesses, least of all on behalf of Africans. The idea that Britain was somehow morally responsible for what went on in that huge and barbarous continent struck him as nonsense. His famous comment to Archbishop Whately that abolition was all 'great folly' and that if he had had his own way he would have done 'nothing at all' was made in jest.[1] Teasing the serious-minded was very much his style. Nevertheless, his conservative instincts were sufficiently well known to make the statement appear not entirely implausible. Nor did he have a high regard for reformers. As it happened he was that summer reading Samuel and Robert Wilberforce's biography of their father. It gave, he told Lord John Russell, a most curious picture of the times and of 'Wilberforce perpetually vexing himself because he amused himself too much . . . One good thing, by the way, is that it shows the great Philanthropist Thos. Clarkson to be a sad fellow.' Why did they feel so much 'discontent and dissatisfaction with themselves'? It was all self-flagellation or, as he put it, 'religious earwash'.[2]

His initial response to Buxton's proposals was equally scornful. 'Buxton has of course sent you his book,' he wrote to Russell from Windsor Castle on 3 September. 'Pray read it without delay. It recommends measures to be taken instantly, and it will form the manual of the saints and dissenters during the next session. I hope he exaggerates the slave trade carried on at present, and I should think it posssible that he does so, as his object is to prove that nothing yet has been effected towards its abolition.' The ostentatious manner in which Buxton had presented him with his work had not impressed him favourable. For his own part he was doubtful that much could be achieved, either by morality or cruisers, so long as a slave could be purchased in Africa 'for a few beads, a yard or two of red cloth, a bad gun and sold elsewhere for a hundred to a hundred and fifty pounds'. As regards the proposal to establish trading posts and settlements in the African interior he could see serious objections. One was the expense of such wars as would inevitably arise from the need to protect them and keep them supplied.

Lord Melbourne as Prime Minister.

Another was the likely loss of life. Whatever Buxton might say, the fact was that when Europeans went to Africa more died than survived. In addition to this there was the hostility which Africans throughout the continent would feel on account of such an incursion. The kind of reaction that might be expected could be gauged by the recent Arab response to the French occupation of Algiers. Finally, there was the jealousy of other powers to be taken into account. They would be no more persuaded that the aim of the British was 'principally for the purpose of suppressing the slave trade than we should believe it of Russia if she were to allege such a motive for the establishing of posts and stations in countries which do not belong to her'. Plainly the Government would need to proceed cautiously. The first essential was to get hold of a really reliable set of figures. It would be embarrassing to the Government if Buxton were proved correct and it was shown that present policies served merely to 'increase the extent and aggravate the horrors of the traffic'.[3]

Discussing the matter with the Queen on 24 September he was more circumspect. He was, she noted in her diary, optimistic about Britain's ability to suppress the slave trade carried out under the Spanish flag thanks to the addition of clauses in the Anglo-Spanish treaty which allowed the navy to seize vessels equipped for the traffic even when there were not slaves on board. He also told her that it was an inopportune time to start establishing posts in Africa in view of the objections Britain herself had raised with reference to French activities in North Africa. Nevertheless, he spoke warmly of Buxton as a friend and associate of Wilberforce's.[4] Evidently the Queen expressed interest in Buxton's proposals for shortly afterwards Melbourne wrote telling him that she had asked to keep his book and would he therefore send another? The book's disclosures, he noted, were appalling and would be dreadful enough if only one quarter of them proved true. But the remedies proposed had serious implications and would need to be considered in the light of general Government policy.

Comparing Buxton's scheme to France's occupation of Algeria was not entirely fanciful, although abolishing slavery and the slave trade there had not been among her aims. She had, nevertheless, sought to justify her actions by invoking much the same principles of Christian philanthropy, commercial interest and national destiny used by Buxton. Such talk, Palmerston had informed Melbourne at the time, was all very well but the practical effect of France's expansion was to give her control of the southern coast of the Mediterranean, a development Britain should take very seriously.[5] Looking at Buxton's proposals from the point of view of Britain's national interest, as Palmerston now told the Prime Minister, there was much to be said for acquiring Fernando Po and making a settlement up the Niger.[6] Like his Cabinet colleagues, he was against acquiring more territories simply for their own sake. Colouring the map red was not his ambition. As the world's leading industrial and commercial power Britain had no need of more formal colonies which, as experience had shown, too often became millstones around the taxpayer's neck. Strategic bases, however, were another matter. Trade, not dominion, was the ultimate aim, but traders would, very properly, look to the Government to promote and protect their interests overseas. With this

HM Brig *Acorn* captures the slaver *Gabriel*.

in mind Britain had already established bases in the Falklands and Singapore and was in the process of acquiring others at Aden and Hong Kong. West Africa lay on the route to India. As navigation turned from sail to steam coaling stations would be needed. West Africa also had commercial potentialities. If Britain did not exploit them others would.[7]

Both Palmerston and Melbourne, however, agreed that Buxton's plan to ring the entire continent with outposts was 'a wild and crude idea'. The problem with it, Palmerston informed Glenelg, was that it was open to precisely the same objections that Buxton himself made with regard to naval treaties and naval patrols, namely that nothing was done until everything was done. Establish a British presence in one place and the traders moved elsewhere; make a treaty with one nation and they began flying the flag of another. To begird the entire coast of Africa with settlements, even if there were no political difficulties involved, would be an expensive and slow process. The point was that it was Europe, not Africa, that held the initiative. Africans wanted European goods and would pay in whatever currency Europeans chose. 'If we insist on having slaves, slaves they will produce; if we prefer being paid by elephants' teeth and gold dust, those articles will be collected and will be got ready for merchants.' Africans, as he was fond of pointing out, were a commercial people, activated by the same desire for gain that inspired Europeans. What they lacked was civilization and the right commercial

26

environment for developing their resources. The problem was the slave trade. If once that scourge were removed, other forms of trade would develop. The slave trade continued not because the slavers escaped the vigilance of the cruisers but because, if they displayed certain flags, the cruisers were unable to intercept them. All that was lacking was treaty power. Lately most of the trade had been carried on under the Portuguese flag but a treaty was now pending that would close that particular loophole. If Portugal refused to put down the slave trade Britain must do it for her, as she easily could. 'We have only to order our cruisers to seize slave traders under Portuguese flag . . . land the crews on a Portuguese settlement, take the slaves to be set free on some settlement of our own, scuttle the ship, and then bid defiance to all claimants.'[8]

This was not at all what Buxton had in mind. The two approaches, however, were by no means incompatible. Unlike his Quaker friends, Buxton was not opposed to using force. In his book he had referred to the need to reorganize and concentrate the efforts of the African Squadron. As regards the desirability of making treaties with native rulers Palmerston had already anticipated Buxton by sending instructions to this effect to naval commanders the previous spring.[9] He was not altogether happy about the notion of paying chiefs to give up the trade, the fear being that they would accept the gifts, sign the treaties, and still go on trafficking. The situation would require careful monitoring. All the same, stripped of its messianic rhetoric, and discounting the claims about the ineffectualness of current policies, in Palmerston's view much exaggerated, there was a good deal in Buxton's pamphlet of which he approved.

How other ministers regarded these matters can only by guessed. Glenelg, unless Buxton was much misled, was a firm supporter. So, too, according to Glenelg, was the Home Secretary, Lord John Russell.[10] Spring Rice, who had previously appeared enthusiastic, was now studiously noncommittal, although he assured Buxton that his ideas were receiving close attention.[11] Nevertheless, as the weeks passed and autumn turned to winter Buxton became increasingly despondent. His great fear, he told Poulett Thomson, President of the Board of Trade, was 'that the subject will be allowed to go to sleep, and that is equivalent to a total defeat'. By mid-November he could restrain himself no longer. 'You ministers,' he wrote to Spring Rice, 'take some liberties with us mere mortals. My whole soul is in Africa and the Slave Trade.'[12] There was also disquieting news that Lord Brougham had seen a copy of the *Letter to Lord Melbourne* and the possibility that he might use it to embarrass the Government in the same way as he had with the apprenticeship issue. Buxton consulted James Stephen, Permanent Under-Secretary at the Colonial Office, the younger son of Wilberforce's old colleague James

Stephen Senior, and thus, like his superior Glenelg, a second-generation Claphamite. Stephen had proved himself an outstanding administrator, being responsible not only for the day-to-day running of the Colonial Office but, it was widely believed, the whole of Britain's overseas empire. He, however, was reassuring, pointing out that if Brougham had seen the book it was no bad thing since it might finally provoke the Cabinet into action.[13]

Eventually, on 28 November, Buxton and Andrew Johnston were summoned to the Colonial Office and there presented with a list of questions the Government wished answered. Returning to Stephen Lushington's house in Great George Street, they discussed these over dinner and then sat up much of the night in their dressing-gowns and slippers drafting replies which Andrew delivered to the Colonial Office the following day. It was now becoming plain that ministers were uncertain as to what exactly was being proposed. Buxton had added further to their confusion by writing privately to Glenelg suggesting that, in addition to purchasing Fernando Po, Britain acquire Mombasa as a base for operations against the Mohammedan slave trade on the East African coast.[14] How grandiose were his plans? It had quickly been established that Mombasa was unavailable[15] and that Palmerston would not countenance any diminution of naval effort. Buxton now hastened to clarify matters by drafting a nine-point statement for Glenelg headed 'Practical Suggestions on Africa'. These provided for a stepping-up of cruiser operations by adding more steamships to the African Squadron, the acquisition of Fernando Po, and a systematic effort to make treaties with the chiefs of the coast and interior. To allay foreign suspicion, settlements should be open to traders of all nations, although British traders should be granted access to the home market on favourable terms. Settlements would, of course, require protection and he hoped the Government would make generous grants towards the education of the native Africans. He himself would prepare an edition of his book for publication, taking care not to reveal any details of the Government's intentions.[16]

That ministers viewed these new proposals favourably soon became apparent. Melbourne received him graciously and said he looked forward to having 'a good long day's talk with him'. Sir George Grey professed to be highly enthusiastic, and Lord Howick thought that there was now little doubt that the Cabinet would accept his propositions.[17]

The news that it had actually done so was broken to Buxton by Glenelg at the Colonial Office on 22 December 1838. Some points, including access to trade by foreign nationals, the physical protection of settlers and the funds available for education, would require further discussion, but otherwise the Government was prepared to go along with everything he had proposed. He returned from the interview jubilant. 'Is not my news delightful?' he wrote to his wife. 'My nine propositions have worked admirably.'[18] His daughter found him in high spirits, eager to press on with practical arrangements.[19] Reflecting on the year's events in more sombre mood he noted that Providence had yet again favoured him. The Government's reservations he regarded as relatively inconsequential.

> So then, Oh God, this mighty work is fairly launched. The Nation is to put forth its strength to save annually hundreds of thousands from slaughter and bondage; a whole Continent plunged in the depths of dark superstition is to be opened for Missionary Labours; a quarter of the Globe visited and blessed with our discoveries – arts, commerce, agriculture – and above all that which is the great Civilizer, the great Improver of mankind, Christianity. Oh God, oh pray heavenly God, leave us not to ourselves in this mighty task.[20]

What part domestic political considerations had played in bringing the Cabinet to its decision can only be guessed, although the circumstances would suggest that, in Melbourne's case at least, they were important determinants. Following his scornful dismissal of the proposals in the summer to have now come around to supporting them represented a significant volte-face. The fact was that the Government's position was perilous and the behaviour of the humanitarians over the apprenticeship issue had been a serious embarrassment. There was no point in alienating them further. Also there was the problem of Lord Brougham whose hatred of his former colleagues, now he had been consigned to the wilderness, knew no bounds. To be driven from office by Brougham and a gaggle of humanitarians would be the ultimate humiliation.

Such an eventuality was not beyond the realms of possibility. By 1839, the Whigs, who had carried through the Great Reform Bill of 1832 and the Emancipation Bill of 1833, had run out of energy and ideas. They had lost heavily as a result of defections to the Tories and two successive general elections and now held a minority of seats in Parliament. That they still contrived to remain in office was entirely due to the support of O'Connell and his Irish followers on the one hand and a miscellaneous rump of radicals on the other. The future behaviour of both remained unpredictable. Either one could put them out of power for the foreseeable future. Conducting business in such circumstances was not easy. 'By one set of people,' Melbourne wrote ruefully to Russell, 'we are told that we are ruining ourselves and losing support by allying ourselves with the Radicals and Roman Catholics; by another that we are producing the same effect by leaning too much to the Tories and Conservatives. Probably both statements are true, and we are losing credit on both sides.'[21] Among their few remaining assets was the support of the Queen.

But that would not prevent their being turned out of office if faced with further defections.

Brougham, for his part, looked forward eagerly to just such an outcome. In his estimation Melbourne and Palmerston were not Whigs at all but Tories masquerading as Whigs. By defending apprenticeship they had 'damned themselves for ever with the Abolition party. They themselves allow that on a Dissolution they would now lose fifty or sixty.... Rely on this, it cannot last thus, Whigs led by Tories is too unnatural a thing to endure or be endured.'[22] There was something almost indecent about the tenacity with which Melbourne clung to office simply to gratify his own vanity by acting as the Queen's mentor. But once Parliament reconvened, the whole ramshackle edifice of Whig rule would come tumbling down.

This was wishful thinking, although it almost came to pass. What is clear is that events were playing into Buxton's hands. The humanitarians needed humouring. During the ministers' panic over apprenticeship Lord Tavistock had written to Russell suggesting that Buxton be given a baronetcy.[23] This was the honour that was eventually granted after the great Exeter Hall meeting of 1840. Nevertheless, it was already plain to the Government by the summer of 1838 that Buxton was not a man to be snubbed. Melbourne, Palmerston and Russell had all noted that his proposals would be high on the humanitarians' future agenda. The expenditure involved did not appear to be large. No great interests of state were involved. There were geopolitical reasons for increasing Britain's stake in West Africa. The administration had few enough new measures for which it could claim credit. Viewed from a purely political standpoint there was much to be said for giving way immediately, at least in principle, so avoiding future embarrassment.

Supposing that he now had the Government's full backing Buxton hastened to London immediately after the Christmas holiday. There he found that Glenelg had already begun taking practical advice as to the type of vessels required. Together with the First Lord of the Admiralty, the Earl of Minto, they pored over charts and discussed treaty arrangements. What most impressed Priscilla, who eagerly recounted these proceedings for the benefit of the ladies at Northrepps, was the change that the Government's decision had produced in her father's demeanour. He was now dealing with ministers 'in a character, new even to him, not bargaining as of old, but as a high member of the Cabinet proposing a plan, asking no favours but bestowing one in giving it to them'.

Only gradually did it dawn on them that the Cabinet's decision was not quite what it had at first seemed. On 13 January the Marquis of Lansdowne, Lord President of the Council, wrote to Buxton expressing unease at the proposal to acquire large tracts of land on the Niger. How would such territories be governed? How would they be defended if not by a large military force? 'It must be recollected,' he wrote, 'that our immense Indian Empire, to which no right-minded English politician would think of adding another of corresponding magnitude, was the work of no deliberate system but of repeated acts of necessity imposed on authorities who professed to be, and I really believe in most instances were, hostile in principle to the plans they were driven to adopt.'[24] If only a fraction of the benefits Buxton envisaged could be attained, then expenses ought not to be spared. But, unless he was much mistaken, the costs involved in governing, defending and supplying what would, in effect, be new colonies in the interior of Africa would far exceed any likely returns. At a time when free-trade ideas were gaining ground and formal colonial rule was very much out of favour, the idea of acquiring yet more possessions did not fit well with prevailing Government policy. The last thing ministers wanted was more colonies.

It was also learned that the Board of Trade would be unwilling to assign the proposed settlements colonial status and thus accept African produce at preferential rates of duty. By far the worst news, however, was the announcement, early in February, that Glenelg had been dismissed and would be replaced by the Marquis of Normanby, newly returned from Ireland where he had been serving as Lord Lieutenant. James Stephen was reported to have shaken his head in disbelief at the choice of his new superior. Buxton regarded it as 'a *very heavy* Blow'. With Glenelg and Stephen at the Colonial Office he had felt he was dealing with friends; with Normanby there he was less sure. Aware that his successor would be unfamiliar with the subject, Glenelg drafted a long memorandum outlining what had been done so far and expressing the hope that he would now press ahead rapidly with the practical arrangements.[25]

In the event, Normanby proved no less welcoming than his predecessor. He had, he told Buxton, read Glenelg's memorandum and agreed with every word of it. He also showed Buxton copies of the draft treaties and instructions that had been prepared. The selection of personnel to go on the expedition could begin in the summer.

Meanwhile Buxton, following Palmerston's advice, had published *The African Slave Trade*. This was an amplified version of the early sections of *Letter to Lord Melbourne*, setting out his findings as regards the character and extent of the traffic but omitting any mention of either his own or the Government's plans. This, as he explained privately, was because he did not want to alarm the Americans about cotton, Russia about hemp, France about grain or anyone else about what they might regard as Britain's expansionist intentions. In particular he did not want to alert Spain to the key role which Fernando Po would play in the whole enterprise while negotiations for its purchase were still continuing.

He also set about gathering together a small group of MPs, deliberately chosen as representatives of both major parties, to serve as a pilot committee to discuss general policy. The first meeting of the Patrons of Africa, as they agreed to call themselves, was held on 20 April 1839, at Stephen Lushington's house in Great George Street. Besides Buxton himself and Lushington, who agreed to act as parliamentary spokesman for the group, it consisted of William Ewart Gladstone, Sir Robert Inglis, William Evans, Edward Buxton and, to advise on financial matters, Samuel Gurney, in short, Buxton concluded, 'an epitome of the State, Whig, Tory and Radical, Dissenter, Low Church, High church, Tip-top High Church or Oxfordism'. All went well up to a point, but he was caught unprepared when Gladstone asked what proof he had that Africa was salubrious. 'Somehow or other,' Buxton reported, 'they take it into their heads that this is a vital part of the question.' He responded by pointing out that he did not intend to send Europeans in large numbers and that those selected would be 'hardy creatures, whom no weather affects and no climate touches'. This was greeted with understandable scepticism. It was, he confessed, a subject on which he had not been properly briefed, so would Anna and Andrew set to at once 'proving that lands about Boussa are as healthy as in Jamaica'? Doubts were also expressed about universal fertility of African soils. Would they therefore provide him with information on that head too?[26]

Much more immediately worrying was the growing realization that most abolitionists, or at all events most antislavery activists, were totally opposed to his scheme. The principal point at issue was the use of force. From the very outset he had made no secret of the fact that force might have to be employed, if only in self-defence against marauding slave traders. In his letters, and in conversations within his family, he had gone much further, suggesting that the success of the whole enterprise would depend on the use of naval power. Although he himself had been careful to tailor his statements so as not to offend the sensibilities of other audiences, word had inevitably leaked out. In March 1838, writing to her uncle, Joseph John Gurney, newly departed on his Quaker mission to America, Priscilla had described her father's plan as being to put down the slave trade by persuading 'France and America to join in a resolution to put it down *by force*, viz. by an effectual blockade of the Coast by settlements at the mouths of and up the rivers and plenty of steamers'. Given Gurney's strict Quaker views on non-violence this was hardly tactful. Unlike Palmerston, Buxton was no advocate of gunboat diplomacy. On the other hand, he was well aware that in dealing with the Government he would get nowhere if he suggested eliminating or even scaling down naval activity. In his 'Practical Suggestions' he deliberately advocated stepping it up. Pleasing both Palmerston and the Quakers was not going to be easy.

Although the immediate issue was the legitimacy of force as an instrument of policy, the split in the abolitionists' ranks reflected disagreements over policy which had begun a decade earlier. In the course of the struggle against West Indian slavery some of the younger and more radical elements in the Anti-Slavery Society had established an Agency Committee to organize popular support and bring pressure to bear on Parliament from without. This body had eventually broken away from the main organization so that in the final stages of the campaign there had been two distinct organizations, one led by Buxton working mainly within Parliament, the other exerting pressure from outside. This latter group, which was notably more extreme in its demands, wanted nothing less than immediate and unconditional emancipation and expressed bitter disappointment when in due course compensation of twenty million pounds was given to the slave-owners and a period of apprenticeship approved. Many of its members believed that Buxton, by demanding too little and giving way too early, had betrayed their cause.[27]

After 1833 the Anti-Slavery Society suspended operations. It eventually wound up its affairs in March 1839 at a meeting which Buxton attended. They were, he observed, a grey-haired remnant. The same could not be said of the Agency Society group from whose ranks Joseph Sturge had now emerged as the acknowledged leader. It was this group, or rather elements from it, for it changed its name and organizational arrangements more than once, that led the campaign against apprenticeship. Sturge himself went to the West Indies to observe the workings of apprenticeship at first hand and it was largely his revelations, together with his skilful mobilization of public opinion, that led to the abrupt termination of that system.

Sturge and Buxton were very similar in personality. Both had worked hard as young men, showed unimpeachable business integrity, amassed large fortunes – in Sturge's case as a Birmingham corn merchant – and thereafter dedicated their lives to promoting social and humanitarian causes. Above all, both were inner-directed, driven by their consciences to undertake ever greater tasks in what they conceived to be the service of mankind. Unlike Buxton, however, who saw himself as being only half a Quaker, Sturge was a Quaker through and through. 'You hold by abstract justice,' Buxton told him on one occasion, 'I hold myself as Counsel of the Negro. I will either speak or hold my tongue, agitate or not stir a finger, as the interests of the Negro require.'[28] But on issues of principle, which in Sturge's case meant most issues, ends could never justify means. For a pacifist he was strikingly pugnacious and, as a moralist, totally implacable.

Sturge never forgave Buxton for agreeing to the compromises of 1833. Even less excusable, in his view, was Buxton's almost total public silence during the subsequent campaign to rectify at least one of those errors by

Joseph Sturge at the Anti-Slavery Convention of 1840.

ending the apprenticeship system. To make matters worse, Buxton had argued, privately at least, against the whole effort to free the apprentices, claiming that it would achieve nothing at home and might well produce disturbances in the West Indies. To the Sturgeites this appeared not only offensive but underhand. Even when, in due course, he revised his views they declined to accept him into their counsels and for a time refused to allow him to speak at their meetings. 'Is it not curious?' he wrote to

34

Hannah. 'The Planters have abused me all my parliamentary life and now the Abolitionists hate me with more than West Indian hatred.' Attempts to heal the rift were unavailing. 'I bless God,' he wrote to Sturge when the final outcome was announced, 'that He who always raised up Agents, such as the crisis required, sent you to the West Indies.' No reply was received and Buxton was pointedly not invited to the grand meeting which Sturge organized in Birmingham to celebrate the triumph of the campaign.

Nor did relations improve subsequently. To Sturge any project which depended on physical force for its accomplishment was anathema. Immediately upon learning of the Government's intention to send an expedition to the Niger he wrote enquiring as to where Buxton himself stood on this question. Buxton replied that he was afraid his views had been misinterpreted. His aim was to substitute a peaceful policy for one which had hitherto relied exclusively on naval force. Responding to a similar query from Josiah Forster, Sturge's principal lieutenant and a Quaker whose views were, if anything, even more rigid than Sturge's own, he affirmed 'with all faithful plainness' that his 'real intention' was to 'rely upon none other than peaceful methods'. The important thing, he assured them both, was that they should now set aside their differences and, acting in concert, bring about the deliverance of Africa.

These overtures were rejected. Sturge, it now transpired, had his own notions about what should be done. To abolish the slave trade in the way Buxton was proposing was not only immoral but, in his view, quite impractical. The only hope was to get rid of slavery itself. To do this the British antislavery movement would have to be remobilized in order to finance and sponsor similar movements, first in the United States and France, then in the slave-importing nations. In the case of the first two there were already indications that this was happening. But British advice and support would be needed. It was to the civilized nations of the world that they should now turn their attention, not to Africa where appeals to principle and morality, the only weapons abolitionists could conscientiously employ, would have no conceivable effect.[29]

Buxton was appalled. There were now three antislavery policies on offer: Palmerston's, his own and Sturge's. While it was perfectly possible for supporters of the first two to work together, or at all events coexist amicably, the chances of reaching an accommodation with the Sturgeites became ever more remote. Sturge, he noted, 'so out-Quakers the Quakers in his doctrines about force' that there was no chance of his swaying any really influential body of opinion in the country and none at all of his influencing the Government. His scheme, in any case, was a wild one. It was also, because of his obsession with first principles, patently inconsistent. While refusing to have any dealings with slave-holders he hoped to win them over by means of persuasion and moral force. He was an opportunist and a manipulator. His real object was to take over the whole antislavery movement. Buxton found it all so aggravating that he had great difficulty sleeping.

One immediate practical difficulty was that as long as Buxton's plans remained secret there was little chance of forestalling Sturge's. The British and Foreign Anti-Slavery Society held its inaugural meeting in Exeter Hall on 17 April 1839. It was attended by several hundred delegates from all over the country. There were at that time still some thirty provincial antislavery societies in existence, all of which had been involved in the recent struggles over apprenticeship. Most now agreed to become auxiliaries of Sturge's new body. Aware of the Sturgeites' hostility Buxton himself declined to attend the meeting. Lushington did, however, and succeeded in toning down a resolution renouncing all forms of physical force, which would have obliged those present to take a public stand against not only the Government's slave trade policies but Buxton's too. 'I knew,' wrote Buxton, 'you would talk so sweetly and craftily to win over their Quakerish hearts.' If abolitionists could not work together there was at least some hope that they would not air their disagreements in public.

Fortunately for Buxton, ministers remained largely unaware of these divisions. Sturge might command the battalions of Quakers, Methodists, Baptists and other religious dissenters in the country at large but, so far as ministers were concerned, Buxton's was the authoritative voice of the humanitarian movement. They were also, that April, more aware than ever of their need for the humanitarians' support. With apprenticeship gone, the Jamaican Assembly had decided that the time had come to invoke its legitimate right to self-rule by ignoring further instructions from London. The Government, concerned about the treatment of the ex-slaves, responded by introducing a bill to suspend the Jamaican constitution. Faced with an improbable alliance of Tories and radicals, both of whom, although for different reasons, deplored the Government's high-handedness, ministers appealed to Buxton. 'If ever there were an issue which the Anti-Slavery party ought to move and act on,' wrote Spring Rice, '. . . the present is one, and *not a moment is to be lost.*' But, unlike Sturge, Buxton had no batallions to mobilize. The bill was carried, although by so small a majority that Melbourne decided to resign. 'Well,' wrote Andrew to Priscilla, 'they have perished in a noble cause fighting for the poor Niggers.'[30]

Then, almost immediately, they were back, the Queen having refused Peel's condition for forming a Cabinet that she dismiss her Whig Ladies of the Bedchamber. Their position, nevertheless, was as precarious as ever. Buxton was relieved at the outcome. Although he had taken care to cultivate Tory support he was far from confident that he could rely on their full backing. Palmerston had offered £50 000 to Spain for Fernando Po and was awaiting a reply. Normanby was as genial as ever, but when practical arrangements were mentioned he seemed curiously uncommunicative. This confirmed Buxton's suspicion that his heart was not really in the undertaking in the way that Glenelg's had been. Nevertheless, it was still assumed that personnel would be selected in the late summer and that the expedition would depart before the end of 1839.

The Patrons of Africa meanwhile expanded its membership. It also acquired offices and a salaried staff consisting of the Reverend John Trew and Robert Stokes, both veterans of earlier campaigns. At meetings of the Committee Buxton did his best to satisfy his colleagues that beyond the coastal belt, admittedly a pestilential area, Africa was both healthy and fertile. The information on both points, it transpired, was too fragmentary and inconclusive to allow firm conclusions to be drawn. Their main concern, however, was to organize the non-governmental side of the venture. Because their aims were twofold, to spread civilization and promote commerce, they agreed that a single organization would not suffice. They would therefore create two bodies. One would be a benevolent society, similar to the now defunct African Institution, with the object of encouraging missionary activity, promoting education, teaching agricultural methods and raising funds in Britain for these purposes. The other would be a trading company to exploit the commercial opportunities which would be opened up. This would require an initial injection of capital, some of which might come from the Government. As Tories, Gladstone and Evans were dubious about this. But even if the Government would not agree to subsidize a private commercial undertaking in that way, the chances were that the necessary funds could be raised in the City. Certainly, once the practicability of African development had been established, merchants would be eager to participate.

Buxton's book was meanwhile attracting attention. Brougham was enthusiastic. Letters arrived expressing support for any plans he might have for expunging such horrors. The Manchester Chamber of Commerce, it was reported, would support any scheme to free them from their almost total dependence on American cotton. Correspondents in the West Indies assured Buxton that he would find no difficulty in raising recruits from the missions there who would be willing to participate in his venture. Everything seemed to be going to plan. The one disquieting factor was the almost total silence of Normanby.

At the Colonial Office, James Stephen and Henry Labouchere, the Parliamentary Under-Secretary, were well aware of Buxton's growing impatience. Since the early spring one of their tasks had been to read and annotate his letters. These, some of them of formidable length and all expressing great urgency, were a characteristic mix of the practical and the visionary. Stephen, although a son of Clapham, was nevertheless a shrewd civil servant and punctilious administrator well able to distinguish between the two. His acerbic notations are much in evidence in the Colonial Office files. Such passages as 'I *have the opinion* that *we shall find* that *there exists...*' elicited heavy underlining and marginal queries. So too did '*call forth and elevate the native mind*' and '*her fertile* soil'. A reference to the Sheik of Bornou attracted the comment '700 miles in the interior!', and the statement 'I entirely disclaim any dispositions to erect a new empire in Africa' much marginal inking and the comment 'This proposal is not so very different in its likely consequences as Mr B supposes.' Notably absent from the files are any observations by Normanby or recommendations for action.[31]

There was consternation, therefore, when a letter arrived on 25 July announcing that Buxton and a delegation of the Patrons of Africa intended to call at the Colonial Office the following Monday to discuss with the Colonial Secretary the progress that had been made to date. More alarming still was the list of specific queries. What was the name of the vessel selected, its draught, tonnage and horse power? Who was its commander and what were his instructions? Were his instructions based on the drafts Buxton had submitted? What decisions had been reached as to the acquisition of sovereignty over the territories to be settled?[32] As Stephen duly noted in a memorandum to Normanby, there *was* no vessel. The Treasury had not even been asked to authorize the expenditure necessary to acquire one. There were certainly no captains, crews, or, so far as he knew, men available. Instructions and sovereignty were Foreign Office matters and Buxton's drafts had been passed on to the Chief Clerk there, James Bandinel, who, lacking ministerial authorization and objecting to receiving orders from Buxton, had resolved simply to sit on them. In fact, Stephen reported, nothing whatever had been done.

Normanby had no alternative but to brazen it out. What he was not prepared for was the composition of the delegation. Informed that thirty gentlemen had arrived he asked first to see Buxton alone. There had been a misunderstanding. He had not seen Buxton's letter. It must have gone to Labouchere who was out of town. At this point Labouchere appeared. Yes, there *had* been a letter but no one seemed to know what had become of it. Finally chairs were found for the delegates – consisting of the Bishop of London, the Earl of Euston, W.E. Gladstone, T.B. Macaulay and some two dozen others, mostly MPs – who were seated in a semi-circle around the minister's desk. At first Normanby claimed there was a vessel, then admitted that there was not. The Government was desperately short of funds because the plans for the new penny postage were proving much more expensive than anyone had anticipated. He had not been properly briefed because ministers were, frankly, run off their feet. These were hectic times. Finally, he agreed to set a date for the following week, when he would see them again and answer all of their questions.[33]

Recounting these events for the benefit of her aunts, Priscilla reported that all agreed that 'the Government have behaved abominably'. Had it been a domestic matter they would have reached a decision in three months; had the directors of the brewery been called on to consider a new undertaking everything would have been resolved in a morning. Buxton was not surprised. Twenty years in Parliament had taught him a great deal about ministers and their ways.

The second meeting was very different from the first. Normanby was now positively servile, yielding submissively to every demand. He was, as Buxton later described it, 'a sheep in the hands of the shearers'. An expedition consisting of a frigate, two or three iron paddle steamers, and commanded by a naval officer would leave before the end of the year. Responsibility for establishing settlements would be in the hands of a group of commissioners who would accompany the expedition. The precise details would need to be worked out jointly with the Admiralty with whom Buxton and his colleagues should begin discussions immediately. All the Colonial Office now required was a list of specific requirements so that they could press ahead with the necessary preparations.[34]

Armed with these concessions, Buxton hastened to the Admiralty. The Earl of Minto, except for some ritual expressions of alarm at the expense involved and protestations about the Government's near-bankruptcy over Rowland Hill's penny postage, seemed reconciled to the notion that the scheme would now go ahead. He suggested that Buxton get in touch with Sir Edward Parry, Comptroller of the Steam Department of the Navy, himself an experienced explorer, who would draw up the necessary estimates. With the assurance that the Government was now behind him, Buxton could now turn his attention to the practical arrangements.

CHAPTER THREE
Preparations and Controversies

In spite of Normanby's dilatoriness the first seven months of 1839 had not been entirely wasted. They had allowed Buxton and his colleagues on the Patrons of Africa Committee to form a much clearer idea of what they wanted.[1] Inevitably this turned out to be rather more than ministers had been led to expect. Three iron paddle steamers were now deemed essential; also an accompanying frigate to carry supplies out from England. The steamers would need to be of shallow draught, suitable for river navigation. In addition, ample stocks of coal would have to be sent ahead and deposited at points along the route and at Fernando Po.

The object of the expedition would be to explore the Niger, make treaties with the local chiefs, acquire land and establish a model farm. It would be led by a senior naval officer who would also act as Chief Commissioner. He would be advised and assisted, particularly in his dealings with the local rulers, by at least three other commissioners, one of whom would be a civilian with experience of Africa. Collectively they would be responsible for advising the Admiralty and Colonial Office on the outfitting of the expedition and the selection of personnel.

For the voyage out the vessels would be fully manned by British crews. Because of the well-known effect of the African climate on Europeans it was proposed that preference be given to black seamen of whom a good number were to be found in British ports. For the same reason there would need to be a larger than normal complement of ship's surgeons. So far as providing for the health of the expedition was concerned no expense should be spared. In addition to the naval personnel on the expedition there would be a number of scientists, missionaries and agriculturalists recruited and paid for by Buxton and his colleagues. More black seamen, together with workers for the model farm, would be taken on board in Sierra Leone and Liberia on the way out; also interpreters fluent in the various West African languages. The whole expedition should be outfitted and ready to sail by late 1839 so as to arrive at the Niger early in the dry season when, it was presumed, the climate would be healthier than after the rains began in June.

Commander William Allen.

That this was a vain hope soon became evident. Nevertheless, preparations were now going ahead. Much time was spent discussing who should lead the expedition. Among the names canvassed were those of Captain Robert FitzRoy, newly returned from his round-the-world voyage with Darwin in the *Beagle*, and Captain Alexander Vidal, who had just completed a geographical survey of the West African coast on behalf of the Admiralty. However, on 17 August, Parry informed Buxton that he had written to Captain Henry Dundas Trotter asking him if he would be prepared to command the force. Trotter's wife had been ill and they had been at Portsmouth on the point of sailing to Malta for a period of

41

recuperation when the letter arrived. Trotter immediately took the coach to London and, after discussions with Parry and reading Buxton's book, he agreed to accept the offer. It proved an excellent choice. A young man – he was only 37 – with aristocratic connections, he had risen rapidly through the ranks, serving at various times in the East Indies, the Persian Gulf and the Caribbean. More important was the fact that he had served for four years with the African Squadron as commander of HMS *Curlew*. He was, Parry assured Buxton, 'in every sense as applicable to our present purpose . . . *a very fine fellow indeed*'.[2]

No time was lost in choosing the other commissioners. As second-in-command Commander William Allen, not to be confused with the Quaker philanthropist of the same name, was ten years older than Trotter and his junior in rank. He was, nevertheless, an obvious choice as the only naval officer with experience of Niger navigation, having served as Admiralty observer on an earlier mercantile expedition which had ascended as far as Raba. It was on his meticulously accurate charts, compiled on that previous occasion, that the expedition was to rely throughout its time on the river. The third naval commissioner was Commander Bird Allen, already known to Buxton through family connections. He was still in his early thirties and, like the others, had served in West Africa. As civilian commissioner, William Cook was thought to be well qualified, both on account of his experience as a merchant captain trading to Africa and because of the resourcefulness he had shown some years before in rescuing the passengers and crew of a burning East Indiaman in the Bay of Biscay, an episode that had made him appear something of a hero at the time.[3]

Buxton professed himself 'abundantly satisfied' and hastened to send word of these appointments to Normanby. Almost immediately, however, two events occurred which once again placed the whole enterprise in jeopardy. The first was the news that Normanby, whose six months at the Colonial Office had shown him to be even less competent than Glenelg, had been dismissed and that he and Labouchere would be replaced by a new team consisting of Lord John Russell and Robert Vernon Smith. This was a much more formidable combination. James Stephen was said to be delighted at the prospect. Buxton was less sure, but came away from his first interview with Russell much mollified by the promise of £3000 to meet the commissioners' initial expenses in finding and hiring vessels.

More alarming was the revelation that there simply were no suitable ships to be found. Trotter and William Allen had visited all the major seaports of England and Scotland only to discover that there was not a single paddle steamer, available or on the stocks, even remotely adapted to their needs. Some were too narrow to accommodate the expedition's equipment, others too highly powered, which meant that too much space was taken up by their engines; all were of too deep draught for effective navigation through the alluvial channels of the Niger Delta. The only solution, they informed Stephen, was to set about building three steamers to the agreed specifications. These would need to be iron vessels – iron being preferable to wood on account of its greater toughness and buoyancy – displacing not more than three to five feet of water. The total cost, Trotter estimated, would be about £26000.[4]

This news was not well received at the Colonial Office. It would mean, Stephen reported, that even if the money were forthcoming the expedition could not leave for at least a year.[5] Buxton assumed he would have to bring pressure to bear by appealing to public opinion.[6] The Admiralty, however, was supportive. Steam was the coming thing. The addition of three steam vessels to its establishment would not come amiss and, whatever the outcome of the expedition, would provide a useful force with which to pursue the slave traders, especially on inland waters. Nevertheless, its own estimates proved to be a good deal higher than Trotter's, amounting to £35000 for the vessels, an annual charge of £10546 for wages and victuals, and a grant of £4000 to cover the expenses of the commissioners, surgeons and chaplain. The Government would therefore need to agree to an initial outlay of £50000 in the full knowledge that it would be called on to provide further sums later.[7]

Considering that the Colonial Office had just refused to increase its annual grant for the support of its West African forts from £3500 to £4000, and had even thought of eliminating it entirely, agreeing to such an outlay would plainly represent a complete change of policy.[8] Russell consulted Minto at the Admiralty who reported that he had spoken to Melbourne and Palmerston who were persuaded that, since the Government had given its word, the expedition should go ahead.[9] To Buxton he suggested that rather than purchase the vessels the Government should merely hire them. This, it turned out, was quite impractical. Finally, Russell agreed to include the Admiralty figures in the Government's Estimates for 1840.[10] This, however, would mean waiting until Parliament reassembled in February. The Treasury, for its part, declined to give any financial guarantee against the possibility that Parliament would refuse the Government's request. Nevertheless, Russell was reassuring. In despair at the prospect of yet further delays Buxton turned to his colleagues in the Patrons of Africa Committee who undertook to authorize William Laird and Son of Birkenhead, a firm specializing in the construction of iron steamers, to begin work on the three vessels on the understanding that Samuel Gurney and Stephen Lushington would pay him 12 per cent of the overall cost should Parliament prove recalcitrant.[11]

Satisfied that everything was now progressing as rapidly as could be expected Buxton prepared to join his family in Rome where his wife had gone in search of better health. Russell wrote wishing him well and warning against 'the very treacherous climate, especially if you sport in the marshes late in the evening'. It was agreed that Lushington could handle political matters during his absence. *The Remedy*, on which Buxton had worked throughout the autumn, was now virtually complete. Sir George Stephen, James Stephen's younger brother and an old antislavery colleague of Buxton's, recently knighted for his services to the cause, had agreed to see it through the press. As the author of *Adventures of a Gentleman in Search of a Horse* and other popular works he was used to dealing with printers. All that was now needed was the Government's permission to publish. As always the problem was Fernando Po. In reponse to the British offer of £50 000 Spain had demanded £2 000 000. Nevertheless, Palmerston, on whom Buxton called en route to Dover, remained convinced that the Spanish would come round. If necessary Britain would increase her offer. On Buxton's urging that she do so, Palmerston 'with a knowing look whispered "the ship timber alone is worth four times the money" '.[12] Now that the Government was intending to lay its plans before Parliament there seemed no good reason for maintaining confidentiality.

The Remedy finally appeared, with the Government's formal consent, on 12 March 1840.[13] It would have appeared earlier had not Buxton continued to have second thoughts. Even in Rome his mind never rested. Lushington, George Stephen and the Cottage Ladies were continually bombarded with letters of advice and queries about developments. More than once he declared himself on the point of returning to England. Nevertheless, he professed himself much reassured by a copy of Russell's submission to the Treasury.[14] If ministers still harboured doubts about the scheme there was no sign of them in the document Russell laid before Parliament on 6 February. The vast scale of the slave trade, Britain's commitment to abolishing it, the ineffectualness of a policy based purely on the use of naval power, the need to encourage legitimate commerce were all set out much as Buxton had described them. 'I do not recollect,' Buxton reported, 'that I ever read a paper that gave me more thorough satisfaction. . . . I think it is a superb epitome of my book. Besides all its other merits, it is a vast relief to me personally. The project is no longer mine; the Government have now taken the task upon themselves.'

This was something of which the officials concerned were only too well aware. Trotter's time was now divided between Birkenhead where the ships were being built and the Commissioner's headquarters at 12 Old Quebec Street, near Marble Arch. Inevitably it turned out that there were many items that had been overlooked in the original estimates. Pay and provisions would need to be found for the seamen and interpreters taken on in Africa; there would have to be longboats, canoes for exploring narrow creeks, stores for the gunners and carpenters, gifts for African rulers. Within weeks of Russell's submitting his proposals to Parliament the Colonial Office was presented with lists of new requirements including the provision for each of the steamers of elaborate ventilating systems.[15] 'You will see,' Stephen wrote to Vernon Smith, 'how the estimate for this service is gradually expanding. Here are two new demands amounting to within a small fraction of £24 000. I do not believe the full charge will ultimately fall far short of £100 000. Such a calculation supposes nothing more than the accumulated inaccuracies of arithmetic and foresight and the average amount of casualties [sic] in such an undertaking.'[16] Smith agreed that the lists were worrying and instructed Stephen to consult Parry at the Admiralty and Bandinel at the Foreign Office. After further discussions a revised estimate of £82 000 was proposed on the basis of which the Treasury would be asked for an initial grant of £62 000.[17]

One issue on which all parties agreed was the need to preserve the health of the expedition. Melbourne's observation that of those who went to Africa as many died as survived erred, at least in the case of those who spent any length of time there, on the side of optimism. The African Squadron lost some 6 per cent of its officers and men annually. They, however, spent their time mostly at sea. Of the 1612 civilian and military personnel sent out to Sierra Leone between 1821 and 1826, 926 died, constituting an overall mortality rate of 56.5 per cent. Among European other ranks sent out there between 1819 and 1836 the *annual* average mortality rate was 48.3 per cent. Similar figures were recorded by the Church Missionary Society. Those who penetrated further into the interior fared even worse. There were no European survivors from Mungo Park's ambitious second expedition of 1805, 87 per cent dying on the overland trek from the Gambia to the Niger, the remainder, including Park himself, in a river ambush near Boussa. Other early explorers met similar fates. Gordon Laing was strangled; Daniel Houghton and Frederic Hornemann simply disappeared; Alexander Anderson, Hugh Clapperton and dozens of others who set out succumbed to the fever and dysentery which to varying degrees affected every expedition that went to Africa. Moreover, these explorers, as their exploits proved, were men of fanatical determination and robust physique, not at all the dissolute ruffians pictured by Buxton whose poor state of health made them succumb at the first touch of river fever. Set against this, however, was the fact that their journeys were undertaken largely on foot and the possibility that the sheer physical exertion involved weakened their constitutions. It did not inevitably follow that fit crews on well-equipped

45

modern vessels would be exposed to the same hazards. All the same, the precedents were far from reassuring.[18]

One notable feature of all these early enterprises was that, although the existence of the Niger had been known since ancient times and was mentioned by both Herodotus and Ptolomy, its lower reaches and where it flowed into the sea, if indeed it did, had until very recently remained a mystery. Unlike the Nile, which was a river without a source, the Niger was a source without a mouth. Some supposed it actually *was* the source of the Nile, others that it flowed into Lake Chad and simply evaporated. Not until 1831, when Richard and John Lander, following the route taken earlier by Mungo Park, made their way overland to Boussa and then managed to float downstream to the sea, was it finally established that the hundreds of small creeks that discharged their waters into the Gulf of Guinea, long familiar to slave traders and palm oil merchants, were in fact the estuary of the great river. Immediately upon the Landers' return a group of enterprising northern merchants, led by Macgregor Laird and Thomas Stirling, determined to explore the commercial opportunities of their discovery. Laird himself, together with Richard Lander, and with William Allen as official naval observer, duly departed in two paddle steamers, specially constructed for the purpose. One of these, the *Alburkah*, was a miniature version of those now being constructed for the Government by Macgregor's brother John. Between October 1832 and July 1834 they succeeded in ascending the Niger as far as Rabba and its Benue tributary to Fundah. Their experiences, as described by Laird and the junior surgeon of the expedition, R.A.M. Oldfield, *Narrative of an Expedition into the Interior of Africa by the River Niger* (1837), were horrific. Of the 39 Europeans who set out 30 died, mostly from fever, but in a few instances from dysentery and in Richard Lander's case from a bullet wound received in a river ambush. In addition, some dozen of their African companions perished mysteriously, probably from poison administered by the Chief of Fundah. Nor did a Rhode Island expedition, which Laird met on the river, fare any better, losing 11 of its 16 members in a mere six weeks. As commercial ventures both expeditions were total failures.[19]

Significantly, Buxton's books contained no mention of these matters although he did draw heavily on the Laird–Oldfield account for geographical information. Yet here, as elsewhere, his penchant for wishful thinking is much in evidence. Laird himself, writing for the *Westminster Review*, drew attention to it by quoting Swift's lines:

> All philosophers who find
> Some favourite system to their mind
> In every point to make it fit
> Will force all nature to submit.

A striking example was the folding map, drafted by MacQueen in Buxton's instructions, which accompanied the joint edition of *The African Slave Trade and Its Remedy*. It was common knowledge that fevers were associated with swamps and night air, as Russell's letter warning Buxton about the perils of the Pontine marshes had indicated. High altitudes and dry climates, by constrast, were assumed to be healthy. In the Laird–Oldfield account, and William Allen's accompanying sketches, the Niger and the Benue were shown to meet at a point flanked by low bluffs beyond which lay a flat savannah country. But on the Buxton–MacQueen map of 1840 the outstanding features of the region, and indeed of the whole of Central Africa, were the towering Kong Mountains, part of a vast range extending all the way from modern Senegal to Uganda.[20]

To those of cooler judgement and less polemical intent it was plain that to avoid a repetition of the 1832–4 fiasco exceptional measures would be required. The problem was that while everyone knew that fevers were associated with marshes, stagnant water and rotting vegetation, and were especially likely to be contracted in the evening or at night, no one knew their precise cause, although the natural assumption was that it must be some sort of noxious exhalation or miasma that entered the body through the lungs. Low-lying evening mists of the kind that rose from lakes and marshes were thought to be especially sinister. Laird had described the lower reaches of the Niger as 'one extensive swamp, covered with mangrove, cabbage and palm trees [from which] the fen-damp rose in the mornings, cold and clammy to the skin, in appearance like the smoke from a damp wood fire'. Unlike poison gasses, however, these miasmas did not attack the system immediately but only after an interval of weeks. One possibility was that, like yeast in the process of fermentation, minute quantities of noxious substance taken into the lungs would gradually propagate themselves and cause illness. It was all very baffling, the more so because, given the current state of medical knowledge, there was no sure way of distinguishing one type of fever from another. For that reason malaria was regarded not as a specific disease but, as the name implies (malaria is simply a contraction of *mala aria* meaning 'bad air'), a set of conditions conducive to producing illness. It was, according to one of the surgeons who accompanied the expedition, 'a certain peculiarity of the atmosphere – call it miasm, malaria, or any other name – which, though inappreciable to chemical agency, operates most powerfully in Europeans'.[21] Many assumed that all fevers were of a common origin. In retrospect it is usually possible, on the basis of contemporary accounts, to distinguish malaria – variously described as African, river, local, marsh, remittant, intermittent or continual fever – from the other principal type of fever met with in tropical countries, namely yellow fever – commonly known as malignant-marsh or bilious fever, or, because of its tendency to produce abdominal bleeding, simply as the black vomit. But as the symptoms of both diseases were quite various and their causes equally mysterious, contemporaries themselves had no way of knowing whether they were dealing with one disease or many.[22]

This was regrettable for it meant that the one proven defence against malaria was seldom used effectively. Cinchona bark, from which two French chemists had recently managed to extract the essential ingredient, quinine, had long been known to offer protection against some fevers. The first recorded use of it was in 1639 when the wife of the Governor of Peru, the Countess of Chinchon, is said to have been cured of an attack of sickness by its administration. She must have been lucky because it is of only limited usefulness once the disease has manifested itself. In the initial stages of infection, however, it does very effectively kill malarial parasites in the bloodstream. It had continued to be employed, often with beneficial results, up to the 1830s. Nevertheless, doctors remained sceptical. In part, this was because of their uncertainty over whether it should be used as a prophylactic or a cure and their inability to control the strength of dosages on account of the varying quality of the bark obtained. But the main difficulty was their natural tendency to classify fevers in terms of their symptoms and associated factors – marshes, rivers, hot climates – rather than, as we now would, in terms of the actual viruses and parasites which induced them.

That fevers were caused by viruses and parasites and that, in the case of both malaria and yellow fever, the vectors were mosquitoes, would not be known for another sixty years.[23] Nor, given the prevailing miasmatic assumptions of medical men, was there any possibility of coming to terms with the very different characteristics of the two diseases. Yellow fever manifests itself in the form of epidemics. Those who contract it will either die in a matter of days or survive, in which case they will enjoy lifelong immunity. They will not, once the fever has subsided, act as carriers. Thus yellow fever will sweep through a population in a short time and disappear until a sufficiently large non-immune population has built up for another outbreak to occur. Malaria, on the other hand, was, and remains, endemic in Africa and many other tropical regions, giving rise to a high infant mortality rate. Those who survive the initial attack will, providing they are frequently reinfected, enjoy a measure of immunity and so suffer only minor inconvenience from subsequent bouts which may recur from time to time. But, regardless of whether or not they are at the time suffering from the ill effects of the disease, they will continue to act as carriers. The African population thus constituted a reservoir of disease against which, as we now know, quinine offered the only effective form of protection then available. Quinine, however, provides no protection whatever against yellow fever. The result was that its advocates in the eighteenth and early nineteenth centuries found their theories under constant attack as news arrived of yellow fever epidemics sweeping through one settlement after another.

Unless they were unlucky, however, and chanced to arrive during such an outbreak the main hazard encountered by new arrivals in Africa, white or black, was malaria. Besides quinine, which might or might not be in favour at the time, there were various traditional prescriptions for preserving good health. On the theory that the sun extracted heat from the stomach, rum, brandy, red pepper and wearing woollen garments next to the skin were frequently advocated. Naval personnel were instructed to change out of wet clothes immediately, not to bivouac on shore overnight, or, if they were obliged to do so, to light fires. Old coasters usually had their own prescriptions, often quite specific as to the types and amounts of liquor that needed to be consumed, which they were happy to pass on to the uninitiated.[24]

Upon the Government's announcement that it intended to dispatch steamers to the Niger, letters began arriving at the Colonial Office offering advice on such matters. Most of the precautions recommended were of a familiar kind but one, from a correspondent in Limerick, contained the novel suggestion that crews be equipped with silk respirators. It was, the author noted, 'a fact ascertained by long experience' that in humid conditions 'the functions of the air cells in the lungs becomes deranged – the temperature of the skin reduced and malignant disease generated'. By filtering out such 'infectious matters' the health of the expedition would be protected.[25] This was, in fact, very much in line with current thinking, although the plan the Admiralty had in mind was altogether more elaborate and ambitious.

Early in 1839, worried about the corrosion affecting the copper sheathing of ship's bottoms in tropical climates, the Admiralty had instructed commanders on the African stations to collect samples of river water. These were then sent to Professor John Daniell of King's College, London, for analysis. Daniell was acknowledged to be the world's leading expert on meteorology and well known as the inventor of the Daniell cell and the Daniell hygrometer, the latter being an instrument already in general use by the navy for measuring the amount of moisture in the air. According to Daniell's report, submitted to the Admiralty in April 1840, the samples contained a variety of elements including chlorine, sulphuric acid, lime, magnesium and sodium. But by far the most notable ingredient in every case was the unusual amount of sulphide gas emitted when the corks of the bottles were removed. So impressed was Professor Daniell by this discovery that he advanced the theory that this was more likely than not the source of the fevers known to be associated with these parts. Hydrogen sulphide is, of course, familiar to most people as the rotten egg smell produced by decaying vegetable or animal matter. The notion that sickness and disease were associated with noxious smells, particularly those caused by putrescence, was already firmly embedded in the Victorian mind. All the samples had been taken from near the estuaries of rivers. By contrast, water collected by William Allen from the upper reaches of the Niger during the 1832–4 expedition and analysed by Professor Michael Faraday had been found to be perfectly pure. Modern science, it seemed, was merely confirming what had all along been suspected, namely that pestilential vapours were the product of decaying vegetation and that the essential ingredient was that most evil-smelling of all chemical compounds, hydrogen sulphide.

That hydrogen sulphide was the sole cause of fever seemed improbable, as it happened, ironically, to be one of the principal ingredients in the waters of Harrogate and other British health spas and was in any case a stench familiar to anyone living in the vicinity of iron-smelting works. Nevertheless, the possibility remained that, acting in conjunction with other elements in the atmosphere, it would induce sickness. Professor Daniell had few doubts that this would prove to be the case. There was also, he discovered, much supporting evidence to be found in the scientific literature. Signor Gaetano Giorgini, a leading Italian authority on fevers, had noted that in the marshes around Genoa 'the mixture of fresh and salt water became corrupt, and spread infection over the neighbourhood of the most destructive kind'. Since the draining of the marshes the health of the population had improved immeasurably. For his own part, Daniell reported to the President of the Royal Geographical Society, 'The evidence of the worst cases of malaria being connected with the decomposition of the sulphates in sea water increases upon me every day.' Further experiments in the laboratory strengthened this conviction. Vegetable matter was placed in two jars; one he filled up with pure river water, the other with a solution of sodium sulphate. Whereas the former remained sweet-smelling, the latter, when the lid was removed, produced 'an insupportable sickening odour' and instantly turned lead acetate paper black. The likelihood was, therefore, that malaria was essentially a coastal phenomenon caused by the action of salt water on decaying vegetation. If he and Signor Giorgini were correct in their deductions, the solution was 'obvious and easy'. All the expedition had to do was 'Steam through the salt waters as fast as possible, and while obliged to be on them make a plentiful use of the chlorine fumigation, which instantly decomposes the sulphuretted hydrogen.'[26]

But, supposing their theory correct, protecting crews from the effects of the air they breathed would hardly be easy. The Niger Delta was one vast swamp, larger than Ireland, interlaced by muddy tidal creeks through which the vessels would necessarily have to proceed with extreme cau-

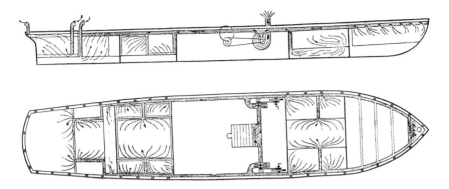

Diagram of David Boswell Reid's air purification system.

tion. During the day at least men would have to work on deck. The best that could be hoped for was to provide a purified atmosphere below decks. Even this would require apparatus of a kind with which no ship in the world had hitherto been equipped.

To solve this problem the Admiralty turned to Dr David Boswell Reid, an Edinburgh chemist who had recently been responsible for installing a ventilation system in the new Parliament buildings in Westminster to protect members from the then prevailing London smog. He was later to achieve fame as head of the United States Sanitary Commission during the Civil War.[27] His solution was to provide each of the three steamers with fanners which could be driven either by the engines when the ships were in motion or by the action of the river currents on the paddles when they were moored. Reid's problems were complicated by the fact that, to avoid the danger of sinking should they be holed, each of the vessels had been divided into five watertight compartments by means of iron bulkheads. To overcome this difficulty he connected the fans to a network of zinc-coated pipes running along the gunwales and extending down into the compartments. In this way it would be possible to draw out stagnant air and expel it through the ship's funnels.

Much more important for protecting the health of the ships' crews, however, was the ability to pump unpolluted atmosphere into the vessels. This could easily be done simply by turning the cocks attached to the pipes and reversing the flow of air. When operating in this way air could be drawn in by means of canvas sleeves attached to a windsail 50 feet above deck level. This could then be passed through an iron tank containing trays of chloride of lime and calcium chloride to remove the

51

hydrogen sulphide and moisture and directed at will to any part of the ship. It did not matter that the decks and hatches were not airtight since the pressure of the air pumped in would prevent the outside atmosphere from penetrating. The contents of the trays in the iron tank or 'purifi-cator' would, of course, need to be changed at intervals. As an added precaution screens or filters could be used to trap any noxious particles which might be suspended in the atmosphere.

As ingenious examples of marine engineering Reid's ventilation sys-tems attracted much attention. Although they added significantly to the expense of the expedition their installation was thought to be well justified. He himself spent much time demonstrating their effectiveness to interested visitors, showing how, by means of turning the various controls, 'medicated' air could be directed to one or another part of the vessel. There was no doubt that he had done what he had been requested to do. Whether it would preserve the health of the expedition remained to be seen. On this point his statements were less sanguine than Daniell's. Nevertheless, as he told John Trew, Secretary of the African Civilization Society, it was all that stood between success and 'what in ordinary circumstances would be a mortality of 80 per cent'.[28]

In spite of his often cavalier statements, the element of risk involved had not entirely escaped Buxton's attention. He had, from the beginning, corresponded at length about his plans with John Jeremie, a protégé who some years earlier had won Buxton's approval by siding with the Mauritian freedmen against their former masters and who was now serv-ing as a judge in Ceylon. Learning that Jeremie had been disappointed at not being appointed Chief Justice there, Buxton suggested that he return to England where, if all went according to plan, he might be appointed 'Governor General of Africa'. Buxton, however, did not want him joining the expedition. 'I know your ardour would prompt you to offer your services, and you might perhaps perish among the mangroves. I am well aware that you are quite prepared for this, but I am not. . . . I want you for higher and more important services respecting Africa.' In the event Jeremie did return to England. Buxton took him to see Russell who agreed to appoint him Governor of Sierra Leone where he perished almost immediately in very much the manner Buxton had feared.[29] With his own 20-year-old nephew, William Edward Forster, the future Liberal statesman and author of the 1870 Education Act, Buxton was firmer. 'Never fear about my health,' Forster had written. 'I have faith the climate would not kill me. (Bye-the-bye "I have a nephew there", would not be a bad *argumentum ad hominem* for thee to use on behalf of the climate).' Buxton, nevertheless, was adamant. 'I have a decided and inflexible opinion that you must not go to Africa. In the first place I really could not bear the anxiety I should have to endure on your account, and the injury I should have been the means of doing your parents. Secondly, I firmly believe you would be of more use to the cause here. . . . In short, to the Niger you go not with my consent.'[30] On similar ground he refused an offer from John Scoble to act as chaplain to the expedition. *Argumenta ad hominem*, it seemed, were not required.

Buxton's own health was meanwhile causing alarm. In Italy his leg swelled up and he found difficulty in breathing. On his return to England in May 1840 his doctors and family urged him to rest. 'I have behaved capitally,' he wrote to Hannah. 'I have told them I cannot work.' But it quickly transpired that there were pressing issues to be settled and soon he was working harder than ever.

The reservations expressed by the Government when they agreed to his scheme were turning out to be more important than he had at first supposed. One issue that caused him particular concern was the question of sovereignty. From the first he had insisted that all settlements should be on territory formally acquired by the British Crown. They should also be large enough in extent for the settlers to feel secure from marauding tribes and the incursions of slave traders. In his *Letter to Lord Melbourne* he had particularly warned against 'savage banditti, instigated by some miscreant from Europe, whose vessel waits upon the shore for a human cargo'; also against runaway sailors who, as in New Zealand, might roam as armed bands through the countryside attacking native villages. Lord Landsdowne was uneasy about the political implications of acquiring territory in sovereignty. To Buxton, however, it appeared not only essential but eminently reasonable that settlers in Africa should be provided with the same kind of protection that people took for granted in Europe. How else would missionaries and traders be persuaded to go?[31]

Glenelg and Normanby had characteristically failed to face up to this issue, but once it became clear that the expedition was going ahead and instructions would need to be drafted, officials in both the Colonial Office and the Foreign Office had taken note of the fact that some decision on the point would eventually have to be made. In September 1839, before the discovery that no vessels were available and when it was still supposed that the expedition would be sailing that November, Stephen sent a long memorandum to Russell outlining the difficulties. Long experience of dealing with Sierra Leone and Cape Colony had made them thoroughly familiar. They were the same problems that arose whenever British settlements in Africa were discussed. 'If we could acquire dominion over the whole of that continent,' he had recently minuted in a mood of exasperation, 'it would be but a worthless posses- sion.' Yet here was Buxton urging the British Government to establish formal agreements to ensure that settlers were subject to British laws rather than the savage customs of the region. Reasonable though this might seem, Russell should 'First, consider the immense extent of our present Colonial Empire, and the demands it makes on us for Troops, Transports, Munitions of War, Salaries, Civil Establishments and the like. Then consider the state of our Revenue and the apparent impossibility of increasing it.' Could Britain really enter into such an open-ended financial commitment?[32]

It was true that the sponsors of the undertaking emphasized its peaceful nature. But on closer examination it became evident 'that the Quakers, who are ready to embark on the enterprise, have a distinction very perceptible to them, however obscure it may be to others, between defending themselves by Arms and being defended by the Arms of the Government – the first being a Crime, the second an Indispensable Privilege'. Holy causes had a way of spawning holy wars. That there would be conflict could be confidently predicted on the basis of all past experience in Africa and elsewhere. Wherever sovereign settlements were situated there were problems with neighbouring sovereignties. This had certainly proved to be the case in Sierra Leone, the Gold Coast and the Cape Coast. Problems would be even more likely to occur in the case of an interior colony which could only be reached through territories over which other rulers exercised jurisdiction. Had Britain even got a right to navigate on the river? What would happen if those who currently controlled commerce disputed it by seeking to impose transit duties and other vexatious restrictions?

Sovereignty would also mean supplying the settlement with an appropriate complement of colonial officials, including a governor. Stephen did not have a high opinion of colonial governors. In this case he would

> unless he be an exception to all other English Governors, be haughty and sensitive to insult in his official character. . . . It seems to me to require no prophetic spirit, but only a very little historical knowledge, to foresee a succession of conflicts in the heart of Africa in which we shall be either Allies or Principals, with a corresponding series of demands for Military aid which, as far as I know, it would be impossible either to meet with common prudence or to refuse without disgrace.

It would, he concluded in true civil service fashion, be agreeable if the Colonial Secretary felt able to grant Buxton's request, but before he did so these were points he should consider.

With the discovery that vessels would have to be built the matter was shelved until the summer of 1840 when Buxton and Lushington returned to the attack. Their aim was not 'enlarging the limits of our Empire' but 'accomplishing an object beyond all others dear to the disinterested benevolence of this Country'. It would be intolerable to establish settlements in regions where slavery existed or 'native superstitions and bloody rites were practised'.[33] Once again Stephen's marginal exclamation marks and underlinings are in evidence, as in the passage 'acceptance of voluntary offers of sovereignty extending over *whole Kingdoms* [!!] will be found the greatest boon which we can confer on Africa...' Russell remained unpersuaded. Rather than replying to Buxton he issued a printed directive to the commissioners informing them that they were not to acquire any land in the Queen's name. He also ruled that further discussion of the question would have to await the expedition's return and a full report on likely defence requirements.[34]

Meanwhile opposition to the Government's plans was beginning to build up in the country at large. For more than two years the public had been kept in the dark as to the specific details of what was being proposed. The Tory opposition, whose support Buxton had been at pains to cultivate, had allowed Russell's request for £62 000 to go through Parliament on the nod. Even at the Exeter Hall meeting there had been scant mention of actual plans and what little there was had been lost sight of in the patriotic euphoria of the occasion. But now that the details had begun to emerge and their implications became apparent voices began to be heard which cast doubt on the wisdom, practicality and moral justification of the entire enterprise.

Among the loudest, as might be expected, were those of the Sturgeites. Since the spring of 1839 the two groups had continued to develop in parallel. The British and Foreign Anti-Slavery Society now had offices at 27 New Broad Street in the City, the African Civilization Society at 15 Parliament Street in Whitehall; both published fortnightly journals: *The British and Foreign Anti-Slavery Reporter* and *The Friend of Africa*. The growing rift between the two bodies was a source of much embarrassment and confusion. Buxton's Exeter Hall meeting had been a triumphant occasion, but it did not, as he had hoped, make 'the Friends forget all their Sturgeism and all nonsensical objection about war, armed steamers and slavery perpetuated'. Indeed, the memory of it was almost immediately eclipsed by Sturge's own World Anti-Slavery Convention which assembled in Freemasons' Hall a fortnight later. Unlike Buxton's meeting, which consisted of a single session, Sturge's went on for two weeks and covered virtually every aspect of the subject with the notable exception of the Government's forthcoming expedition to the Niger. It was, in fact, the first *international* conference of a non-governmental nature to be held and attracted large numbers of delegates from overseas including 53 from the United States. On the fifth day Buxton managed to make a brief statement only to find himself immediately embroiled in a wrangle with one of the American delegates, James G. Birney, over whether he supported the American Colonization Society. This was a

Sir Thomas Fowell Buxton at the Anti-Slavery Convention of 1840.

sore point with American abolitionists who claimed that colonization was a rival movement, the object of which was to remove· free blacks from America. Buxton replied that, while he had no objection to what colonizationists were doing in Liberia, he did not approve of what he understood to be their policies in the United States. On the ninth day, Sturge ruled out of order a speech by Dr Thomas Hodgkin, President of the Aborigines Protection Society, regretting 'the animosity which has separated the best friends of the coloured people'.[35]

The most that could be hoped for, Buxton concluded, was to avoid public recriminations. Yet even this proved difficult. Sturge denounced the Niger expedition at the Quakers' London Yearly Meeting. 'If the plan had been written by William Penn himself,' Buxton observed, 'he would find some reason for disapproving it.' There were also attacks on his personal integrity. 'You are quite right,' he replied to one Sturgeite, 'in the supposition that I am a Porter Brewer. I assure you that were I convinced on conscientious grounds that it were better for me to desist I hope that I should yield to the dictates of my conscience, but as yet I have met with no arguments sufficient to bring me to such a conclusion.'[36]

The African Civilization Society worked in close collaboration with Trotter and his group at Old Quebec Street. But in the provinces, where the Sturgeites were now firmly entrenched, they found their attempts to establish auxiliary bodies systematically frustrated. Meetings in Manchester, Liverpool and elsewhere were poorly atttended. In Buxton's native Norfolk, where Sturgeites were not to be feared, the inaugural meeting of the Norwich auxiliary was broken up by Chartists who swarmed on to the platform claiming that the workers of England were 'slaves working for idle Gentlemen' and demanding universal suffrage, an equal division of property, an end to kingcraft and priestcraft and the destruction of the workhouses. Katherine Fry, Elizabeth Fry's daughter, compared the scene to the outbreak of the French Revolution, men shouting and women screaming. What most impressed her was the uncouth appearance of the intruders, the passion registered on all their faces and the 'true *prison* countenances' of the ringleaders, all notorious troublemakers; also the way their womenfolk, led by 'three well-known Socialist sisters, the vilest of the vile', actively egged them on. Having taken over the platform they proceeded to pass their own resolutions, concluding with three times three cheers for Feargus O'Connor and three times three groans for the Bishop of Norwich and Mr Gurney, while 'Uncle Buxton and Uncle Joseph sat in the centre, looking so patient and so sad.' The ladies in the party returned to Earlham much shaken, where they were later joined for dinner by their menfolk, including the Bishop who, it was reported, had been mobbed on his way from the hall.[37]

So far as the Sturgeites were concerned, Sir George Stephen reported, people were baffled 'deciding which of us is the real Simon Pure'. No less embarrassing was the necessity of explaining these disagreements to the expedition's supporters, including the Government, who were as unfamiliar with the warring tribes of Exeter Hall as with those of the Niger. On Buxton's urging Stephen wrote a pamphlet, *A Letter to . . . Lord John Russell*, published in August 1840, setting out the historical and ideological background of the controversy. In private letters to Trotter and others Buxton did his best to put a good face on the matter.[38]

Another challenge came from a group whose interests both Buxton and the Government had confidently supposed that they were promoting, namely the African merchants. Their principal spokesman was Robert Jamieson, an enterprising Liverpool trader who had recently dispatched a thirty-horse-power paddle steamer, the *Ethiope*, with the intention of establishing regular commercial links with the tribes beyond the already well-known Oil Rivers of the Delta. Its commander, John Beecroft, knew more than anyone about trading in West Africa and had been among those whom Buxton had earlier consulted.

In February, immediately upon learning that the Government intended to despatch an expedition, Jamieson wrote to Russell enquiring whether it was intended to be a commercial venture conducted at the public expense. Russell replied that although it would be Government financed its aims were benevolent rather than commercial.[39] Jamieson responded with a pamphlet, *An Appeal to the Government . . . Against the Proposed Niger Expedition*, pointing out that, whatever the original intention, one of its principal objects was to promote legitimate trade. To that extent it represented unfair competition and would inevitably prove counter-productive. Genuine traders would be compelled to withdraw. Even if, as he confidently believed, the whole undertaking turned out to be an abject failure it would prove difficult subsequently to re-establish links with Africans to whom merchandise had simply been given away as largesse or as bribes for future good behaviour rather than exchanged on a strictly commercial basis. Buxton's figures on slave exports were much exaggerated.[40] By no stretch of the imagination could they be seen as representative of what was happening on the Niger where the exporting of slaves had long since given way to trading in palm oil, of which Liverpool happened to be the major importer. But even leaving aside the damage that would be done to established traders the whole approach was wrong-headed. The first essential, as everyone with experience of Africa knew, was to establish trading relations. Trade must precede agriculture. To set about building fancy model farms and the like in the expectation that somehow trade would then develop was to tackle the problem the wrong way round. Africans were quite capable of producing what was required. This was something that philanthropists, given their paternalistic assumptions, simply could not bring themselves to admit. 'Sierra Leone stands a melancholy monument to the total futility of such settlements for the objects in question.' Its exports were derisory compared with the palm oil, valued at £350 000 annually, which Liverpool currently imported from the Oil Rivers. 'So much for private enterprise (the soul of British commerce) *when let alone.*' It was not the slave trade but philanthropy that drove out legitimate commerce. More Sierra Leones? In the interior of Africa? It made no sense. If Buxton and his associates wanted to practise their philanthropy they should go south of the equator where the slave trade was still carried on. They would not do any good but at least they would do no harm.

Responding to these charges on behalf of the African Civilization Society, Sir George Stephen, in his *A Second Letter to . . . Lord John Russell in Reply to Mr Jamieson*, argued that they derived entirely from self-interested motives. The alarm expressed by the Liverpool merchants reflected their belief in the extreme lucrativeness of African trade and to that extent supported the Society's case. The fact was that a small group of entrepreneurs wanted to keep Africa to themselves. The object of the Society, by contrast, was to open up the interior to a much larger number of traders. The proposed expedition was not itself a trading venture. The commercial articles it carried would serve merely as examples of British manufacture. Moreover, those for whom Jamieson spoke were not interested in redeeming a continent where 'all is demoralization, barbarity and murderous oppression . . . and man is degraded to the level of the beast of the forest'. They were interested merely in profits. A British colony based on 'an African bill of rights' would be quite different. There trade and humanity would go hand in hand: Africans would flock to such a settlement. Enjoying British protection and under British tutelage, they would be taught the value of civilization, Christianity and how best to exploit their indigenous resources. Why was Sierra Leone always thrown in their teeth? In reality Sierra Leone was not the unmitigated failure that was claimed, although its development had been hampered by poor management and an unfortunate site. The trade figures for 1836, which were the latest available, showed that she had exported goods worth £71 927. This was no small achievement given the difficulties under which the people there laboured. But Sierra Leone was merely a first attempt and provided no basis for judging the benefits that might now confidently be expected from a well-equipped and properly planned expedition designed to develop the resources of the African hinterland.

Jamieson replied with a point-by-point rebuttal.[41] While it was perfectly true, as Stephen claimed, that the value of exports passing through Sierra Leone's customs houses in 1836 were valued at £71 927 he had failed to note that £60 223 of that sum related to timber and palm oil not originating in the colony but brought down from the back country or gathered along the coast and that the actual value of the goods (mostly groundnuts) produced by the settlers was a mere £11 704. Given the great expense that had been borne by Britain in establishing the colony and maintaining it for some fifty years this represented a poor return on investment when compared with the £300 000 to £400 000 derived from the Gulf of Guinea where Britain maintained no civil establishment at all. The members of the African Civilization Society were dreamers. He compared Buxton to Don Quixote and repeated his claim that the Government had no business encouraging such knight-errantry. Trade should be left to merchants, not dabbled in by governments and philanthropists.

In this he was supported by Professor Herman Merivale of Oxford who in his lectures to undergraduates that year described Buxton's scheme as 'the chimerical speculation of civilizing Africa, by establishing a legitimate commerce with her inhabitants, through the force of government bounties'. The truth was that Africa's future depended on impersonal economic forces far too powerful for any humanitarian body or even national government to control. What was most striking about the proposed Niger expedition was 'the utter disproportion between the means and the object. . .'[42]

The major challenge, however, came not from merchants, Sturgeites, Chartists or academics but from *The Times*. 'The Thunderer', as it was already known, was radical Tory in its sympathies and, with a circulation approaching 60 000, was acknowledged to be the most powerful journal in the country. Along with other newspapers it had hitherto confined itself, as in its coverage of the Exeter Hall meeting, to factual reporting. But on 11 November the proprietor and joint editor, John Walter, attended a meeting in Reading, chaired by the Marquis of Downshire, at which the principal speakers were Sir George Stephen and Sir John Jeremie, the latter newly knighted after his recent appointment but not yet departed for Sierra Leone. This was one of many sponsored by the African Civilization Society, the purpose in this case being to establish a Berkshire auxiliary. The proceedings had not progressed far before Walter rose to object to the way the event was being stage-managed. Were they meeting simply to ratify proposals which had been agreed in advance or were they genuinely anxious to engage in discussion? If the latter, they should begin by taking note of the truly disastrous consequences for the country of the devious, dishonest and ill-conceived policies of the abolitionist party to date.[43]

Attempts were made to rule him out of order but in spite of this he ploughed inexorably on. He was not, he emphasized, a supporter of slavery, still less of the slave trade. Nevertheless, the meeting should take account of the chicanery practised in the past by the supporters of the present scheme. They had misled European emigrants with false promises and sent them to parts of the world where they had perished. They had abolished slavery in the West Indies at a cost of £20 000 000 with the result that they had cut sugar production by 30 per cent and doubled the price paid for the article by British consumers. And they had spent £15 000 000 on trying to suppress the slave trade, the total effect of which, if Buxton's book was to be believed, was only to exacerbate its horrors. Everyone knew that the climate of Africa was lethal to Europeans. Whole regiments that were sent there simply melted away. Yet here were the same people who had misled the British public in the past proposing a new and even more improbable enterprise that would eat up more money and more lives. How could sensible men, on this evidence, honestly give their support to an undertaking so plainly destined for failure?

Unprepared for such an assault, George Stephen's response was flustered. Those present would recognize the unjustified nature of the claims being made; many leading Tories had given the scheme their support; 'prudent men' had little to fear from the West African climate; Christianity and commerce were the answer.

The Times published a verbatim account of the meeting; also a lengthy editorial regretting that the Prince Consort's advisers had allowed him to become associated with the scheme without first enquiring into its details or assessing the trustworthiness of its sponsors. 'To say the truth,' it declared, 'there is a large degree of charlatanism in the whole [Exeter Hall] system, which, as carried on in the present day, bids fair to supersede the office of the church in religion, and of the state in civil government.' Self-appointed, inconsistent, showy, playing on public sentiment, impervious to rational argument, above all irresponsible, these societies were quite unfitted to perform the tasks they were attempting. Here was 'the benevolent baronet' proposing to send brave men off to 'new death-swamps like Sierra Leone'. And to what purpose? 'The absurdity of a handful of European adventurers expecting, as if by an enchanter's wand, to change the face of the great African continent, and to stop the slave trade, *on the principles of political economy*, surpasses anything which the imagination of Swift was able to conceive.'

The Times returned to the subject frequently in the weeks that followed.[44] Having raked the Buxtonites with its fire, it next turned on the ministry, demanding to know why it had agreed to back the enterprise and, in particular, why it had behaved so secretively. Surely so important a matter ought to have been thrown open to public discussion? Large sums of public money were involved. Yet the selfsame Whig ministry that was intent on ending outdoor relief for the poor of England, preferring instead to herd them into workhouses, was lavishing funds on ridiculous schemes for faraway Africans dreamed up by 'self-styled philanthropists who deliberately propose to sacrifice thousands of their countrymen at the shrine of self-conceit'. It was 'stark staring absurdity'.

Matters were not helped by this erratic behaviour of Sir George Stephen who took these jibes as an attack on his personal integrity and dashed off yet another pamphlet which he described to Buxton as a 'storm against that miserable ass Walter – Oh it is genuine fun when one has a decent opposition.' Buxton had already warned his colleagues that Sir George needed careful handling. He was a prickly character, emotional and indiscreet, and had lately annoyed them by laying bare, in his *A Second Letter to . . . Lord John Russell*, the disagreements that had divided the old antislavery societies which, as Priscilla Johnston noted, they had hitherto been at pains to conceal. Fond as he was of Sir George, Buxton firmly refused to pay for the publication of his latest effusion. Why, he asked, should he publish 'papers to abuse the Times – in which said papers "the bloody old Times" is about the mildest passage?' Incoherent with rage, Stephen responded by challenging him to a duel. Duelling was by that time virtually obsolete in England. Two abolitionists fighting over a pamphlet! Fortunately *The Times* never got hold of the story. Aware of the ludicrousness of the situation Buxton tactfully ignored the challenge and the incident was eventually forgotten.[45]

His own view was that there was no point in declaring war on *The Times* in the certain knowledge that it would simply lead to more fulminations. The beast had been aroused. To goad it further would be counter-productive. This was aptly demonstrated when Stephen, ignoring all advice, published *A Third Letter to . . . Lord John Russell* at his own expense, thereby provoking *The Times* into reflecting that he must be 'a very funny sort of person'. The chiefs of Africa were like the 'artful Dodgers' and 'flash Neds' of London. How much effect would moral suasion have on those gentry? It was hard to credit that these were the dreams of grown men and not of some young Quaker lady in Mr Gurney's drawing-room. As a parting shot it printed some verses that had lately appeared in *John Bull*:

> The fact, my dear Philanthropy, is this –
> You're now like one upon a precipice,
>   Or on the giddy top of some high steeple:
> Your dizzied thoughts are carried so far out
> 'Tis clear you know not what you are about:–
>   Come down, come down, look after your own people.[46]

These exchanges confirmed Buxton in his belief that the only possible course was to keep quiet and wait for it all to blow over. There was little danger that at this late stage the Government would abandon the expedition because of criticisms in a newspaper already notorious for its opposition to ministerial policies. Nevertheless, it was all very awkward, not least because it impeded fund-gathering for the model farm which, for a time, it was feared might have to be abandoned. 'I find folks here,' Buxton wrote from London, 'very much dejected. The Times and the Chartists and the . . . resolutions published by the London Anti-Slavery Society, the stoppage of anything flowing into our coffers and the rapid expenditure we incur, all these and a dozen other things render us rather a downcast and forlorn squadron, and we are just in this hobble, we dare not hold meetings thro' the Country and we are bankrupts without them.'[47] In the event sufficient funds were raised, mainly from family and friends, for the model farm project to go ahead, although on a much reduced scale. The commercial company, of which Buxton had initially had such high hopes, was reluctantly shelved. These events, together with worries about Buxton's health, which was showing ominous signs of collapsing under the strain, cast a shadow over the proceedings.

In February the issue was rather belatedly taken up in the Commons by Viscount Ingestre, who 'trusted . . . that the Government would not, for the sake of pleasing a few benevolent men, turn its attention so exclusively to the improvement of Africa as to forget the welfare of the men [on] the expedition'. Was it not the case that they would be entering the river at the very worst time of year? Joseph Hume wanted to know what the Government was thinking of sending sailors, of all people, into the middle of Africa? Was the object to foster trade, plant colonies or explore the African interior? Whatever it was, sailors were hardly the men to accomplish it. The Government had behaved shamefully in failing to submit to Parliament the full details of the plan.[48]

Not all comment, however, was hostile. During the early months of 1841, as more became known, there was plenty of evidence to be found in the Press to show that the expedition had caught the public imagination. Articles continued to appear describing the outfitting of the ships and the special care that was being taken to safeguard the health of their crews. The first of January 1841 was designated a day of prayer for the success of the expedition and special services were held in a number of churches. *The Times*, having said all it had to say, contented itself with sporadic explosions of Olympian wrath.[49] Meanwhile various correspondents were writing to Russell with what were intended to be helpful suggestions. One of these, Paul Read of Stroud, Gloucestershire, sent him a pamphlet stating that 'It has so long been the fashion to let our benevolent hearts expand so wide at the distresses of the Negro that the miseries of the famishing factory slaves of our own country are lost in the abyss.' What could be done to compensate for such dereliction? The solution, rather surprisingly, was to establish penal colonies along the Niger. Whatever happened to the convicts it would be much better than employing them in the hulks to do work which could be better done by the honest unemployed. It would also be much cheaper than paying double wages to the members of the present expedition. Samuel Carson of Pimlico proposed equipping the steamers with inflatable leather bags to increase their buoyancy. These and other suggestions Russell forwarded either to Buxton or Trotter. One letter, however, got no further than the Colonial Office.[50]

This was from Thomas Stirling of Sheffield, the original instigator of the 1832–4 expedition who had introduced Richard Lander to Macgregor Laird. He was by far the most knowledgeable of all the correspondents; also the most pessimistic in his conclusions. The actual size of the Atlantic slave trade, he correctly estimated, was about 50 000.[51] Buxton's figures were far too high and in particular did not make adequate allowance for the substantial success of the policies the Government was already pursuing. He realized that the Government's mind was already made up but he felt he could not let the expedition sail without registering a personal protest. Ministers had 'succumbed to the morbid impatience of commencing operations without a defined object or fixed plan. The improvement of one quarter of the globe is not the enterprise of a year.' Model farms, schoolmasters, missionaries, treaties, legitimate trade, civilization – it was 'not right to lead gallant men to almost certain death' for the attainment of such an ill-thought-out jumble of objectives.

The principal hazard, of course, was malaria. To judge from past experience the settlement at Fernando Po was just as unhealthy as the mainland. It was also doubtful if the interior was any more healthy than the coast. The climate of the low hills further inland – and there were no high ones – was arguably the most lethal of all. Malaria seemed to prevail throughout Africa except, he noted with extraordinary perceptiveness, in areas above 4000 feet. If Britain wanted settlements she should aim to establish them above that level, either high up in the volcanic interior of Fernando Po or in the mountains of the Cameroons to the south. On the other hand,

> if the present Expedition sail, it will not be difficult to prophesy the result. Captain Trotter will ascend the River in July. He will survey no more than has been surveyed before. If his object be to make Treaties of Commerce or obtain grants of Land, he may procure them in abundance – but they will be of little use unless it be arranged that a continual succession of

Expeditions shall follow. He will return to the Coast in November – his people struck down with disease – and a deeper gloom will close over Africa.[52]

'I suppose,' minuted Stephen, 'this should be communicated to Captain Trotter.' Vernon Smith demurred: 'I see no use in sending him these evil auguries.' Russell agreed. 'It is difficult,' he noted, 'to find any pertinent suggestions in all this.' The letter was quietly filed.

CHAPTER FOUR
Africa Encountered

From the first it was intended that the expedition should sail in December so as to begin the ascent of the river well before the onset of the rainy season in June. Everyone agreed that the unhealthiest time of the year was in October and November when the lands were drying out after the rains. The *Reliance*, a brigantine carrying 225 tons of coal, did, in fact, depart on 11 December. The rest of the expedition, however, was still busily outfitting.

Trotter's flagship, the *Albert*, left Birkenhead in 11 January and after successful sea trials docked at Deptford on 3 February. Meanwhile a report from Jamieson had arrived at the Colonial Office relaying the news that Beecroft had ascended the Niger the previous summer. After exploring various creeks leading into the Delta the *Ethiope* had finally managed to reach the main river by way of the Nun branch. It had then gone upstream almost to Boussa, the furthest point reached by steamer so far. The people were friendly and anxious for trade. In all, the *Ethiope* had spent six months in the interior during the course of which all the Europeans had been sick and a third of them had died. It was, Stephen reported, 'far from encouraging'. Of more immediate concern, however, was Jamieson's claim that owing to the shallowness of the water during the dry season it would be impossible to gain access to the river before July.[1]

Immediately upon seeing Jamieson's letter Trotter wrote to the Admiralty and Colonial Office requesting permission to delay his departure until April. As with the ever-increasing costs, Stephen received this new request with weary resignation. 'I shall not wonder much,' he told Vernon Smith, 'if at last we are punctual as to the month and inaccurate only as to the year.' Russell was for ordering an immediate departure, but further enquiries established that on account of the difficulties encountered fitting the ventilating apparatus the steamers were unlikely to be ready to sail much earlier. There seemed no alternative, Russell noted, but that the expedition ascend the river in the very worst season.[2]

HMS *Albert* at Deptford.

By mid-March all three steamers had arrived at Woolwich. Paddle boats were already a familiar sight on the Thames by the early 1840s although most were still built of wood.[3] The Diamond Steam Packet Company had started a service between London and Gravesend in 1836. Larger ocean-going steamers were also beginning to make their appearance. In 1840 Samuel Cunard had introduced a regular transatlantic service between Liverpool, Nova Scotia and Boston, bringing, among others, several dozen delegates to Sturge's World Anti-Slavery Convention. Nevertheless, Trotter's three vessels attracted a good deal of attention and a stream of distinguished visitors. Buxton inspected them on 19 March, Prince Albert on the 23rd and Russell on the 29th. All were intrigued by the ingenuity that had gone into their construction.

The two larger vessels, the *Albert* and the *Wilberforce*, each carried a crew of 57. They measured 136 by 27 feet, weighed 457 tons and had a draught of 4 feet 9 inches. Care had been taken to ensure that they were in every respect identical so that spare parts would be interchangeable. Each was powered by twin 35 horsepower engines adapted to burning either coal or wood. These had been kept deliberately small so as to reduce weight and allow for the additional crew and cargo to be taken on board along the African coast. The third steamer, the *Soudan*, carried a crew of 40. It was smaller, driven by a single 35 horsepower engine and, drawing only 3 feet of water, was especially designed for penetrating shallow creeks. For purposes of defence, the vessels were provided with brass twelve-pounders, swivel guns and a variety of small arms.

Much attention had also been given to detail. Compared to other naval ships of the day their outfittings were luxurious. The whole of the decks below, with the exception of the engine room, were covered with oil-cloth; and, to protect the crews from extremes of temperature, the insides of the iron hulls were lined with wood almost throughout. The officers were all white, but of the 95 seamen, 28 were coloured, mostly West Indians or Africans, although with a few East Indians and North Americans among them. They at least, it was presumed, would escape the effects of the African climate. In addition to the seamen, there were 22 marines and 8 sappers, the latter lately returned from a course at Chatham on methods of blasting rocks underwater, arranged on the expedition's behalf by the navy. In view of the acknowledged dangers, particularly from the African climate, the personnel on the expedition, all of whom were volunteers, would draw double pay from the time of leaving England.[4]

On his visit to the vessels the Prince almost came to grief when his pinnace was swept under a mooring rope, but he took it all in good part. He was particularly interested in the technical arrangements. These included retractable keels, essential for ocean navigation or when the vessels were under sail, and the compasses, which had been corrected by means of adjustable bar magnets according to a system devised by Professor George Airy, the Astronomer Royal, to compensate for the attraction of the steamers' hulls. What proved most intriguing, however, was the operation of the ventilating systems. Dr Reid was on hand, showing first how he could extract smoke from the *Albert*'s lower deck, and then, after turning the valves, suffuse the vessel with a succession of sweet-smelling perfumes. The Prince was delighted by his visit and presented each of the captains with an appropriately inscribed gold watch.[5]

A large party of Buxtons and Gurneys had lunch on the *Albert* and went for a cruise up the river. 'It was,' one of the nieces reported, 'the first time Uncle Buxton had seen the ships. . . . It *was wonderful* to look around and to think that *he* had been the instrument of all this mighty preparation.' In return, the officers were entertained to dinner at the brewery and at Samuel Gurney's home in Essex where Elizabeth Fry gave them her blessing. They should all take care, she told them, 'to keep a very single eye to their Lord; not to depend on the arm of flesh but continually to look upwards'. Evidently they took it in good part. 'Betsy's sermon, or as they were pleased to call it Lady Fry's speech, delighted them,' Buxton told Anna, 'and so did the champagne and so did the cordiality of the welcome.' Some thought Captain Trotter looked anxious and, according to Catherine Buxton, everyone felt sorry for 'poor, dear Mrs Trotter looking so woe-begone and poorly'. But the rest seemed in good spirits. The younger ladies were particularly taken by Lieutenant Fishbourne and Commander Bird Allen, both looking very handsome in their uniforms, while the officers, in turn, were much impressed by the grandeur of the occasion.[6]

No less intriguing than the 'Niger heroes', at least to the younger ladies, were two young Asante princes, William Kwantabisa and John Ansah, nephews of the current ruler of Asante, who were to accompany the expedition as far as Cape Coast Castle on their way back to Kumase. They were, in point of fact, black hostages, brought to England by the Colonial Office in 1836 and enrolled at a school in Clapham where they had received a grounding in reading, writing, arithmetic and Gospel history. Latterly they had been touring the country under the tutelage of the Reverend Thomas Pyne to learn more of its character and achievements. Stephen thought 'the word "princes" a little extravagant' to describe the sons of a former Asantehene and preferred his own term 'black youths'.[7] Nevertheless, they had captured the public imagination and were presented at court almost as if they were visiting royalty. Buxton, who had taken a paternal interest in them, was delighted at the progress they had made. According to his daughter-in-law Catherine, 'they, particularly Ansah, are amazingly improved – a tall, genteel, elegant young man.' Both were wished well in their future role as emissaries of British culture to the Kingdom of Asante, in furtherance of which the Government was to provide each of them with a stipend of £100 annually.[8]

The Buxtons and Gurneys attended a farewell service at Woolwich at which Elizabeth Fry distributed 'copies of her text books, of which she had brought sufficient for the whole expedition'. The men were reported to be pleased and the officers delighted. Trotter was presented with £1000 by the African Civilization Society to use in whatever way he deemed appropriate to further the objects of the expedition together with three trunks containing 36 copies of *The Slave Trade and its Remedy*, 17 Arabic and 12 Hebrew bibles, J.J. Gurney's *Portable Evidence of Christianity*, a selection of coloured handkerchiefs and petticoats, a cock hat and feathers, a brass helmet, and an array of 50 different kinds of seeds for use on the model farm. The vessels then departed for Plymouth battling against a stiff easterly breeze and with high seas running. Off Sheerness the *Wilberforce* ran foul of the *Albert*, crushing her own longboat and unshipping the *Albert*'s jib-boom. This caused some delay. At Plymouth they took on coals and enjoyed the hospitality of the local gentry. The *Soudan*, being slower than the other vessels, left on 17 April, accompanied by the *Harriot* transport carrying the model farm implements and other

The *Wilberforce, Albert* and *Soudan* at sea.

expedition effects. After further delays caused by strong southerly gales the *Albert* and *Wilberforce* sailed from Devonport on the evening of 12 May. The British battle fleet was drawn up at Spithead and as the two small steamers passed in the twilight each was given three hearty cheers.

The voyage to Madeira proved uneventful. Clear skies and a northerly breeze enabled the vessels to make good time. Keeping abreast, under full canvas, with engines beating and paddles turning, they went cheerfully across the Bay of Biscay which for once proved smooth as a lake.

On board much time was spent experimenting with the ventilating apparatuses to familiarize all hands with their operation. The various valves on the tubes leading from the fans and the slides controlling the flow of air into and out of the cabins were labelled and numbered and their functions explained. Everything was found to work admirably. By following Dr Reid's instructions, adjusting the controls and inserting the appropriate trays into the medicator, they were able to reduce the temperature below decks by several degrees and also to lower the humidity significantly.[10]

Dr M'William and his medical colleagues were also at pains to impress on all Europeans the importance of conforming to the strict regimen laid down by the Surgeon General once they reached the tropics. This obliged them to wear flannel underclothes and stomachers, protect their heads from the sun with straw hats and padding, or, in the case of officers, white service caps, change immediately out of wet clothes, sleep below decks, dose themselves regularly either with rum or lemon juice, and drink coffee before going on duty. In addition they should take care to exercise regularly, avoid drinking river water that had not been boiled, eat cranberries, pickled cabbage, fresh meat and vegetables and take wine and quinine as prescribed.[11]

The commissioners were required, under the terms of their appointment, to keep individual records to be submitted to the Colonial Secretary at the conclusion of the expedition. In addition, however, several others, conscious of the historic nature of their quest, had also begun keeping private journals. One of these, William Simpson, had already formed an unfavourable view of his shipmates. A man of stern, even morbid, piety, he had first heard of the expedition while attending chapel in Liverpool. He held strong antislavery views, acquired while working as a clerk in the Caribbean, and had promptly volunteered for the post of Assistant Secretary to the Commissioners. He had no previous experience of Africa and, being under the impression that he might encounter Jews there, had taken the precaution of arming himself with letters of introduction from the Chief Rabbi and the Rabbi of the Portuguese community in London. On joining the *Wilberforce* at Woolwich he found himself assigned to quarters on the lower deck where the conversation of his messmates, all much younger than himself and less well educated, contrasted markedly with the high endeavour to which they were committed. He found peculiarly apt the chaplain's choice of text on their first sabbath at sea, Zachariah 8 and 13, as 'applied to the sailor, hitherto a curse and a pollution to the lands he visited, but now, he hoped, to prove a blessing to them', although whether it would have much effect on his companions Simpson doubted. But whatever the outcome it was the Lord's will. He suffered much from headaches and consoled himself reading 'the Word'.[12]

John Duncan, aboard the *Albert*, took a more robust view of his situation. As the former sergeant-major of the 1st Battalion of the Life Guards he was unlikely to be impressed by the salty talk of sailors or, for that matter, by evangelical notions of idealism and spirituality. Quite simply he was in search of adventure and Africa seemed a likelier place than most to find it. That was why he had chosen to leave the cavalry in order to become the expedition's master-at-arms. Six feet three in height, with an aquiline nose, full beard and broad shoulders, he was an imposing figure. Strength, manliness, courage and fighting ability were the qualities he admired. Yet, for all that, he was an acute observer with a sharp eye for detail. He was also an accomplished artist, having taught himself to draw while in the army. Compared to the others, his journal, written in a plain straightforward style reminiscent of William Cobbett

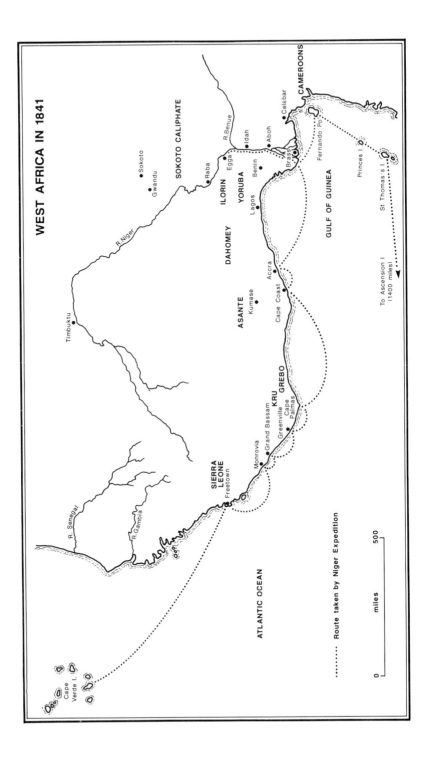

WEST AFRICA IN 1841

ATLANTIC OCEAN

Cape
Verde I.

R. Senegal

R. Gambia

Timbuktu

R. Niger

SOKOTO CALIPHATE

• Gwandu

• Sokoto

• Raba

R. Benue

Egga

Idah

Aboh

Calabar

CAMEROONS

ILORIN

YORUBA

DAHOMEY

Benin

Lagos

Brass

Fernando Po

Princes I.

St Thomas's I.

GULF OF GUINEA

ASANTE

Kumase

Accra

Cape Coast

GREBO
KRU

Grand Bassam
Greenville
Cape Palmas

Monrovia

SIERRA
LEONE
Freetown

To Ascension I.
(1400 miles)

·········· Route taken by Niger Expedition

0   500
miles

John Duncan.

(another former sergeant-major), gives a distinctly down-to-earth view of events.[13]

Their arrival at Madeira on 21 May allowed the scientists in the party to begin their investigations. Dr Theodor Vogel and Mr John Ansell, the expedition's botanist and plant collector, lost no time in departing for the mountains from where they returned laden with specimens, including some thought to be genuinely new to science. Together with Dr William Stanger, the geologist, Mr Charles Gottfried Roscher, the minerologist, and Mr Lewis Fraser from the Zoological Society, they had all been recruited and were being paid by the African Civilization Society.[14]

While the ships were taking on coal, Commander William Allen of the *Wilberforce* went on shore to experiment with his transportable magnetometer. This was a newly invented instrument, obtained from

Göttingen with the assistance of a grant from the Royal Society, designed to measure variations in the earth's magnetic field. The Admiralty had recently embarked on a global survey requiring simultaneous readings to be taken from vessels at different latitudes. Since fluctuations in the magnetic field occur not only from season to season but according to the time of day, organizing his affairs so that he could take readings at the pre-arranged times was to be one of Allen's principal concerns throughout the expedition.[15]

After spending five days in Madeira they departed for Cape Verde, where they found the *Soudan* and the *Harriot* waiting. It transpired that they had had a stormy passage across the Bay of Biscay and had put in at Lisbon for repairs. They had also shipped a good deal of water so it was found necessary to unload and re-stow their provisions. While this was being done, John Morley, a carpenter's mate, fell overboard and was drowned in full view of the assembled ships' companies. His body was recovered and the following day buried with military honours. The marines and sappers who had come out in the *Harriot* provided an escort and fired a volley over his grave. This was the expedition's second casualty, the *Soudan* having lost its purser's steward overboard near Tenerife. Morley had been a popular man and the abrupt manner of his death, Simpson was pleased to note, had a sobering effect on his messmates.[16]

St Vincent, everyone agreed, was a miserable place. 'Anything more comfortless than the view of this island, I never beheld,' noted Vogel. 'One might believe that after the formation of the world, a quantity of useless surplus stones was cast into the sea, and that thus the island of St Vincent arose.'[17] The island also provided members of the expedition with their first glimpse of tropical poverty. Porto Grande, its name notwithstanding, proved to be a dusty collection of stick and mud huts, its inhabitants naked or in rags. 'The meanest pauper in England,' wrote Duncan, 'is a King compared with the best and most opulent of them.' When the wind blew off the land it was as if it had passed through a furnace. Even the water at eight fathoms was at 87°F. They spent two weeks checking the inventories, swabbing out the holds and accustoming the crews to working in the sun. Some of the younger officers amused themselves stalking wild goats and the scientists made forays into the mountains which turned out to be almost entirely barren.[18]

For those who had not previously visited southern latitudes the voyage southward along the African coast brought various novelties – flying fish, sharks, the extraordinary phosphorescence of the sea, which at night cascaded off the revolving paddles like liquid silver, and the sight of a vast flight of locusts.[19]

Approaching Sierra Leone on 23 June they encountered a tropical tornado, the first of many. Like all such storms on the Coast it came rolling out of the east, visible in the distance as a towering arch of cloud, flickering with light and audible as a low rumbling like distant surf. It bore down on them bringing violent squalls and incessant thunder and lightning along with torrential rain. The vessels followed the standard procedure of hauling down their canvas except for a single head-sail and running before it. The storm lasted only a short while but was followed by several hours of heavy rain which poured through into the cabins, the planks of the decks having shrunk as a result of the baking they had received during the preceding weeks. But once the skies had cleared Dr Reid's fans were put to work and proved remarkably effective in drying out the lower decks.[20]

After the barrenness of Cape Verde, Sierra Leone, refreshed by the first summer rains, its vegetation bursting into leaf, looked green and spring-like. Those who knew it only for its charnel-house reputation were surprised to find well-laid-out streets, substantial stone residences, chapels, taverns, retailers' shops and a general air of settled well-being. On first encounter Freetown appeared more West Indian than African. Most Europeans lived on the parallel streets extending up from the harbour, although some had built themselves secluded villas in the hills around. There was, they discovered, even a Turf Club, with a race course, where fashionable dinners, balls and fêtes were held.[21]

At the time of the expedition's visit Freetown was almost exactly fifty years old, having been founded in 1792 as a settlement for some 1200 blacks from Nova Scotia, mostly former slaves from the thirteen colonies. They had been followed in 1800 by a party of 550 captive Maroons from Jamaica, runaway slaves and their descendants who had established communities in the mountains there. But these original settlers were now outnumbered by the African recaptives (that is, slaves freed by the British cruisers), brought in by the cruisers, several hundred of whom arrived annually. On landing they were normally apprenticed for a period of six months after which they were expected to support themselves. Some became farmers, others artisans or retailers; a few rose to become leading merchants and wholesalers in the colony.[22]

Yet, in spite of appearances, it was borne home to the visitors that the place's reputation as a plague spot was well deserved. On docking they were greeted with news of the death of Buxton's protégé Sir John Jeremie. He had arrived in the colony the previous December full of schemes for growing cotton and establishing a postal service and savings bank. Mindful of the Government's wish to negotiate antislavery treaties he had lost no time in departing for the interior to confer with the local Africans. There he was quickly made aware that affairs were much more complicated than was imagined by those who attended rallies in Exeter

Hall. The colony had long been troubled by frontier wars with the result that he found his well-meaning approaches rebuffed. In his one and only report to the Colonial Office he quoted the Chief of the Mandingoes as saying 'this was always the way with white men, they first sent quiet people to do them good, then merchants, then as their numbers increased they built forts and brought guns and at last they took away your country.' He did make one treaty, with the Chief of the Timmanies, before being struck down. Evidently he had made a good impression on the colonists during his brief administration. William Allen records a market woman as saying, 'Gubberna Jeremy dead – fever catch him – he werry good man.' People in Freetown were used to a high turnover of Governors.[23]

The expedition had been expected in March and many in the colony had begun to wonder if it would arrive at all. Since Jeremie's death, responsibility for the colony's affairs had devolved on the Queen's Advocate, John Carr, a young Trinidadian who had studied at University College, London, and been called to the Bar. He was, as it happened, the brother of Alfred Carr, the Supervisor engaged by the African Civilization Society to organize the model farm who had travelled out in the *Wilberforce*. In the expedition's official reports Alfred Carr is listed as 'a West Indian gentleman of colour' although in dealings with Africans he is referred to as white. He at once set about selecting personnel for the farm from among those recommended by the local missionaries. In the event he engaged ten: one mason, three carpenters, one sawyer, four farmers and a personal servant, all recaptives who had learned their trades in the colony and who were willing to take their wives and children with them. To transport these families and their effects the expedition acquired an 80-ton brigantine, the *Amelia*, a former slaver, which they hastily set about refitting for the purpose.[24]

Meanwhile the ships' officers were engaged in recruiting African deckhands. Most were members of the Kru tribe, accustomed to working on vessels up and down the coast as a means of earning wages with which to acquire more wives and so increase the size of their households, upon which, as was commonly the case in West Africa, their wealth and status depended. Many came wearing articles of British naval dress – captains' tunics with epaulettes, Wellington boots, even cocked hats – obtained from the sales of dead officers' effects. They went by curious nicknames such as Jack Sprat, Pale Ale and Prince of Whales. Krumen had their own headmen and hierarchies of command. They were especially skilled at manoeuvring vessels through surf or up shallow estuaries, but they were also accustomed to performing most of the tasks which it was thought inappropriate for whites to undertake in the tropics. River work on steamers was not popular, however, on account of the woodcutting involved, so it was only by agreeing to pay above the regular market rate that the additional hundred-odd personnel were eventually persuaded to join the expedition. William Simpson noted that after the Krumen had arrived the British seamen showed little inclination to bestir themselves.[25]

With so many liberated Africans in the colony there was no problem finding qualified interpreters. The task of selecting them had been given to the Church Missionary Society which had shown keen interest in the expedition's plans. The CMS had accordingly written to two of its representatives, the Reverend Friedrich Schön and a native catechist, Samuel Crowther. They were instructed to travel with the expedition and to report on the suitability of the Niger as an area for future missionary activity. Both were later to publish accounts of their experiences. Schön was one of several Germans employed in Sierra Leone by the CMS and was already a seasoned missionary having worked for nine years in the colony. During that time he had lost two wives and at the time of the expedition's arrival, a third, whom he had married only a few months previously, was already ailing. Crowther, now in his early thirties, was a Yoruba recaptive, originally from the interior north of Lagos. His story was typical of many. He had been enslaved as a boy when his town was overrun by a mixed force of Fulani and local Mohammedans during the religious struggles of the 1820s. After changing hands no less that five times he had eventually been sold to a Portuguese slave ship from which he had been freed by a British cruiser and carried to Freetown. He had subsequently become a pupil and eventually a tutor at Fourah Bay College, the nearby Anglican training establishment.[26]

During the nine days that they spent in Freetown members of the expedition were able to explore the colony. John Duncan encountered a former member of his old regiment whom he introduced to the Asante princes as having fought against their late father. The princes impressed the colony's Anglican chaplain by 'their amiable and polished manners, as well as with their pure and Christian sentiments'. They were, he concluded 'encouraging specimens of what can be effected in the African character'. William Simpson lost no time in introducing himself to the local Wesleyans and expressed himself much gratified by the strictness with which the sabbath was observed. At St George's Church he heard a sermon, 'an eulogium on England, what she had done and was about to do, for the African race'. He was heartened by the enthusiasm with which the black congregation entered into the spirit of the service, clapping their hands and stamping their feet.[27]

Not all the recaptives were converts. On the night of 28 June the town experienced a storm unusual even by Sierra Leone standards. The commissariat building was damaged and much other mischief caused.

While it was in progress, some Yoruba, worshippers of the thunder-god Shango, appeared in their doorways beating on tom-toms and shouting. Elizabeth Helen Melville, the wife of the Registrar of the Mixed Commission Court, describes how, as crash succeeded crash, they could be heard making 'such horrid yelling noises that I could believe a herd of wild beasts were prancing through Freetown in full cry'. Two of them, a man and a woman, were struck by lightning and in the stillness that followed the storm's passing the lamentations of their fellows could be heard across the town. When the ships' officers visited the scene the following morning they found the blackened bodies, still lying among the wreckage of their hut and already covered in flies. What made the incident especially sad, William Allen believed, was the assumption of those of their cult that to be struck by lightning was an 'especial mark of the favour of their gods, who had thus translated them by the agency of a fluid which they worship as a deity.'[28]

With its numbers now swelled from 160 to over 300, the flotilla proceeded southward in heavy seas. The decks were crowded with new passengers, many of them seasick. This, combined with the almost incessant rain, made life miserable for everyone. To make matters worse, it was discovered that the coals taken on at Freetown were of such poor quality as to be almost useless and proceeding under canvas against the prevailing headwinds proved painfully slow. One of the few consolations was that the rain had swelled the deck planks sufficiently to keep the cabins below tolerably dry. Along the way they met HMS *Ferret* in much worse straits with many of the crew down with fever and the ship's doctor already dead.[29]

Arriving at Monrovia on 5 July they found three American vessels anchored in the harbour and the stars and stripes flying over the Governor's residence. The Governor himself, Thomas Buchanan, came on board the *Albert* to greet them. Monrovia was the largest of the Liberian settlements with a population of just under a thousand, almost all former slaves or black freemen brought over by the American Colonization Society. What most intrigued the visitors was the extent to which these settlers, in spite of being refugees from the slave republic, had preserved their Americanness, and the sheer novelty of finding a black fragment of the United States thus embedded in Africa. A particular case in point was the discovery that, although Monrovia had been founded as recently as 1822 and the entire settler population was less than one-tenth that of Sierra Leone, it already had two newspapers, *Africa's Luminary*, which spoke for the Methodists, and the *Liberia Herald*, representing the Baptists and the incumbent Buchanan administration. The main bone of contention dividing the parties was the question of whether missionaries should be required to pay customs duties on imported goods, a proposition which the Methodists bitterly opposed.[30]

One reason for putting in at Monrovia was to recruit more workers for the model farm. Carr was particularly anxious to encourage the cultivation of cotton. After some hard bargaining he managed to secure the services as head overseer of Ralph Moore, who seemed to be familiar with the way cotton was grown in Mississippi, and of John Jones, another black American immigrant, who agreed to act as his assistant.[31]

In the event the crew of the *Wilberforce* saw more of Liberia than they had intended. Soon after leaving Monrovia they ran out of coal. They first attempted to put in at Bassa Cove where the Philadelphia Colonization Society had a small settlement but the sandbar, even at high tide, proved too dangerous to attempt. They therefore proceeded further down the coast to Grand Bassa where they anchored offshore. Here they remained for six miserable days watching the rain fall and the Krumen ferry wood through the surf in their canoes. At one point a band of marauding Fulani appeared, clad in monkey skins and armed with muskets and spears. They, it turned out, were at war with the local Grebus, or Fishmen, whose own attitude towards the woodcutters was less than friendly, a situation not improved when one of the naturalists in search of specimens accidentally peppered one of them with lead shot.[32]

The wood thus obtained served to carry them only as far as Cape Palmas, the southernmost extremity of Liberia. There they found a sheltered anchorage opposite a large village of Grebus, its thatched roofs looking, it was remarked, very much like British haystacks. The village headman came aboard, resplendent in an old scarlet coat with rusty epaulettes, and after some bargaining agreed to provide men to help with the woodcutting.[33]

While this was being done William Allen went in search of his old servant Jack Smoke, who had accompanied him, and on occasion nursed him, on the previous Laird expedition. Smoke was not at home but was soon sent for and when he arrived expressed delight at the reappearance of his former master. He readily accepted the offer of the position of second head Kruman aboard the *Wilberforce*, and after a few brief words with his wife, who seemed not at all put out, departed taking with him no more possessions than the loincloth he was wearing.[34]

Allen and some of the other officers also visited nearby Harper, named after General Robert Goodloe Harper, a prominent Baltimorian. This was a settlement recently established by the Maryland State Colonization Society under a black Governor, John Brown Russwurm, a Jamaican-born graduate of Bowdoin College in Maine. They found the ground around largely cleared and the settlers busily harvesting rice. Proceeding on they arrived at a palm grove in which there was a school house from which there came the sound of hymn singing. This proved to be a quite separate establishment belonging to the American Board of Commissioners for Foreign Missions and run by John Leighton Wilson and his wife, both from South Carolina. Mrs Wilson had inherited some thirty slaves whom they had freed and brought to Cape Palmas with them. Their main concern, however, was to win the confidence of the nearby tribes. This had put them at odds with Russwurm and his fellow black settlers whom the Wilsons charged with high-handedness and lack of civility in their treatment of the local Africans. There had certainly been trouble, which gave rise to another issue, namely whether the Wilsons' black assistants should serve in the militia force which Russwurm had organized for the defence of the settlement, a problem which they passed on to their respective boards back in America. Allen found the couple in poor health, saddened by the opposition their efforts were encountering, but determined to persevere.[35]

The *Wilberforce* again ran out of firewood, this time just short of Cape Coast Castle, and was towed in by the *Soudan*. The *Albert* too had had a troubled passage and been obliged to put in for wood at Greenville on the Sinoe river, yet another American settlement, this one belonging to the Mississippi State Colonization Society.

While they were there they witnessed a ritual performed by the local Grebus of which Schön gives a detailed account under the heading 'Remarkable Heathenish Ceremony.' In a large open space in the centre of the village a crowd had gathered. A fire had been lit in front of which sat two musicians endlessly repeating the same combination of notes. Next to them was an array of charms made of horns, claws, teeth, the skins of animals and filthy pieces of calico. A woman appeared, her legs encumbered with iron rings almost to her knees, and was ritually smeared with the contents of a pot in which leaves, herbs and earth had been mixed. She then began dancing in a trance-like way, occasionally blowing on a large horn. Two white fowls were handed to her by an old man. These she held up to the assembled crowd and then offered them a few grains of rice which she scattered among the charms and which they promptly ate. They were then released. The exercise was next repeated with a young kid which, having refused the rice, was handed to the old man who beat it to death against the ground. The people then walked off and the ceremony seemed to be over. Did the pot contain a drug or a poison? Had the woman been accused of some crime and was this a form of ordeal? Or was she perhaps a female witch doctor who had in some way benefited the old man who now offered her the fowls and the kid as a form of ritual payment? Schön had no idea.[36]

William Allen, who also records the incident, was in no doubt that the woman had been obliged to drink 'Sassy water', that is to say poison which, not having proved fatal, had demonstrated her innocence of whatever it was that she had been accused. On what ground he based this judgement he does not say. Perhaps he had consulted someone knowledgeable in such matters. John Ansah, recounting the same events in a letter to the Reverend Thomas Pyne, described his personal revulsion at the spectacle of the Krumen's 'barbarous custom in dancing' and their 'tormenting a goat for their idols awfully. I did not like the sight; I withdrew from them.'[37]

Here, as elsewhere, the voyagers' comments on African customs are no less revealing for what they tell us about European attitudes, which Ansah was at pains to show that he had adopted, than for what they indicate about African behaviour. Writing, mostly in rather stilted prose, for audiences they perceived as high-minded and ethnocentric, Victorian commentators were not much inclined to go to the trouble of understanding other cultures, particularly when, as in this case, they were seen as manifestly inferior to their own. Moreover, unlike earlier travellers in West Africa, mostly lone individuals dependent on those they encountered for protection and sustenance, the members of the Niger expedition had remarkably few opportunities for observing, and no need whatever to adapt to, the everyday patterns of African life. Viewing the passing scene from the decks of their ships – essentially travelling microcosms of British society – venturing on shore only during the hours of daylight, fearful of the very air they breathed, it is not to be wondered at that their portrayal of African life is less than fully rounded. Well intentioned though they unquestionably were, risking their lives on what was plainly a perilous quest, they nevertheless subscribed to the conventional prejudices of their day.

What he had seen on the Laird expedition had confirmed William Allen's view that Africans were capable of believing the most extraordinary things. They lived surrounded by spirits which had to be placated and their favours sought. As a result they set great store by charms and attributed all sorts of magical qualities to inanimate objects. Some even claimed to have the capacity to turn themselves into any shape they chose. He viewed African priests or Ju-ju men with particular hostility. 'But,' as he noted, 'where the whole religion is but a tissue of palpable imposture, the principal requisites must be great cunning and boldness.' In reality they were mere charlatans exploiting the blind superstition of their votaries. William Simpson regarded the Grebus's custom of decorating their burial grounds with objects belonging to the deceased as a misguided attempt to 'carry with them their wealth, even to the grave'. Any deviation from European norms he put down to devil worship. Dr M'William, as a scientist, took a more detached view. If, as he had been given to understand, Africans believed that God was capable only of good, propitiating the devil, who was plainly capable of evil, made excellent sense.[38]

What is notably lacking from all such speculations is any willingness

81

on the part of the commentators to question their own beliefs and practices. Apart from drawing consolation from the fact that Africans too claimed to believe in a supreme being, no attempt was made to examine the parallels between so-called 'native superstitions' and European modes of religious behaviour. It would have required little reflection to note that Europeans too decorated their churches, placed objects on graves, appealed to their deity through intermediaries and in innumerable other ways made obeisance to systems of thought depending for their justification on the unknowable every bit as much as those found in Africa. Had they thought back to the Hebrew Bible – in which goats were frequently sacrificed – they would have found the similarities even more striking. But these were issues to which the voyagers' minds were closed. If anyone had such unsettling thoughts they are not recorded.

Still further from their minds was any suspicion that the Africans themselves might find such Eurocentric attitudes harsh and threatening or that they might harbour a belief in divine providence that came close to equalling that of Elizabeth Fry herself. Was not Christianity the most humane of all religions? Were not their own intentions of the best? How could one take seriously the practices of those who appeared to worship idols, and such poor idols at that, made as they often were of little bits of cloth, rusty nails, splinters of bone and other pathetic fragments? The notion that West Africans were deeply religious beings who believed in the omnipresence of the supernatural and sought divine guidance, help and comfort from their deities was not one that commended itself to the members of the Niger expedition. Pure though their intentions were, they had come to teach, improve, convert, not to have their own views confounded.[39]

At Cape Coast they took on coals, provisions and stores. Among the latter was a generous supply of cowries, small white shells of a kind often used for ornamenting horses' bridles in England, that had been sent ahead by the Admiralty. Cowries had long served as a form of specie in West Africa, having originally been introduced by traders travelling overland from the Red Sea. With 6.5 million of them, packed in 583 bags and weighing over seven tons, there was little danger of the expedition's running short of currency. Nor, judging from the quantity of agricultural equipment that they found themselves obliged to load on to the steamers' decks, would the model farm be in need of further supplies for many years. In these, as in other material respects, the expedition was not merely well but munificently provided.[40]

Cape Coast Castle proved a conspicuous landmark, a whitewashed fortress, built in baronial style with towers and battlements, standing on a granite promontory overlooking the bay. Access from the sea was by way of a watergate, flanked by two small bastions, from which a tunnel led to the main courtyard. To the rear, beyond the castle walls, stood a town of some 5000 inhabitants consisting of a number of two-storey traders' houses, mostly stone built with wide verandahs, various retail shops, a central marketplace, and, radiating out into the surrounding bush, clusters of whitewashed clay huts shaded by palm and tamarind trees.[41]

At one time this whole stretch of coast had been dotted with European forts, essentially slave warehouses established with the consent of the local rulers, of which Cape Coast Castle remained the largest and grandest. Since Britain's outlawing of the slave trade, however, and with the stepping up of cruiser operations, most had been abandoned. Apart from some illegal slaving, trade was now mostly in gold dust, brought down from the interior, and palm oil, which were exchanged for rum, tobacco and gunpowder. For this purpose the Dutch and Danes still maintained a number of small trading posts. During the 1820s, following a series of costly wars with the Asantes, the British Government had resolved to evacuate all its remaining forts but had in the end relented to the extent of agreeing to hand them over to the resident British merchants while continuing to pay annual contributions towards their upkeep. This was a compromise of which James Stephen strongly disapproved, blurring as it did the distinction between public and private enterprise and leaving wholly indeterminate the area of British authority. In a characteristically biting minute he was later to describe the forts as 'factories kept up at the expense of the nation at large for the profit of half a dozen inconsiderable merchants'.[42]

The commander of Cape Coast Castle and its three dependencies, Dixcove, Anomabu and James Fort, Accra, was George Maclean, a taciturn, hard-headed Scotsman, formerly of the Royal African Colonial Corps. He came bobbing out in a canoe paddled by forty pull-a-boys to greet the new arrivals. He already knew about the expedition having been consulted by Buxton while in London on his last furlough. He had held his present post since 1830. Officially he was President, which is to say chairman and chief executive officer, accountable to a local Council of Merchants by whom he had been elected and to whom he was responsible for creating the conditions necessary for the promotion of trade. This involved not only seeing to the administration and defence of the forts but preserving peace in the area. For this purpose he had at his disposal a force of some hundred and twenty African regulars and roughly half as many militia. These scarcely sufficed to garrison the forts. They could not have stood up in pitched battle even against one of the coastal peoples let alone the massed power of Asante.

Yet in spite of this, and of Stephen's misgivings, the Gold Coast had remained remarkably peaceful during the twelve years he had been in office. There had been no repetition of the desolating intertribal wars of the 1820s that had persuaded the Colonial Office to abandon its responsibilities in the area, indeed virtually no armed conflicts at all. This was almost entirely due to his willingness to accept the political realities of the situation and to his skill as a mediator. The basis of his strategy was to create an alliance of coastal peoples to offset the power of the inland Asante, whose own interests he undertook to respect by permitting direct access to the coastal trade and agreeing to return fugitives.[43]

Members of the expedition were able to observe Maclean in his role as peacemaker when two chiefs arrived at the Castle seeking his help in a case involving the killing of one of their subjects during a local dispute. Each came borne on a litter and attended by sword-bearers, cane-bearers and other followers. After hearing their depositions the President imposed a fine on both, a judgement which they accepted without demur. After paying tribute to his sagacity they departed with much shouting and beating of tom-toms.[44]

This display of feudal authority and the grandeur of the castle greatly impressed the visitors. What they did not know, although the senior officers may have had some inkling of it, was the suspicion which the possession of such power by a solitary official, not even answerable to the British Government, aroused in the minds of people back home. This was something which Maclean himself, isolated as he was, had not yet fully grasped, although the evidence was accumulating. One example was the plethora of stories that had begun to circulate concerning the circumstances of his wife's death.

While in England two years previously he had met and married Letitia Landon who, under the pen-name 'L.E.L', was well known as a prolific writer of sentimental verse. For any white woman, let alone a literary figure of some note, to settle on the Gold Coast invited comment. Her death some two months after her arrival, not from fever as might have been expected but from a sudden seizure, naturally gave rise to much gossip among her literary friends. Amelia Opie relayed to the Buxtons an account she had received according to which Maclean had kept his new bride locked up in one wing of the castle where she had been poisoned on the orders of a Fanti wife by whom he was reputed to have had five children. For Europeans to have African wives was considered quite normal on the Coast. Kenneth Macaulay in Sierra Leone had several whom he selected from among the recaptives brought in by the cruisers, producing thereby a large number of progeny whom his English relatives found themselves obliged to support after yellow fever carried him away. In Maclean's case, however, there is no evidence of any such involvement. Europeans in West Africa knew a great deal about one another's personal lives. Had the stories about his marriage which circulated in England had any basis the facts would quickly have leaked out. His biographer concludes that Mrs Maclean probably died of a heart attack.[45] What is striking about this episode is not the evidence, prosaic as it turns out to be, but what people unfamiliar with the Gold Coast and Maclean's situation there were willing to believe.

Much more damaging to his reputation, at least in British Government circles, was the charge of involvement with slavery and the slave trade. During their brief stay the officers of the expedition, William Cook in particular, became uneasily aware that distinctions which seemed obvious to people in England were a good deal cloudier in Africa.

This was brought home to them when Maclean applied to Trotter for the release of John Dick, a local blacksmith whom Alfred Carr had hired to work on the model farm and who had already taken up quarters on the *Amelia*. The request was made on the grounds that Dick belonged to a Mr Barnes, one of the British merchants at Anomabu. It transpired that Barnes had agreed to take Dick as surety for a loan made to Dick's father some years previously. In conformity with local practice, therefore, Barnes was entitled to Dick's services until such time as the debt was paid off. Technically speaking, Dick was a 'pawn' rather than a slave, but to those untutored in West African practices the distinction was hard to perceive. Being in need of a blacksmith and reluctant to see Dick returned to what looked remarkably like slavery, Carr agreed to pay Maclean the sum necessary for his release. As Cook later informed the Colonial Secretary, 'Capt. McLean, throughout this business, acted more like the advocate of the slave-holding Mr Barnes than the representative of Her Majesty.'[46]

This story was the more damaging because the owner was a British subject. Similar tales of suspected wrongdoing by British nationals had been reaching the Colonial Office for some years. Sir John Jeremie, on his arrival at Freetown, had been shocked to hear that Maclean had assisted in winding up a merchant's estate which had involved his disposing of no less than three hundred slaves. He had responded by announcing that the holding of slaves by British nationals anywhere on the Coast was illegal under the terms of the 1833 Emancipation Act. This alarmed Maclean. The proclamation appeared to him to be based on a misreading of the 1833 Act and total ignorance of local conditions. Having left Britain before the great antislavery upsurge of the 1830s he failed to grasp the intensity of feeling on the subject. As he saw it nothing but mischief would come of applying to Africa notions of law and status derived from England, or, for that matter, the West Indies. The Gold Coast was not a British colony. If Europeans were to have any influence there they had to fall in with the ways of peoples to whom the distinction between free and slave was largely meaningless. In West Africa there simply was no freedom, at least not in the European sense. He had much more import-ant things to occupy his attention than worrying about such social niceties.[47]

He was also unhappy at what he saw of Kwantabisa and Ansah, whom Trotter now returned to his care. Giving them the elements of a British education was one thing; treating them as visiting royalty was quite another. It was little wonder that their heads had been turned. They impressed him as so absurdly conceited and puffed up by their experience that he resolved to keep them at Cape Coast until their egos had deflated. Returning them to Kumase in their present state, he informed Russell, would 'put them in a very false position with respect to the King and Chiefs of Ashantee'.[48]

The missionaries on the expedition found their visit to the Gold Coast a depressing experience. Always, it seemed, the tidings were of failure and death. The Wesleyans had planned to promote a major missionary effort among the Asante, but of the ten missionaries sent out four had died and three others had been invalided home, all within the space of three months. Through his porthole Schön gloomily contemplated the mists brooding over the hills, giving them 'an aguish appearance'. On the streets of Accra he observed 'a large Fetish, made of clay, in the shape of a human being, painted white on one side and red on the other, which is worshipped by the Natives', and returned to his cabin on the *Wilberforce* 'with a heavy heart because of the misery, degradation and superstition of the inhabitants'. Here a letter from his wife awaited him with the reassuring news that she was recovering from her fever but announcing the loss of yet another close friend. 'I am ever led to reflect on the deaths of Missionaries,' he noted in his journal, '. . . and my unbelieving heart seems at times to discover nothing in them but discouragement.' William Simpson was equally despondent, feeling himself 'but as a speck in a great creation or system of things for whom it was a delusion to think the Almighty might care'.[49]

Anxiety increased with the appearance of the first cases of fever among the crews. Henry Halbert, a black stoker taken on in England, fell ill shortly after the *Wilberforce* left Cape Palmas and died four days later. The other cases appeared to be mild and were confined to the coloured members of the *Wilberforce*'s crew, who, it was noted, had spent time wooding at Grand Bassa. The expedition had meanwhile suffered two other losses: Samuel Johnson, a sailor aboard the *Albert*, who fell from the yardarm while furling the sails, and a Kruman taken on at Sierra Leone, who died apparently from apoplexy.[50]

At Accra the British, Dutch and Danes occupied adjoining forts, each with its national flag flying. John Duncan went on shore to purchase a supply of straw hats for the crew of the *Albert*, which persuaded him that the local inhabitants were 'a set of accomplished rogues'. The expedition's scientists were entertained by the Danish Governor, Mr Dall, who arranged for them to visit a nearby coffee plantation. Unlike Britain, Denmark had not yet abolished slavery. They found the superintendent's house 'arranged with European accommodations, where [they] were surrounded with all the luxury of the civilized world, and had for dinner French asparagus'. The slaves seemed to Vogel a cheerful group, little different from the free blacks except that they were possibly more shameless in demanding money for drink.[51]

Accra was the expedition's last port of call before entering the Niger. From there to the Nun estuary was only a short sail. But the weather now turned stormy. In driving rain and with a heavy swell running they soon lost sight of one another and were obliged to make their individual ways to what they hoped would prove to be the right stretch of coast. After several days of this buffeting visibility improved sufficiently for them to rendezvous and begin transferring a final supply of coals from the *Harriot* to the steamers. This they did under the watchful gaze of HMS *Buzzard*, the cruiser responsible for patrolling that stretch of coast. In the distance the land, or what they could glimpse of it through squalls of rain, looked sullen and uninviting, in fact much like many another stretch of coast except that twice a day, as the tide turned, a mighty gush of brown water came frothing and foaming outwards from the shore to where the vessels rode at anchor, tossing them about and splashing on to their decks. 'The ebullition,' Allen noted, 'was indeed so great that the water came in at the cabin windows which had not occurred before, with all the heavy swell we had experienced on this coast.' It was their first premonition of what awaited them beyond the distant line of breakers.[52]

CHAPTER FIVE
The First Ascent

On Friday, 13 August 1841, the *Albert*, piloted by Lieutenant Levinge of the *Buzzard*, followed closely by the *Soudan* and the *Amelia*, crossed over the bar of the Niger into the Nun estuary. A large leafless tree looking, it was thought, very much like a gallows, marked the point where the breakers gave way to the smoother water of the river. Rain was still falling accompanied by intermittent thunder and lightning. It was hardly an auspicious moment to have chosen for their arrival. Nevertheless, after the gales and buffeting of the previous week, it was a relief to be able to stand on deck and take in the view without having to cling to the rigging.

Not that there was a great deal to see. From where they anchored, some three-quarters of a mile beyond the bar, the Nun had more the appearance of a lake than a river. Terns and wading birds flew past, also swallows and the occasional kingfisher. Parties of pelicans sat bobbing on the water. Through their telescopes they could see that the banks were covered in dense thickets of mangroves. At high tide these appeared to cluster along the water's edge, much like alders along the Thames, but at low tide were revealed to be standing high above mud banks to which they clung precariously on their skeleton-like roots. Further away, well back from the river, were clumps of taller trees, baobabs, cotton trees and various types of palm.[1]

All three steamers had lost their rudder fins in the heavy seas. Leaving the *Albert* and *Amelia* riding at anchor, Trotter departed on the *Soudan* to find a shelving spot where they could be beached and repaired. He quickly discovered that the stories about the perplexing nature of the Delta were well founded. On every side were creeks, lagoons and broad stretches of water that looked inviting but led nowhere. After grounding several times the vessel finally stuck and was not got off until the following morning.

Doctors M'William and Stanger had meanwhile begun testing the water and were pleased to report that no evidence of hydrogen sulphide could be found. Less reassuring was the death, shortly after their cross-

Crossing the bar.

ing the bar, of the expedition's mathematical instrument maker, John William Bach. He was the first European on the expedition to have contracted fever and his death cast a shadow over the proceedings. However, it was noted that his symptoms suggested that the malady was of a 'non-endemical' variety; also that prior to joining the expedition he had been much given to drink, a serious handicap, one would suppose, for one of his profession. Further reassurance was found in the fact that those blacks aboard the *Wilberforce* who had first been taken ill were now well on the way to recovery. Bach's body was taken on shore in one of the *Albert*'s longboats and buried on a spit of land near the river mouth.[2]

Opposite this spot, but some little way down the coast, stood the village of Akassa. Since the expedition's arrival groups of villagers had been seen in the distance observing its movements. At first they had run away when officers approached, but on learning that the vessels were British they became more friendly and conversed readily in Spanish. They were primitive-looking figures, armed with long spears and crudely shaped iron machetes. They had their hair brushed up to form crests and their faces were heavily marked with perpendicular cicatrices. Apart from loincloths and strings of blue beads, they wore nothing at all.

Walking along the shore with a group of them, the officers came across

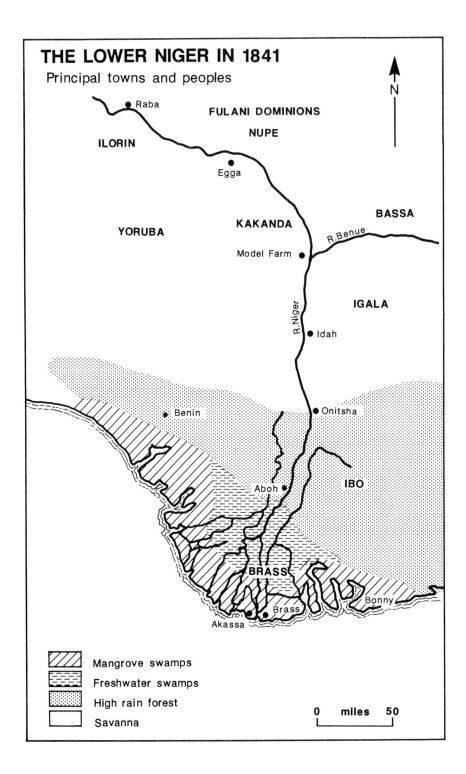

THE LOWER NIGER IN 1841
Principal towns and peoples

N

Raba

FULANI DOMINIONS

NUPE

ILORIN

Egga

BASSA

YORUBA

KAKANDA

R.Benue

Model Farm

R.Niger

IGALA

Idah

Benin

Onitsha

Aboh

IBO

BRASS

Bonny

Brass

Akassa

Mangrove swamps
Freshwater swamps
High rain forest
Savanna

0   miles   50

the body of a woman washed up by the tide. She was not long dead and had a length of rope looped around her waist. The villagers supposed she had been sacrificed somewhere up river and had floated down with the current. They laughed and seemed amused at the officers' concern. They themselves, according to William Allen, admitted to making human sacrifices on certain occasions, pointing out that the victims were merely slaves. Reports of other bodies further along the shore prompted the officers to wonder if 'some great Fetiche tragedy had lately been enacted', and, if so, whether it might in any way have been connected with their own arrival.[3]

The village of Akassa, which they later visited, impressed them as very poor. It consisted of some sixty bamboo huts, quadrangular in shape and roofed over with palm leaves. Among the villagers who flocked around them, Dr M'William noted several with scabs, ulcers and other cutaneous eruptions. He presumed these were caused either by syphilis or yaws. There were also several cases of leprosy. The village headman, Chief Emmery, readily agreed to the doctors' proposal that they be allowed to vaccinate the village children. In this respect, as they were to find elsewhere, Africans proved remarkably trusting, ascribing to British doctors even greater powers than those possessed by their own Ju-ju men. Emmery was aged about 50 and had donned a regimental drummer's jacket and a top hat, both the worse for wear, in honour of their visit. He seemed flattered by their attention and happily accepted their invitation to inspect the ships.[4]

Enquiry revealed that Emmery and his people were tributary to Ammai-Kunno, or King Boy as he was known to the British, the principal ruler of the central region of the Delta. In former times they had acted as his agents, keeping a lookout for British cruisers and providing pilots for the incoming slave ships on their way to the barracoons higher up the estuary. But since the tightening of Palmerston's blockade policy few slavers came this way and they had reverted mainly to fishing for their livelihood, along with some trading in palm oil which they exchanged with passing vessels for tobacco and rum.

King Boy's capital, Brass Town, lay some thirty miles to the east. A messenger was sent informing him of the expedition's arrival but he replied that he was too busy to attend a conference. Instead, he sent a nephew, Jack Fire, who came bringing a 'dash' of three sheep and an offer to sell them palm oil. Jack Fire boasted greatly of his uncle's wealth and power saying that he had a hundred and forty wives and eighteen large canoes, each with forty men, employed trading between the coast and the interior.

King Boy was already well known to the leaders of the expedition on account of his evil reputation. It was common knowledge that the slave trade was still carried on from Brass Town, where the Spanish firm of Pedro Martinez had an establishment.[5] In 1831 he had purchased the destitute Lander brothers and attempted to sell them to a passing Liverpool palm oil trader who, in the event, tricked him into parting with them without payment. Eighteen months later, when Richard Lander returned with Macgregor Laird and his steamers, he had done everything in his power to obstruct their operations. The pilot he provided, Laird suspected, had been instructed simply to lose them in the labyrinth of creeks running parallel to the shore. Louis, the pilot who eventually took them through the narrow passage leading to the Niger, was, according to William Allen, subsequently put to death on Boy's orders.[6] Laird describes Boy as an 'ill-looking fellow' with a 'disagreeable sulky cast of countenance', and Oldfield goes so far as to call him 'a wicked designing and treacherous villain'.[7] Trotter notes that he had 'long been notorious for dishonesty'.[8] When Buxton spoke of the degraded, corrupted natives of the coast it was the likes of King Boy he had in mind. In short, he was seen as greedy, treacherous and cruel, epitomizing all those deplorable traits of character associated with those who habitually dealt in human merchandise.

Being persuaded by the purity of their own intentions it was natural for these observers to judge the behaviour of Africans in moral rather than political or economic terms. Viewed from King Boy's standpoint, however, it was plain that the steamers, or 'Devil Ships' as he referred to them, represented a potent threat both to himself and to the Brass people. Indeed the entire thrust of British policy since the abolition of the slave trade could be seen as a deliberate attempt to destroy the livelihood of the Delta's inhabitants.

That problems of economic adjustment would arise had, of course, been foreseen. That was why Buxton had placed so much emphasis on the need to encourage legitimate commerce. The difficulty, so far as the lower Delta was concerned, was that its soils were too poor for anything of value to be grown there. For that very reason, until the coming of the Age of Discovery, this whole region had been uninhabited except for a few small settlements of Ijaw fishermen. There had, of course, been thriving societies in the interior, but they had looked to the north and east for their trade and to the long caravan routes leading across the desert to the Mediterranean coast and the Red Sea. The arrival of the seaborne Europeans had reversed this alignment, drawing migrants southward to found Brass, Bonny, Calabar and the other coastal settlements whose names are familiar from the annals of the slave trade. These were not tribal capitals in the traditional sense but small city-states with mixed populations whose trader-princes met Europeans as equal partners in trade and commerce.[9]

The danger now was that what had become a frontier of opportunity would again become an economic backwater. Britain's campaign against the slave trade had already succeeded in driving much of that particular traffic south of the line. However, as Jamieson had pointed out, slaving had now largely been replaced by the trade in palm oil. This was something to which the coastal peoples could well adapt. Palm oil, like the slaves and virtually everything else exported from the Gulf, came from the interior and could not be disposed of without their assistance. The real challenge to their position therefore came not from the cruisers but from the steamers. For once Europeans were able to trade directly with the interior there would no longer be a role for middlemen; the whole delicately balanced system of river commerce, built up over centuries, would instantly disappear. Goods would no longer pass from merchant to merchant and town to town as they had done. The old relay system would be superseded. In short, what confronted Brass, Bonny and the other coastal states was the prospect of a technological revolution that would leave them not only without trade but bereft of any alternative means of sustenance. Then what would become of Boy's eighteen canoes? As Jack Fire explained to the officers, they were employed bringing from up-river palm oil, yams, fowls, goats, sheep, rice and black beans, and taking back rum, cowries, cloths, shirts, hats, knives, looking-glasses, hook and line, scissors, tumblers, wine glasses, muskets, powder and ball.[10] Without the rum and muskets they would be unable to obtain the palm oil; more important, they would lack the yams, bullocks and other foodstuffs on which they depended for their very existence. They would, in fact, find themselves reduced to the same miserable condition as the people of Akassa.

This explains why King Boy trailed abjectly behind Laird and his steamers all the way up-river to Aboh and his embarrassing intrusion into the subsequent negotiations with its ruler. When Laird remarked on his fawning attitude towards the Aboh leader he replied, 'King Obi too much palm oil, King Boy too little.' It also explains the very different account which Oldfield heard him give to the Brass people on his return from Aboh: 'Devil ship no will! King Boy no will! Devil ship no will! King Boy no will! King Boy all same as King Obi! King Boy big, all same as King Obi! Palaver set – palaver set!' But King Boy was not as big as King Obi. There was no hope that any palaver would dissuade the people of Aboh from trading directly with the steamers if the opportunity arose. Boy's position, for the moment, looked desperate. How much he knew about the ambush in which Lander lost his life is not revealed. One doubts that the news of that event, or of the expedition's subsequent débâcle, caused him anything other than joy. His only regret, possibly, was that he had allowed the Lander brothers to emerge from the Niger, so bringing about this new challenge to himself and his people.[11]

The *Wilberforce* had meanwhile completed its loading and joined the other vessels. In a final despatch to Lord John Russell, entrusted to Lieutenant Levinge, the commissioners reported that the *Harriot* was now on its way to Fernando Po and that the rudders were being repaired. When that had been done the expedition would begin its ascent of the river. Except for a few minor cases of fever they were in excellent health and good heart.[12]

During the week that they spent in the estuary heavy rain, accompanied by thunder and lightning, fell every day. Nevertheless, the crews pressed ahead with scraping away the barnacles and seaweed that had accumulated on the ships' hulls, adjusting the retractable keels and fitting new rudders. To protect themselves from the worst of the storms they erected a marquee acquired from the sponsors of the famous Eglinton Tournament of 1839, designed in the form of a knightly pavilion and suggestive of jousting and chivalry, that would have looked very well on the tented fields of Agincourt but appeared decidedly out of place and rather forlorn in its present surroundings. In the evenings they lit fires to repel the night mists rising from the nearby swamps.

By 19 August all three steamers had been refloated. After a formal prayer by the expedition's chaplain, asking God to 'give success to our endeavours to introduce civilization and Christianity into this benighted country', they got up steam and set out. The *Albert*, with the *Amelia* in tow, led the way with the *Soudan* and the *Wilberforce* following. The skies had finally cleared and with the sun shining and the river sparkling they headed northward up the estuary. Along the way they passed the spot, now deserted, where King Boy's barracoons had formerly stood. Away from the coast the Nun narrowed, taking on more the appearance of a river, although, broken up as it was by mud banks and with branches leading off in all directions, it was impossible to tell, except from the strength of the current, where the main channel lay. Further on, as they approached Louis Creek, it seemed as if the Niger's waters were being choked by the accumulations of silt carried down from the interior and so compelled to seep downward as though through some giant sponge, soft and porous. Occasionally whole chunks of it would break off and come floating by with vegetation attached.[13]

Louis Creek itself, when they reached it, proved to be set at an angle to the main body of water and only some thirty yards wide. The *Wilberforce*, approaching with too much caution, failed to get its head into the stream and was swept back by the unexpected velocity of the current. Fortunately there was room enough to turn and make a second attempt. Under the shade of the trees, with no breeze to stir the air, it was suffocatingly hot. The mangroves grew so closely that they brushed the sides of the ships as they passed. Mixed in with them were bunches of orchids and festoons of purple and white flowering creeper. Troops of small monkeys hopped from tree to tree keeping pace with the vessels.

Little by little the channel widened until it finally gave way to another broad sheet this time of fresh water interspersed with many small islets. They were now beyond the influence of the tides. Up to this point they had seen no sign of human occupation, but presently lines of fishing stakes were observed extending out from the shore and nearby the occasional fishing hut. Further along were small cultivated patches. A native in a very tiny canoe appeared and, catching sight of them, instantly vanished into a nearby creek. By the late afternoon they were passing small groups of mud huts. When the *Albert* anchored opposite one of these small settlements the villagers fled into the bush. They were persuaded to come out by a visiting Ibo pilot whom the expedition had met earlier in the estuary. Captain Trotter offered to hire him but he wanted more for his services than they were prepared to pay. In the village was a Ju-ju house containing the wooden likeness of a crocodile.

They anchored for the night near a larger village. The inhabitants gathered on the bank armed with muskets and cutlasses, but it soon became evident that their intentions were not aggressive and that they had merely turned out to defend themselves. Assured through interpreters that no attack was intended they laid aside their weapons but refused to approach any closer.

Throughout the day, observing the passing scene from under the canvas awnings, members of the expedition had been struck by the silence of the swamps. Except for the noises of the ships, the pounding of the engines, the churning of the paddles and the rhythmical chanting of the leadsmen, no sound reached them. After the surge and swell of the sea it seemed strange and slightly eerie. But now, as night fell, their surroundings sprang to life with a strident cacophony of frogs and insects. As it grew darker the air was filled with myriads of fireflies. Anchored in mid-stream with the water rippling under their bows, the current was strong enough to turn the paddles and circulate air through the medicators and ventilating tubes, but away from the coast there was no evening breeze to swell the windsails, now hanging limply from the mastheads. Below deck the atmosphere remained as hot and humid as it had been all day.

Resuming their progress the following morning they passed more small settlements. Here they observed stacks of puncheons and other evidence that palm oil was being actively collected. The people were still very timid. A number were observed earnestly arming themselves with sticks and billhooks and running along the banks to warn neighbouring villages of the vessels' approach. Towards the afternoon, however, others less fearful came paddling out in their canoes to offer poultry, goats, yams, plantains and bunches of bananas. None wore more than a loincloth and many wore nothing at all. As if to make up for this lack of opportunity for self-decoration they had their hair shaven into chess-board patterns or plaited and piled up in crests, ridges, pyramids and other fantastical shapes. For amusement the officers began dropping coloured handkerchiefs overboard to watch the canoeists race to pick them up. One woman, who had retrieved several, overtook the *Albert* to offer them back under the impression that they might have fallen by accident.

The river was now three hundred yards or more wide and confined between well-defined banks. Since their passage through Louis Creek the mangroves had been replaced by palms and cotton trees growing up to the water's edge and reminding William Simpson of the rain forests of South America. As on the previous day, the doctors continued testing the air and water, but could still find no trace of hydrogen sulphide.

At intervals they passed large canoes deeply laden with palm oil bound for Bonny. These had iron cannon lashed to their bows and their crews were well armed with muskets. Most appeared to belong to King Boy.

After a second night on the river, the *Wilberforce* took a divergent route leading off to the west. Here the giant trees almost met overhead and trailing creepers became entangled in the rigging. The air was damp and suffocating. Chattering flights of parrots criss-crossed the river and herons, disturbed by their approach, flew ahead on heavy wings. No white man, they learned, had previously passed this way. In one village they were offered some young Yoruba captives, little boys aged 9 or 10. Their owner agreed that the slave trade was a bad thing but could see no hope of its ever being given up. In another village they found people firmly persuaded that slaves sold to whites were killed and eaten. This, as Mungo Park had discovered during his travels along the headwaters of the Niger, was a widely held belief in the West African interior. That the exporting of slaves still continued in spite of this, Schön reflected, was sad evidence of Africa's fallen state.[14]

The *Wilberforce* rejoined the main channel ahead of the rest of the expedition. Rather than wait for it to catch up, they left a message with the headman of a nearby village and continued on upstream.

Their arrival at Oniah market produced a considerable stir. Oniah was the principal trading centre between Aboh and the coast and marked the dividing line between Brass and Ibo territory. Like Onitsha, Gori and Buddu markets, which the expedition would visit later, it was regarded as neutral ground where even those who were at war with one another could meet and exchange goods.[15] The *Wilberforce* was quickly surrounded by dozens of canoes of all types. Among the occupants, Marquis Granby, the

Scene on the lower Niger.

Brass interpreter, a recaptive whom they had taken on at Sierra Leone, recognized Ukasa, the brother of his former owner. Ukasa was invited on deck and was so astonished that anyone sold to the slave ships should return, a thing that had never been known before, that he volunteered to guide them to Aboh, mainly, it would seem, in order to hear the full story of Granby's adventures.

It emerged that Ukasa had at various times had Granby in his charge and had taken a parental interest in his development. However, Granby had subsequently proved such a troublesome slave, continually running away, that the brother had sold him down the river. After his recapture by a British cruiser he had served for some years on board a British man-of-war. This enabled him to impress Ukasa with his knowledge of the wider world. Interpreters were key figures on the expedition. When they spoke to their fellow Africans it was as the representatives of the world's leading maritime power. It was a role Granby relished, as his superiors had already noted. Only the previous day, pressed by some of the officers to reassure a nervous village headman as to their peaceable intentions, he had rounded on them with the retort 'I done tell him this already. I tell him "Suppose you go fire one big gun, him whole town go broke."' For a former slave, and a disgraced one at that, he had arranged his return in style![16]

It turned out that Ukasa remembered William Allen, also Brown, the coloured clerk taken on at Cape Coast, from their visit to Aboh with Laird. According to Ukasa the Obi greatly lamented Laird's failure to send back the steamers as had been promised.

The rest of the expedition was meanwhile making slow progress. Trotter had been sufficiently alarmed at the *Wilberforce*'s disappearance to take the *Albert* back to the point where she had turned off, firing the guns as a signal. Failing to get any response and guessing what had happened he resumed his ascent. All the villages within earshot of the gunfire, including those they had passed earlier, were now deserted and their canoes hidden. Further on they found the *Soudan* aground. She had picked up the *Wilberforce*'s message and turned back, but, misjudging the swiftness of the current, had found herself swept onto a sandbank. After towing her off it was the turn of the *Albert*, with the *Amelia* once again in tow, to run aground. A crowd of good-humoured villagers promptly turned out and helped push her off.

Beyond Oniah they found themselves accompanied by a growing flotilla of canoes of all types. Those who had missed seeing the *Wilberforce* on its passage upstream now flocked out in such crowds to see the other vessels that their progress took on the appearance of a regatta. Excited groups of children ran along the banks. A man in a canoe alongside the *Soudan* got to his feet and danced to the rhythmic beat of the paddles. Some of the more venturesome swam out to get a better view and to compete for the pocket handkerchiefs tossed overboard.[17]

They anchored off Aboh late in the afternoon of Wednesday, 25 August, to find the *Wilberforce*, which had arrived the previous evening, surrounded by canoes and a royal visitation in progress. But being late in the day it was decided to postpone any formal negotiations until the following morning.

The Niger was now some half a mile wide, muddy brown in colour, and fast flowing. The land on either side was low and swampy and, because of the height of the river, much of it was under water. The town of Aboh itself, screened from view by trees, was set back from the main river on a parallel creek. A good deal was already known about the place from the accounts of Lander and Laird. Laird had put its population at between five and six thousand, making it by far the largest settlement in the northern Delta. It owed its size and influence principally to its strategic location at the apex of the network of creeks connecting with the coast which enabled it to command the entire trade of the Niger valley. Canoes from the interior needed to pass by before branching off to Bonny, Brass or Benin. So far as its own trade was concerned, Aboh could play off one coastal state against another by virtue of having direct access to the Gulf at many different points. Any military challenge to its position could readily be dealt with. In an exceptional emergency, according to William Allen, Aboh could muster as many as three hundred war canoes armed with muskets and cannon.[18]

Yet, strong though Aboh's position appeared, there was every prospect that it could be strengthened still further by opening up direct trade with Europeans, thereby cutting out the coastal middlemen. Laird had been in no doubt that the aim was to establish a monopoly. This was precisely what King Boy feared. There was, of course, a danger that Aboh itself might be bypassed, but that appeared negligible. The demand was now for palm oil and Aboh was in the centre of the palm-oil-producing region. Whatever might be found higher up the river, among the Igala, Nupe and Fulani, it would not be palm oil. All things considered, it was plausible to suppose that Aboh stood to gain more than it would lose from direct trade. This had certainly been the view in 1832. No trader, in Laird's view, was ever more eager for custom than the Obi.[19]

On the morning after the *Wilberforce*'s arrival a deputation appeared led by the Obi's eldest son, Ejeh, who immediately recognized Allen from his earlier visit. After breakfast in the officers' quarters he returned to the town in company with Charles Roscher, the mineralogist, and shortly before noon the royal flotilla emerged from Aboh creek to the accompaniment of much blowing of horns and beating of drums. The Obi himself was immediately identifiable, standing amidships in his canoe under a large crimson parasol held over him by an attendant. He wore a red coat, baggy white trousers of Turkish dimensions, and a black conical hat which he sported at a rakish angle and from which there dangled a gold tassel. His canoe, flying a makeshift Union Jack, was enormous, hewn out of a single cotton tree and propelled by forty pull-a-boys.

On reaching the deck he welcomed Allen as an old friend. This, at least, is the account Allen gives of his greeting, and subsequent events bear out its accuracy. But what is striking about the descriptions of this and other encounters with Africans is the sharply contrasting impressions they made on different observers. Allen reserved his particular animus for Ju-ju men, whom he describes as 'easily distinguished by their keen, insidious look and overbearing manner'. Other Africans, however, he judged on what he took to be their individual merits. In the case of the Obi he found 'his features . . . pleasing and his countenance expressive of kindness, with an air of dignity and self-possession like one used to command'. He was, Allen judged, 'not much under fifty'. By way of contrast, William Simpson, describing the same encounter, saw the Obi as 'a short, ill-favoured looking man, of about sixty years of age . . . clothed in . . . a cap, not unlike a fool's cap . . . no shoes, but anklets of ivory and wild beasts' tusks'. As it happened he was on this occasion angry at having had his waistcoat purloined by one of the Obi's sons who

Aboh Creek with war canoes.

'paced the deck with all imaginable satisfaction with himself, leaving me to compensate myself for the loss of my garment'. But, this misadventure aside, he could see no virtue in what he regarded as savagery and viewed his superiors' anxiety to impress their visitors with deep Methodist distrust.[20]

Even Allen was put out of countenance by the appearance of the Obi's wives and daughters, clad in ivory bracelets and anklets and very little else, inappropriate dress for a visit to a British man-of-war at any time but especially in view of the formal nature of the occasion. Long dresses were promptly rustled up from the stores and presented to the visitors, who donned them with reluctance, looking, as Allen himself was forced to admit, less than entirely comfortable.

The Obi himself was meanwhile showing great curiosity about the ship and its fitments. He was particularly fascinated by the twelve-pounder long-gun which the crew fired for his benefit. He professed himself disappointed to find that the *Wilberforce* was not a trade ship but brightened up considerably at the mention of gifts. He was, he said, willing to trade in palm oil, ivory and slaves. This last was not well received. Allen and Commissioner Cook duly explained that the English were averse to the slave trade. To this the Obi responded by saying that he intended to give up that particular traffic. Unperturbed by the abruptness of this conversation, Cook urged him not to judge white men

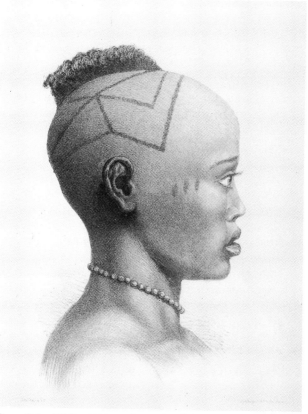

One of the Obi's children drawn by John Duncan.

by the colour of their skins. Many white men did wicked things but they were Spaniards, not Englishmen. It was the English who, by means of their cruisers, were trying to put down the slave trade. At this point the Obi grew restive and asked to see more of the ship. On being shown a lithograph of Queen Victoria and Prince Albert he surprised his hosts by enquiring which was which. It was remembered, however, that he had never seen a white woman. He left at sundown, although some of his entourage remained at dinner with the junior officers until later in the evening.[21]

Official negotiations began early the following morning. The Obi arrived as before in his state canoe, only this time in a scarlet outfit and bringing with him a gift of two bullocks, two sheep and a large quantity of yams. He and his retinue were piped on board the *Albert* by the ship's crew and there received by the four commissioners in full dress regalia complete with cocked hats and feathers. They were then escorted to the quarter deck and seated under the awnings. It was done, according to Duncan who supervised the event, using precisely the same rules that would have applied had they been receiving the Lord High Admiral of England.

Trotter opened the proceedings[22] by explaining that he had been sent by his Queen to negotiate a treaty for the abolition of the slave trade. Quite apart from the moral issues involved, it would be very much to the Obi's advantage to retain as many of his people as possible for the purpose of gathering palm oil, ivory and other commodities instead of selling them to traders for trifling amounts and so losing their services for ever.

The Obi said he understood. However, he did not sell his own people, nor did he make war to get slaves, although sometimes the captives he took in the course of his struggles with neighbouring rulers became slaves. If, however, the English would bring him other kinds of commerce he would be happy to give up the slave trade. What he wanted were cowries, cloth, muskets, powder, handkerchiefs, coral beads. What else? Hats. Would he be interested in salt? Yes, in that too. In return he would sell palm oil, ivory, dyes such as camwood and indigo, indeed whatever the English wanted and he could provide. As Trotter was later to report, the attitude that emerged as a result of their close questioning 'was more that of a keen trader than of a sovereign chief of an extensive country'.[23]

This is hardly surprising. The Ibo were not a monarchical people. The Obi's position, therefore, was more akin to that of the trader-princes of Brass and Bonny than to that of traditional tribal chiefs such as the Attah of Igala whom the commissioners were to encounter later. What the transcript of their discussion also reveals, however, is his impatience with their attempts to interfere in what he regarded as domestic matters and their irritating habit of going back and forth over the same ground. This became apparent early in their discussions when Schön attempted to read him the African Civilization Society's (in fact Priscilla Johnston's) 'Address to the Chiefs of Africa'. He had, he said, already promised to give up the slave trade and wished to hear no more about it. He and his people would do what they could. If, however, the English wanted him to intervene in the traffic carried on by others they would need to provide him with the necessary arms for it would certainly involve him in war with his neighbours.

Alarmed at the direction the discussion was taking, the commissioners asked the Obi to retire for a few minutes. The idea of engaging Africans in an armed struggle against the slave trade was a notion too outrageous even for the fertile imagination of James Stephen. Yet now that it had been drawn to their attention it did look very much like the logical corollary of what they were proposing. Plainly it was not an issue to be decided on the spur of the moment.

On the Obi's return, therefore, the commissioners turned to a different line of questioning. Did he, in fact, have the authority to make binding agreements on behalf of all his people? Indeed he did. Whatever might be the case in England there was only one King in Aboh. He would also be happy for the English to travel freely through his dominions, establish trading posts, practise their religion, cultivate the land and would punish any of his subjects who interfered with their right to do so. To all such proposals he responded with an emphatic *makka* ('it is good') and by snapping his fingers as a sign of approval.

He was less impressed by the Reverend Schön's attempts to explain the Christian religion. In response to the statement 'There is only one God', he replied, rather mysteriously, that he had heard there were two. (Father and Son? God and Devil? – the matter was never clarified.) He also flatly contradicted much that had been gleaned from Ukasa and members of his own entourage who had visited the *Wilberforce* the previous day. Human beings were not sacrificed, only animals. He had never heard of the practice of leaving newborn twins in the bush to die. Finally, rising to his feet, he declared he was tired of so much talking and wished to go on shore.

It was now mid-afternoon. At his invitation a group from the *Albert* returned to Aboh with the royal party. The river, they were told, was higher than for many years. It seemed that this must, indeed, be the case since much of the area was under water. As they approached closer they could see clusters of dishevelled huts strung out along the creek to which they were connected by a system of narrow canals, bridged over here and there by fallen trees and broken remnants of canoe. Heavy rain, which had been falling ever since they arrived, added to the dismal prospect.

The Obi was borne from his canoe to the royal residences on the back of a sturdy attendant. The visitors, declining an invitation to be carried in the same way, waded along behind. The royal residences themselves proved to be a rambling assemblage of buildings built of stick and clay, with wide overhanging roofs of palm leaves, and raised above the surrounding morass either on strong wooden stakes or earth mounds.[24]

On arrival the visitors were shown into an interior courtyard and offered calabashes of palm wine. From what they could see of them the adjoining apartments appeared surprisingly dry and clean. No doubt, Schön reflected, had they arrived at a different time of year they would have formed a very different impression of the town. At one end of the courtyard he noted a large idol armed with a sword and pistol. This was the god of war. Various of the Obi's wives appeared, bursting into uncontrollable fits of giggling at the odd appearance of their visitors.

The Obi and his wives.

The Obi himself, anxious to repay their hospitality, insisted that his guests sit on his throne, a clay elevation set under the eaves and covered with elegantly woven grass matting. He was in an ebullient mood and described for the benefit of his wives the events of the day, after which he retired to consult with his headmen and practise his ritual observances. Some of the officers later glimpsed him, surrounded by his attendants, touching with the point of a sword a series of iron rings strung out along a pole, rather as if he were conducting an experiment in magnetizing.[25]

The Obi's departure left his guests free to join other members of the expedition who had already begun exploring the town. William Simpson was with a party that met a large procession of townspeople led by the King's trumpeter, whom he characteristically describes as 'a mirth-exciting personage' blowing into an enormous horn, hung with a string of human teeth, by means of which he produced a braying noise like an ox. The people themselves seemed friendly enough, inviting the visitors into their homes and offering fruit and palm wine. Nevertheless, some of what they saw suggested that the Obi had been less than frank.

Several later reported having seen captives in chains. One group that wandered into the bush came upon a large earthen idol, placed in a thicket surrounded by high trees, from which they were driven away by priests with cries of '*Tshuku-Tshuku*'. *Tshuku* meant God. Was this where

104

human sacrifices were offered? Their suspicions were strengthened by the discovery of a boy, chained by the neck, with two headless goats nearby which, they were told, had recently been sacrificed. On returning to the ships and hearing the sound of tom-toms accompanied by much shouting it was hard not to suppose that barbarous rituals were being practised.[26]

When, however, Simon Jonas, the Ibo interpreter, who had remained in the town overnight, returned to the *Albert* the following morning, he reported no such events. True to his word, the Obi had proclaimed his intentions of giving up the slave trade and of abiding by the other terms proposed. Jonas did report, however, that the suspicions of some of those who had visited the vessels had been aroused by what they had seen. Peering into one of the medical officers' cabins they had observed a human skull which, they could only suppose, had been taken from some poor African. This, in fact, was not far off the mark. In the 1840s, craniology, the study of skulls and, in particular, the measuring of the size of the brain capacities of those belonging to different races, was seen as an exciting new science whose exponents claimed to have found an objective basis for the study of mankind. Among the papers passed on by the Admiralty was one from the distinguished anthropologist Dr James Cowles Pritchard asking the scientists on the expedition to study the character of the different races they encountered and 'if possible to get some of their skulls, well ascertained to be such'.[27] What the origin of this particular skull was is not revealed. But these were scientific matters which, it was assumed, Africans could not grasp. Visitors to the ships also expressed puzzlement at the way Europeans spoke out against *arrisi* or idols while surrounding themselves with votive images and ritualistic objects of their own – crosses, bibles, lithographs of The Saviour and of the royal couple – which they treated as if they were *arrisi* and which differed from those of Aboh principally by virtue of finer manufacture. 'We can hardly believe,' Schön noted, 'how ignorant they are and what singular conclusions they will draw from things they see or hear.'[28] Cultural relativism was not a viewpoint that commended itself to the minds of Victorians.

For an alarming moment it even seemed as though this mutual incomprehension might prevent the signing of the treaty. As on the previous evening the Obi was in an expansive mood. Upon being seated on the quarterdeck, however, he quickly made it plain that he was not disposed to listen to any further sermons on the subject of the slave trade. While the final draft of the treaty was being prepared, therefore, Trotter proposed that they pray for the blessing of God. The Obi obediently fell to his knees along with everyone else but on rising appeared greatly agitated, evidently fearing some form of sorcery, and called for his Ju-ju man. Unwilling to allow a pagan rite on a Christian vessel his hosts quickly intervened, explaining that no harm had been intended. He was eventually calmed down with the help of a tumbler of port and taken to Trotter's cabin. There Duncan helped pass the time by drawing his portrait and playing tunes on the Jew's harp, which the Obi accompanied by clapping his hands.[29]

After the treaty had been signed and witnessed he was presented with a double-barrelled flintlock, a pair of silver-mounted pistols, a ceremonial sabre, a sergeant-major's dress uniform, several lengths of cloth and a great many mirrors, pocket knives and other gewgaws. The value of all the gifts together was about fifty pounds. He was, he said, delighted with them although what he wanted was not presents but regular trade. Aboh always had plenty of palm oil. He would be happy to have a mission established there and hoped that in the meantime Simon Jonas would be allowed to remain, a request to which the commissioners promptly assented. Altogether it was regarded as a very statesman-like performance. Before leaving the ship he displayed his resolution by stoically holding on to the leads of a galvanic battery for a full minute, something none of his entourage had been prepared to do, a feat that impressed both them and the Europeans present.[30]

After the departure of the Obi and his followers the steamers resumed their ascent of the river, accompanied as before by a flotilla of excited canoeists. The visit to Aboh, it was felt, could hardly have gone better. The commissioners were particularly reassured by the Obi's request to have Simon Jonas remain, something he would scarcely have proposed had he not intended to keep to the terms of their treaty.

Spirits were also raised by the reappearance of the sun. After the almost incessant rain of the preceding week everything above and below deck was sodden. Dr Reid's fans had been kept running night and day but the effect had been slight. Indeed, on the lower deck, where the crew slept, apart from producing a strong smell of chlorine, they seemed to have no effect at all. Plainly, to cope with the steamy atmosphere of the Niger, a much more powerful system of air-conditioning was needed.[31]

But with the sun shining and a blue sky these problems were soon forgotten. At every turn the river became more majestic. On occasion it appeared to be as much as two miles wide, perhaps more, although it was difficult to tell on account of the numerous islands and the fact that it had overflowed its banks in many places. The river also revealed various novelties: crocodiles, an enormous floating python, rafts of flowering waterlilies, exotic water birds, flocks of parakeets, gaudy butterflies. Once a body came floating by. Occasionally their progress was interrupted by having to avoid whole trees borne downward by the current, their roots and branches sticking up out of the muddy waters, showing that the Niger was very much in full flood.

Beyond Damugu, which they passed at noon on their third day, the appearance of both the country and the people began to change. For the first time they saw areas of rising ground which presently gave way to low hills. This was Igala territory. The houses now were circular in shape with high conical roofs. At one point they glimpsed a walled town. The people wore robes and turbans and impressed Duncan as looking much more civilized than those they had seen earlier.

They anchored off Idah, the Igala capital, just as the sun was setting. The town was set high up on a sandstone bluff overlooking the river, here a mile-and-a-half wide. It was a clear night with a bright moon. From where they lay close in shore they could hear the sound of voices and music and see fires burning in various parts of the town. It was an idyllic scene.

Rain set in early the next morning. A deputation consisting of M'William, Schön and William Johnson, the Igala interpreter, departed to wait on the Attah. On landing they learned that strangers could not approach so eminent a personage without having been formally introduced. They were therefore taken through a maze of narrow streets to the residence of Amanda Bue, a sister of the late ruler, a large woman with a shaven head, who offered them palm wine and goora nuts. After questioning them about the expedition and its aims she sent a eunuch to announce their arrival to the Attah. They then settled down in her piazza to await a summons to the palace.

News of their presence had spread. Inquisitive crowds came to peer at them. So too did dogs, sheep, hens and goats which, like the townspeople, seemed to have free access to the establishment. A row of scraggy-necked vultures eyed them from a nearby rooftop. No one appeared in the least concerned about the passage of time or at all perturbed when, after three hours, they announced their intention of visiting the market.[32]

They were hungry on account of having left the ships before breakfast. The market was bustling. Unfortunately, they had neglected to bring any cowries with them, but a good-natured townsman gave them enough to buy peanuts and coconuts. What they saw bore out Duncan's view that the Igala were more civilized and certainly far more adept as craftsmen than the people lower down the river. Islamic influences were much in evidence. Laid out under the trees they saw saddles, bridles, whips, armlets, sandals and various other items of leatherware. They were much struck by the cotton goods, made up of narrowly woven strips stitched together and dyed in bright colours. Also on display were swords, daggers and spearheads, many nicely engraved or with inlays of different coloured metal. Everything they saw, they were assured, was of local manufacture. There were, they noted, almost no European wares to be seen. It all went to show that the Igala were an intelligent, industrious

The landing place at Idah.

people with well-developed commercial instincts whose friendship would be well worth cultivating.

Back at Amanda Bue's they were given a meal of stewed meat and yams served up in wooden bowls. The princess showed them how to eat it with their fingers, first sampling a piece from each bowl herself to demonstrate that it was not poisoned. What sort of meat it was they were not sure. Then, shortly after midday, word arrived from the Attah and they were taken to the royal residence. This was a cluster of conical-shaped dwellings set apart from the rest of the town, protected on one side by the cliff edge, and on the other three by a clay wall the entrances to which were guarded by the Attah's personal bodyguard armed with spears and muskets. They were escorted to an interior patio where they were left for another four hours. It was not, they were told, the Attah's custom to receive visitors while it was raining. This seemed an odd excuse, particularly since it was not raining at that particular moment. Finally, on their declaring that they would return to the ships and depart up-river, attendants appeared carrying carpets and a bamboo throne.

The Attah's arrival was heralded by a procession of between forty and fifty eunuchs, led by a group of musicians, who arranged themselves cross-legged in front of the throne facing the visitors. The Attah was then borne in on a litter by eight slaves. A screen was temporarily erected while he was seated on his throne and his dress adjusted. On its removal he was revealed as a large, portly man in his middle years and of rather sluggish appearance flanked by his priests and ministers. Throughout most of the proceedings he remained impassive while a spokesman expressed his views.

Johnson, it turned out, was a distant relative of the Attah's. After describing his experiences since leaving the Niger he briefly outlined the expedition's purpose and invited the Attah to visit the ships. Everything he said was repeated word for word by the Attah's spokesman in a louder tone of voice. Replying on behalf of the Attah the spokesman said that Johnson should be pleased to see a member of his family now on the throne. The Attah was delighted to welcome white men, but they must not be impatient. He liked his guests to stay for several days and eat with him. Also, he did not like going out in the rain. When they insisted on seeing him he presumed that they could stop the rain, but he observed that rain was still falling. As Attah he ruled the river north and south. God made the Attah to be very much like himself and no Attah ever went on board a canoe. If strangers wanted to see him they would need to come to Idah. Next time he wanted the captain of the expedition, not his messengers.

It was a kingly speech. Whether he actually believed they could stop the rain was left unclear. Schön, never notable for his sense of humour, supposed he did. Africans, Schön was persuaded, were so conscious of white superiority they could believe them capable of almost anything. During their subsequent discussions the Attah himself occasionally intervened. Was it the British who were interfering with the slave trade along the coast? Did they, in fact, *have* land and houses like other people or did they live perpetually on board these floating towns by means of which they travelled about? It also emerged that the delays they had experienced had been deliberately arranged as a way of learning their intentions and that every detail of what they had said and done during the day, including the gift of cowries, had been promptly reported to the palace. It seemed a curiously Byzantine method of conducting business.

It was immediately clear to the commissioners that meeting in Idah would put them at a disadvantage. At Aboh the steamers themselves had provided all the testimony that was needed of the wealth, power and ingenuity of the nation they represented. Anyone who doubted that in another, far-off part of the world Progress and Christianity were on the march need only look about him. The Igala, as had been amply demonstrated, set great store by ceremony and display. But they were a land rather than a riverine power. Up-river, it was noted, canoes were not armed with cannon and swivel-guns. Since passing Damugu they had glimpsed groups of armed horsemen. Impressing the Attah would require mobilizing all their resources.

The next day was sultry but fine. At the appointed hour each of the

The Attah and his attendants.

steamers fired a five-gun salute. The commissioners and their party in full regalia clambered into the paddle-box boats and departed for the shore. There they found a group of musicians waiting along with six horses. Duncan was assigned the largest of these, in his opinion a poor creature more like a New Forest pony than a horse, its saddle and bridle not worth five shillings. For a man of six feet three inches, with cuirass and helmet, it was certainly a diminutive mount. The musicians led the procession, followed by Duncan, his knees up to his chin and carrying a boarding pike with a Union Jack attached; next came the marines and sappers trying not very successfully to keep in step occasionally blowing on their bugles, while the commissioners and chief clerk brought up the rear on the remaining horses.

The procedure was much as on the previous day, only this time the entire town turned out to witness their arrival. First they were taken to see Princess Amanda Bue, who recognized Commander Allen from his previous visit. After some desultory talk they made their way to the royal compound, rather prematurely it turned out as no preparations had yet been made to receive them. Gradually, however, the dignitaries began to arrive, making their way through the crowd of spectators that had gathered outside. Some were men of striking appearance. Particularly imposing, it was thought, was Lobo, the chief judge, a tall figure enveloped in a light blue robe, who strode in accompanied by a young

attendant carrying the ceremonial sword of justice. 'His whole appearance', according to Allen, 'was extremely commanding, and his features
expressive of intelligence, dignity and benevolence.'

The same could not be said of the Attah who on arrival proved to be
even more fantastically dressed than on the previous day in layers of
gown, scarlet trousers, huge leather boots decorated with bells, and a
conical hat not unlike the Obi's but ornamented with feathers. The whole
assemblage, Duncan thought, made him look not unlike Guy Fawkes on
bonfire night. As before, the Attah relied on his spokesman to answer on
his behalf. He himself remained impassive throughout most of the
proceedings but when, as occasionally happened, he laughed, his fan-
bearers swiftly extended their fans to cover his face, apparently on the
principle that it was unbecoming for a personage of his eminence to
betray his emotions in front of strangers.

The negotiations, if they can be called that, proved very perfunctory as
the Attah, or rather his spokesman, immediately agreed to everything
that was asked. This was the more surprising as William Johnson the
previous day had outlined their aims only in the most general terms.
Perhaps more had been learned through Amanda Bue and the spokesman's responses merely reflected what the Attah and his advisers had
already decided. More disturbing was the possibility that no thought had
been given to these matters at all and, knowing what had happened to the
Laird expedition and with the prospect of gifts, they regarded the formal
part of the negotiations as merely an exchange of airy promises for which
they would never be called to account. But, whatever the explanation, the
Attah instantly agreed to prohibit the slave trade, discontinue human
sacrifices, allow a Christian mission to be established, provide a portion
of land near the Niger–Benue confluence for the model farm, and collect
trading goods for exchange with the steamers which, he was assured,
would henceforward be making regular visits to his kingdom.

As each of these undertakings was agreed his attendants gave a loud
shout of approbation, taken up by the crowd outside, as if some major
stroke of statesmanship had been accomplished. Eager to enter into the
spirit of the occasion, on the mention of their sovereign's name the British
contingent rose to their feet baring their heads while the buglers played
'God Save the Queen'. This brought the Attah to life, who asked if he
could examine one of the bugles. He also enquired about John Duncan
who, as Master at Arms, commanded the buglers and whose Life
Guards' finery came closest to rivalling his own. How many such soldiers
did the Queen have? On being told the size of Her Majesty's forces he
expressed great astonishment.

It was now growing dark. No lights being produced, the deputation
took its leave, explaining that the following day would be Sunday, and

therefore a day of rest, but that they would return on the Monday with the treaty.

They went back to the ships pleased if a little puzzled by their encounter, not least by the readiness with which all their demands had been met. It was an error, Allen reflected, to think of the Igala as uncivilized. They were deft craftsmen. Their ceremonial robes, dyed in striking colours and intricately embroidered in silk, were garments of great magnificence. Plainly they were not savages. But could they really mean what they said and agree to alter their whole way of life without discussion or question simply because some white visitors urged them to do so? It seemed improbable. Yet there was no denying that they were an able and industrious people with an elaborate, albeit autocratic, system of government. They were also, so far as could be learned, capable of raising a formidable army. Whether, on this account, they would be much susceptible to European influence time would show. But whatever the outcome they were clearly not the children of darkness yearning for spiritual light dreamed of by Buxton and the African Civilization Society. Abolishing slavery or otherwise interfering in their internal affairs would require tact and perseverance if it was not to end in bloodshed. Europeans would have to learn to work with what they found. They could not expect to influence Africa for the better by blundering in with their own preconceived notions.[33]

This was also a thought that occurred to Schön. The CMS had instructed him to work for 'the evangelization of desolated and benighted Africa'.[34] This part of Africa was not desolated; whether it was benighted was a matter of opinion. As regards evangelization he had particularly noted that there were no idols on display in Idah, the result, he presumed, of Islamic influence. Would this prove a serious barrier to future activity by Christian missionaries? So far as he could see the commitment to Islam did not go very deep. Certainly much went on in Idah of which the Prophet himself would hardly have approved, including human sacrifice, a topic on which Amanda Bue was a storehouse of information. As for the mallams (or local Islamic priests), they impressed him as a poor lot, able to recite a few verses of the Koran which they had learned by heart but otherwise quite illiterate, as was shown when their leader, presented with an Arabic Bible, studiously examined it upside down. They practised certain rituals, circumcision and, as was clear from the number of eunuchs, castration, although their ministerial labours seemed mainly to consist of selling charms to the people, most of whom remained basically pagan.

Whatever the extent of the mallams' influence it plainly did not include any enforcement of Mohammed's prohibition on consumption of alcohol. This had been evident on both visits when wine was freely offered. It was most dramatically illustrated when William Johnson, having remained in Idah overnight, returned drunk, fell out of the paddle-box boat, and was drowned. In Sierra Leone, Schön recalled, he had always been a regular communicant and had never shown any sign of insobriety. No doubt his reunion with his relatives had proved too much for him. But if the CMS did decide to send African catechists to Idah they would need to be chosen very carefully.[35]

The commissioners' final interview with the Attah went off as planned. This time there were no delays. The Attah himself was very affable, agreed to all the provisions in the treaty and mainly seemed impatient to hurry matters along so that he could receive his presents. These were rather grander than those given to the Obi, being valued at some hundred pounds.[36] This was in recognition of what the commissioners perceived as his higher status as the leader of a relatively advanced people.[37]

They sailed the following morning taking with them two of the Attah's advisers with whom they were to negotiate the lease of the land, yet to be selected, for the model farm. Before departing they buried John Peglar, the *Albert*'s armourer, the first victim of a fever epidemic which, since their arrival at Idah, had broken out simultaneously on all three vessels. 'Oh God!' wrote Simpson, 'our times are in thy hands; may we improve by what is taking place around us, so that when it is thy will to call us, we may not be unprepared.'[38]

CHAPTER SIX
A Devouring Pestilence

The fever was immediately diagnosed as being of a particularly virulent kind, similar to that which had attacked the Laird expedition on its ascent of the river. The premonitory signs were feelings of lassitude, dull aching pains in the back and limbs, headaches and giddiness. At that stage crew members commonly denied feeling unwell, though what was happening might well be evident to those around them from the lethargic way in which they moved and a heavy somnolent look about the eyes. These symptoms seldom lasted for more than a day.

The symptoms of the next stage were unequivocal. These occurred when the plasmodia infesting the red blood cells caused them to burst releasing toxic agents into the bloodstream. Sufferers' faces then became suddenly pale, their hands and feet white and their nails blue. They also complained of giddiness, nausea, difficulty in breathing, dryness of the mouth, above all, a strong sensation of coldness. But however many blankets were wrapped around them, and however hot the day, this feeling of penetrating cold would persist for up to four hours. Then, quite suddenly, it would be replaced by a pervasive sensation of heat as they broke into a profuse sweat. This third stage normally lasted for between eight and twelve hours, accompanied by a rapid pulse rate and an urgent thirst. It would then give way to the feelings of languor and exhaustion characteristic of the fever's fourth, or remittent, stage. Patients would now profess that there was nothing wrong with them, only to be seized after an interval by another paroxysm as the cycle repeated itself.

This, at least, was the general pattern although, as the surgeons were later to emphasize in their reports, no two cases were exactly alike. Some patients had experienced no warning symptoms at all. Aboard the *Albert* the periods of remission were generally short, lasting for at most twelve hours, whereas on the *Soudan* the seizures tended to occur on alternate days, suggesting that different forms of the malarial plasmodium may have been involved. Generally the attacks became increasingly severe until around the tenth day when they either began to subside, and the intervals between them lengthened, or the patients fell into a comatose state eventually leading to death. Others, however, in the final stages of their illness, suffered violent convulsions. Most alarming were the cases of those who, on account of a blockage of the blood vessels in their brains, ran amok and had to be roped to their hammocks.

The methods employed for dealing with this epidemic were standard and are well exemplified in the treatment given in the case of John Peglar. Peglar was 22 years old and hitherto in good health. On the day after the expedition's arrival in Idah he complained of general uneasiness. This was immediately diagnosed as a premonitory symptom of river fever and he was given a dose of mercurous chloride and James's powder (a mixture of antimony oxide and calcium phosphate), the first to induce salivation and the second sweating. This was done on the principle that the initial paroxysms of the disease, when the mouth became parched and the skin dry, were the most critical and that the return of saliva and profuse sweating that followed represented an improvement in the patient's condition. By artificially inducing these symptoms, therefore, it was hoped to alleviate, and possibly shorten the seizures and thereby hasten recovery. It was, of course, recognized that mercury was a poison which, administered in excess, would harm the patient. The recommended dose of five grains (0.32 grams) administered at three-hourly intervals was quite enough to prove lethal if continued for much more than a day. But set against this was its supposed usefulness as a specific for relieving what was, plainly, a dire condition.

This was the effect it was perceived to have had on Peglar who was accordingly sent to rest in his quarters in the lower deck. When, however, the surgeons visited him the following morning he was found to be in a state of high fever with a rapid pulse rate, a condition not improved by the fact that he was lying in sodden bedclothes, his hammock having accidentally got wet. He was duly given more mercury together with opium to help him sleep. Later in the morning he was bled. This made him comatose. Further doses of mercury and opium were administered at intervals during the day.

By the third morning he was found to be very weak and scarcely capable of speaking or even swallowing. His breath smelled so strongly of mercury that doses were discontinued and he was given quinine and red wine instead. His head was also shaved and a scalding poultice applied to the nape of his neck to produce a skin blister. Like bleeding, blistering was intended to release poisonous humours from the body. Peglar's blister, it was later noted, had risen well. But his general condition rapidly worsened and on the fourth day he appeared largely paralysed, incapable of doing anything more than open his mouth when he wanted to drink. He died that evening. On cutting him open his liver and spleen, surprisingly, were pronounced healthy, but there were signs of ulceration and bleeding in his intestines. The same symptoms were also found, along with unusual quantities of bile and mucus in the stomach, in the cases of other patients who died. In most instances, however, enlargement of the spleen and abnormalities of the liver were also noted. But what actually *killed* these patients (damage to the liver, kidneys, lungs and brain caused by acute anaemia and restricted blood flow) remained, like so much else, a mystery.

Given the nature of the treatment, the surprising thing, perhaps, is that so many – roughly two-thirds – eventually recovered. Quinine may marginally have helped alleviate the paroxysms in some cases, although, as previously noted, it would have been much more effective if administered as a prophylactic. Most often it appears to have been used as a tonic during the period of recuperation, for which purpose it was virtually useless. Otherwise, none of the remedies employed was capable of doing any good and most – bleeding, the raising of skin blisters, purgatives and diaphoretics – were positively harmful. This applies particularly to mercurous chloride, nowadays commonly used as an insecticide and fungicide. From the account of the symptoms and the autopsy report it would appear more likely than not to have been a contributory cause of death in Peglar's case.[1] It is hard to avoid drawing the conclusion that the members of the Niger expedition would have fared better had they received no medical treatment at all.

By the time the expedition left Idah eight crew members were down with fever and there was little doubt that others would soon follow. Some, indeed, were already exhibiting symptoms. To add to their misfortunes another problem promptly arose. Returning from wooding on the opposite shore the *Wilberforce* was swept onto the sandy point of an island against which the current ran so strongly that there appeared no way of getting her off. Unloading part of her cargo and moving the rest about did no good. Nor did the *Albert*'s attempts to tow her off: the howsers were too weak and parted under the strain. Moreover, every movement of the vessel simply embedded her deeper in the sand silting up around her hull. The situation was the more alarming as the river was now at its seasonal height. Should it begin to fall the likelihood was that the *Wilberforce* would remain where she was until the next rainy season, as had happened to the *Quorra* on the previous expedition. How many of her crew would survive such an experience was problematical. After two days of futile effort and just as the situation looked hopeless, a torrential downpour of rain raised the level of the water sufficiently for her to be winched free. It was a lucky escape. Nevertheless, the possibility of finding themselves stranded somewhere deep in the African interior until the following summer was a

The hills below the Confluence.

fear that haunted their imaginations throughout the remainder of their time on the river.[2]

Proceeding upstream the crews were heartened by the sight of hills. They were not, to be sure, very high hills, and certainly nothing like Buxton's Kong Mountains, but any increase in elevation was seen as evidence that they were moving into healthier territory. It was also noted that although daytime temperatures became steadily higher as they proceeded up-river, rising well into the eighties by early afternoon, the atmosphere was less humid. This too was regarded as a hopeful sign.

For those with an eye for it the scenery was certainly magnificent as forest gave way to savanna and the river wound its leisurely way between flat-topped hills intersected by wooded valleys. They passed numerous villages, each surrounded by patches of well-cultivated land. Women working in the fields interrupted their labours to watch the vessels pass. Around Kiri market, which they passed in the late afternoon of their first day, a great many canoes were to be seen passing to and fro, heavily laden with produce, some with goats and bullocks, others with small horses aboard. It was a peaceful and industrious scene.

But by degrees the villages on their route became more thinly scattered until they found themselves entering a wide gorge flanked by conical hills rising abruptly 400 feet or more from the river banks. On the summits of one or two could be discerned small villages, presumably put there for

117

defensive purposes. The scene reminded Schön and Vogel of their native Rhine except that it had an altogether wilder and more unkempt aspect. Huge boulders dislodged from the surrounding hillsides littered the shore and river-bed making navigation hazardous. Confined between these precipitous banks the current was now so fast flowing that even at their full six knots the steamers had difficulty making headway. According to the Attah's representatives the water was higher than it had been for the previous twenty years.[3]

Approaching the confluence with the Benue they stopped to gather wood near a small village perched on a hill overlooking the river. These people, they learned, were Kakanda from Adda Kudu who had been driven from their lands by marauding Fulani. This was disquieting news since Adda Kudu was precisely where they had intended to establish the model farm. The villagers were dirty and in rags, having evidently suffered from their displacement, but brightened up considerably at the mention of white protection and the prospect of being allowed to return to their lands. From their hilltop they pointed out several other refugee villages, indicating that something like a general exodus from the area of the Confluence must have taken place.[4]

Further on the expedition encountered more such settlements, all in a similar state of wretchedness. In one of the largest of these, which had upwards of a thousand inhabitants, the headmen responded to Samuel Crowther's explanation of the expedition's purpose with incredulity and had him repeat it to make sure that their ears had not deceived them. Nevertheless, the chief agreed to accompany the steamers, bringing with him three eunuch attendants whose task it was to fan him; also a group of musicians. Their playing disturbed the sick, whose numbers since leaving Idah had been swelling daily.

The Confluence, when they reached it on 11 September, looked not at all like the future New Orleans of Africa. Adda Kudu was in ruins and already much overgrown with shrubs and creepers. When Laird had called there nine years before it had been a bustling river town and a centre of the local cloth-dyeing industry. Its population he had then put at about 5000. Now the place was totally deserted. Cutting their way through the underbrush they found dozens of large earthenware pots or vats sunk into the ground, formerly used by the dyers, some with traces of dye still in them. At every step they were startled by the movements of snakes and lizards. From the amount of charred timber wood they concluded that the town had been systematically burnt, but the clay walls remained and here and there they came across a hut with its roof still intact. In what he took to have been the chief's residence John Duncan caught a scorpion which he took back to the *Albert* to show the naturalists.[5]

Intending to take advantage of what remained of the town's amenities the crews began unloading the carts, ploughs, harrows and other pieces of equipment belonging to the model farm. They erected the Eglinton marquee next to a large breadfruit tree where they supposed the town elders had formerly congregated. Before the unloading had been completed, however, word came that a better site had been found some three miles further up the shore and that everything would have to be reloaded. This caused grumbling as it was suffocatingly hot and the crews were weary.

The following day was Sunday and so a day of rest. Aboard the *Wilberforce*, Schön's sermon was punctuated by the sound of loud hammering from the carpenters' quarters as they prepared a coffin for James Kneebone, a seaman who had died the previous night. Bodies, they found, decomposed quickly in these conditions. Once the doctors had completed their autopsies the remains had to be disposed of promptly. Some pigeons John Duncan had shot the previous day were found to be smelling by the evening.[6]

On Monday they finished reloading the farm implements and began discharging them at the new site. There being no depth of water close in shore they were obliged to manhandle them on to the paddle-box boats and then on to the marshy bank. Some proved heavy and cumbersome. In the course of the operation the *Wilberforce*'s paddle-box boat broke loose and sank in midstream taking with it the farm's cotton gin and palm oil press. The machinery, which would not have been required for many years, was seen as no great sacrifice but the loss of the boat was much regretted. To add to their discomfort the steamers experienced an invasion of snakes, dislodged from the nearby reedbeds by the high waters, which had swarmed up the paddle wheels and mooring ropes in the night. The Krumen took great delight in hunting them down and shouts of triumph could be heard as yet another was discovered.[7]

The new site was close to Mount Stirling, a 200-foot hill named by the Laird expedition after one of its sponsors, Thomas Stirling of Sheffield, whose predictions about the present enterprise have already been noted. The land did not appear to be particularly fertile but was possibly marginally superior to any other that was to be found in the vicinity. It lay at the foot of Mount Patti, a 1200-foot sandstone escarpment from the top of which the expedition's scientists were able to obtain a panoramic view of the whole area. In terms of sheer scale it far surpassed anything they had encountered so far. All around, extending as far as the eye could see, were range upon range of bench-shaped hills, those in the distance faintly blue in the early-morning haze. Emerging out of the east, winding its way between these, came the Benue, every bit as majestic as the Niger itself. There was a striking contrast between its clear, dark current and

The confluence of the Niger and Benue.

the Niger's muddy brown, clearly evident where the two mingled to form a broad expanse of water a full two miles wide. On the near shore of this lake, the steamers, still busily discharging their farm implements, looked exceedingly diminutive. Away to the south the waters narrowed as they entered the defile through which the expedition had just ascended. It was all very grand and not a little daunting.

Apart from three Kakanda villages at the top of Mount Patti itself the near side of the river appeared uninhabited. However, there were small cultivated patches near Mount Stirling, indicating that those who had fled to the opposite shore were in the habit of returning. Of the dreaded Fulani there was no sign.

It had to be admitted that as a base for future British operations in Africa the area looked decidedly unpromising. In fact, apart from its scenic grandeur and its being at the junction of two important rivers, which was what had caught the attention first of MacQueen and then Buxton, there was almost nothing to be said for it. Poor soil, political turmoil, malarial marshes, it could hardly have been worse. And then there were the snakes and insects, not to mention the various epidermal complaints from which most of the whites were now suffering. 'Every one of us, who is not sick,' wrote Vogel, 'is plagued with itching of the skin, and eruptions: this affliction, together with the mosquitoes . . . does not let us sleep at night. In short, it is a wretched existence for a European.'[8]

Yet what alternative was there? The farm would have to be located somewhere. In any case it was too late now to change their plans. The commissioners duly set about purchasing from the Attah's representatives a strip of territory sixteen miles long by some five miles wide, extending along the western bank from Mount Patti in the north to Mount Saracte in the south and encompassing what remained of Adda Kudu. The fact that this whole tract had lately been depopulated could even be regarded as an advantage since it reduced the likelihood of future territorial disputes arising. Those who subsequently wished to move there could be told on what terms they would be allowed to settle. In return for ceding the land the Attah was to be paid 700 000 cowries, the equivalent of £45, one-fifth immediately, the remainder in instalments over a period of not more than five years. This transaction completed, Alfred Carr then formally applied for, and was granted, a tract of 500 acres at a rent of one penny per acre to be paid annually to Her Majesty's Treasury by the Model Farm Society of Mincing Lane, London.[9]

By the time Carr and his workers had been landed and the Eglinton marquee re-erected there had been three further deaths. More alarming still was the rapidity with which the fever was spreading. Of the expedition's 145 Europeans, 63 were now on the sick list. Several of the coloured personnel taken on in England were also ill. William Allen had been unwell for some days. His was proving a relatively mild case, but William Simpson's was more serious. Having prepared himself spiritually for Death and Judgement, Simpson experienced severe abdominal pains and began vomiting, after which he lost consciousness and could subsequently recall nothing that happened during the next two weeks. To allow them the benefit of the breeze the sick were accommodated on deck, giving the vessels, as Vogel noted, the appearance of 'so many lazarettos'. On 17 September the *Albert* lost its assistant surgeon and gunroom steward. At service that evening the crew sang

> Why do we mourn departing friends,
> Or shake at death's alarms?
> 'Tis but the voice that Jesus sends.
> To call them to his arms.

Schön was pleased to note that even the most hard-bitten sailors joined in the singing with unaccustomed fervour.[10]

The following morning the four commissioners met to consider what to do. One option was carrying the sick to the top of Mount Patti where the air might prove more wholesome. On the other hand it might not. Dr M'William professed uncertainty as to the matter. Plainly getting them there would be back-breaking work and there was reason to doubt if the crews were up to it. William Cook took the view that to press on in present circumstances would jeopardize the whole enterprise. The sensible course would be to return to the sea and try again when the sick had recovered. William Allen agreed and wanted it clearly entered into the record that he believed the entire expedition ought immediately to head for the Gulf. The river would soon begin to fall, exposing the mudbanks from which, as was well known, the most fatal maladies arose. Bad as things were, the sickly season had not yet begun. Bird Allen felt that to abandon their efforts now would be premature. They ought at least to press on for another week or so. However, the sick, who were a liability, should be sent at once to the coast, preferably aboard the *Soudan* which now had only four crew members fit for duty and plainly was in no condition to proceed further. Dr M'William agreed that the climate up-river might prove healthier. On the basis of this advice Trotter ruled that the sick should at once be transferred to the *Soudan* and taken down-river. Meanwhile he and Bird Allen in the *Albert* and Cook and William Allen in the *Wilberforce* should prepare to ascend the Niger and Benue respectively.[11]

The *Soudan* departed early the following afternoon, her decks festooned with the hammocks and cots of the sick. In addition to her own invalids she carried thirteen from the *Wilberforce* and six from the *Albert*, making a total of more than forty. Any idea of following the Surgeon General's instructions about keeping below decks at night had by this time been abandoned. With only two doctors and a scratch crew there simply was no way of carrying them out, besides which conditions in the crews' quarters were not only suffocatingly hot but too cramped for the sick to be satisfactorily attended to. Some were demanding water, others vomiting or crying out in delirium. Even on the quarterdeck administering to one meant climbing over or stooping under another.[12]

It had taken over a month to reach the Confluence. But with the current behind her, pausing only during the hours of darkness, the *Soudan* managed the return voyage in under three days. Along the way they buried three of their number, the last, William Marshall, the *Soudan*'s medical officer, alongside John William Bach on the spit of land near the sandbar.

Across the bar they found HMS *Dolphin* waiting. Thirty-five of the sick were immediately transferred to her quarters, leaving behind two who were thought to be on the point of death and seven others who appeared to be recovering. The *Dolphin* then departed bound for Ascension and the bracing airs of the mid-Atlantic, while the *Soudan* and what remained of

its crew embarked on the two-hundred-mile crossing to the island of
Fernando Po.

While the *Soudan* had been preparing to descend the river more cases of
fever had been occurring by the hour. Following her departure a special
meeting of the commissioners was convened at William Allen's request.
The situation, he informed his colleagues, had changed since the previous
day. To press ahead with Trotter's plans for ascending the Niger and
Benue would simply mean sacrificing more lives, conceivably those of the
entire expedition. And to what purpose? Appearing in front of Raba in
their present sorry state would merely prejudice their cause in the eyes of
its rulers. He was the only officer present with previous experience of the
river. During the past few hours two of the *Wilberforce*'s three engineers
had reported sick, bringing the total number of cases aboard his vessel to
thirty-two. As her commander it was his duty to state that with only three
officers and ten men fit for duty she was in no condition to ascend the
Benue or indeed do anything other than return to the sea with all due
despatch.[13]

It was a tricky situation. Removing the wounded from the field of
battle was one thing; no one could object to their having sent the sick to
the coast. But for the commissioners themselves to abandon their quest at
this stage looked uncommonly like cowardice in the face of the enemy.
Yet for Trotter to insist that a vessel undertake duties contrary to the
professional advice of its commander was a decision not to be taken
lightly. There would be recriminations. Someone's reputation would
suffer. Allen had made his views abundantly clear. So too had Cook. Both
were bent on leaving the river. And plainly the situation aboard the
Wilberforce had worsened since the previous day. By way of compromise,
therefore, it was decided that the *Albert* should continue on up the Niger,
as previously agreed, but that the *Wilberforce* should return to the sea and
there, once the health of the crew permitted, begin negotiating treaties
with the coastal rulers, a secondary objective recommended in Lord John
Russell's instructions.

By the time the *Wilberforce* departed on 21 September, taking with her a
further contingent of sick from the *Albert*, she was little more than a
floating hospital.[14] During the nine days it took her to reach the bar
it rained incessantly. The main difficulty, however, was lack of fuel.
Although the current, swollen by the rains, carried her along, often at an
alarming pace, without steam her helmsman lacked all capacity to steer,
giving rise to the possibility that she would end up on a mudbank from
which it would be impossible to get her off.

They anchored off Aboh where they enquired if any wood was to be had there but were told that the river had risen so much since their departure that the entire town was now under water. Those who were not engaged in salvaging their possessions had gone to market. Further on they came upon two villages with stacks of firewood ready cut. But this was King Boy's territory and the villagers steadfastly refused to sell. They thus found themselves with no alternative but to anchor while the Krumen, often standing in water up to their hips, cut down trees and ferried them back to the vessel to be sawn into lengths small enough to be fitted into the ship's boilers. It was remarkable, Allen notes, how cheerfully and willingly they set to work.

For the Europeans, suffering in their hammocks or sitting idly on deck, watching the curtains of rain sweeping across the river and surrounding forest, it was a frustrating business. At the entrance to Louis Creek the vessel collided with a projecting tree-stump, ripping away her galley and much of her rigging. But the most anxious time of all was the four days they were obliged to spend in the estuary collecting enough wood to carry them the two hundred miles to Fernando Po. Fortunately, it proved a smooth crossing so that, by the evening of October 1, they were safely anchored in Clarence Cove and able to begin transferring the sick to quarters on shore.

With the *Wilberforce* gone and Alfred Carr and his assistants busily at work, the *Albert* got up steam and headed up-river, leaving the *Amelia*, manned by a scratch crew of Sierra Leone blacks, to stand guard over the settlement. The *Albert*, in fact, was in no better state than the *Wilberforce*. Of the six original occupants of the gunroom, only Stanger and M'William remained. Theodore Müller, the expedition's chaplain, had departed and been replaced by Friedrich Schön. Theodor Vogel, Roscher the geologist, and Frazer the naturalist had also gone. The crew, too, was much depleted and of those who remained a good half were already ailing. Nevertheless, it was reassuring to be on the move. The throb of the engines and the beat of the paddle wheels helped to revive flagging spirits as they trudged gallantly onward. Whatever lay ahead, they supposed, could hardly be worse than what they had already experienced.[15]

Their first day's journey took them through gently undulating country. Much of the land on both sides of the river was flooded, sometimes over an area of several miles, giving the Niger a lake-like appearance with here and there clumps of trees or occasionally a solitary palm protruding from the waters. Along the way they passed villages marooned and deserted. Further on they encountered yet more encampments of refugees. These had fled the right bank, not on account of the waters, but because of an army of nine hundred Fulani horsemen who had lately been scouring the neighbourhood and who were reported to be still camped nearby.

Formerly this whole area had been within the domain of the Attah, whose suzerainty the villagers, most of whom were Kakanda, still acknowledged. But times were changing. Over the past ten years their land had repeatedly been overrun by Fulani, whose demands for tribute they professed to be quite incapable of meeting. As a result captives and cattle were taken and sold. It was later learned that over the previous three months the Fulani force operating in the area had sent back to Raba no less than 4000 captives and 1000 black cattle as well as a large quantity of cowries.[16]

The Kakanda did not hesitate to put the blame for the slave trade on the Fulani. But that they were not averse to trading in slaves themselves became evident when James Macaulay, one of the expedition's interpreters and a Nupe by birth, met a former owner, a stout little woman who laughed a great deal and professed to see nothing wrong in the practice. She had purchased him from the Fulani, who had taken him on a raid higher up the river. Her husband had subsequently sold him to the Obi, who sent him to King Peppel of Bonny. Peppel had then sold him to a Spanish slave ship from which he was rescued by a British cruiser.[17] From the attitude of the woman and others around it appeared that such transactions were regarded as part of the normal life of the river. But what the Kakanda plainly did not regard as normal, and deeply resented, was the recent enslavement of their entire nation by conquerors from the north leaving them with no effective recourse other than a mass flight to the east bank where the Fulani, lacking canoes, were incapable of pursuing them.

Thanks to his knowledge of Hausa, which served as the *lingua franca* of the river, Schön was able to gather a good deal of additional information about the Fulani empire's southward advance. Besides the horsemen, the region had lately been visited by various itinerant mallams seeking converts. Regarding themselves as already Mohammedan, the Kakanda resented being treated as infidels. The mallams, who came from Raba, Egga and other towns further north, taught Arabic prayers, the meaning of which the Kakanda professed not to understand. They also sold charms and circumcised the boys, a service for which they took payment. The changing balance of political influence in the region was aptly revealed at Gori market, a large two-day affair held every fortnight, which was in full swing when the expedition arrived. On being questioned in the presence of Igala representatives the Chief of Gori affirmed his allegiance to the Attah to whom he paid a tribute of one horse a year. As the acknowledged overlord the Attah theoretically had the right to levy troops in the area in return for which he offered military protection. But that this was a purely formal and long-outdated arrangement immediately became apparent when, in response to further questions, the chief revealed that Gori was also obliged to pay an annual tribute of 360 000 cowries to the Fulani rulers of Rabba.[18]

The leaders of the expedition already knew a certain amount, thanks to earlier travellers' accounts, about this powerful predatory empire whose borderlands they were now entering. In 1824, travelling overland from Tripoli, Hugh Clapperton had visited Sokoto, its capital. There he had enjoyed the hospitality of its ruler, Caliph Bello, who had talked expansively about his wish for commercial relations with the British and the possibility of their establishing a consulate there. Intrigued by these reports, the British Government had hastened to mount a second expedition, setting out this time from Badagri. On its arrival in Sokoto, however, Clapperton found his approaches rebuffed, the Caliph having meanwhile become suspicious of Britain's imperial intentions and the overtures she was simultaneously making to his arch-rival, the Sultan of Bornu. Bitterly disappointed, Clapperton died on the return journey, but his journals were preserved by his manservant, Richard Lander, and later published along with Lander's own account of their expedition.[19]

From these descriptions it was possible to piece together a fairly coherent account of the Fulani empire's origins and early history. Its founder, Shaikh Uthman dan Fodio, a Muslim scholar, preacher and reformer from the northern kingdom of Gobir, having gathered around himself a band of dedicated supporters, in 1804 declared a jihad, or holy war, against the Fulani's Hausa overlords. In the course of the struggles that followed, animated by longstanding grievances and the prevailing religious excitement, the Fulani, hitherto a peaceful and largely pastoral people, had transformed themselves into a formidable fighting force, which, by the time of the Founder's death in 1817, had established ruling Fulani dynasties in most Hausa states and controlled much of what is now northern Nigeria. He had meanwhile divided his empire between his son, Caliph Bello, and his elder brother, the Emir of Gwandu, who continued to press their crusade southward into Nupe and Yorubaland. But although the Fulani provided most of the initial impetus behind this movement their success owed much to their ability to recruit jihadists from other tribes and their capacity to ferment local rebellions.[20]

This had been the case in Nupe, whose capital, Raba, the expedition planned to make its next major port of call. Initially, at least, what happened there was not unlike what had happened in Hausaland. Mallam Dendo, an itinerant Fulani preacher, had succeeded in installing himself as adviser to Majia, the Nupe ruler or Etsu. He had also assembled around himself a heterogeneous following of Fulani pastoralists, discontented Nupe merchants and Hausa mercenary soldiers. The political situation within the Kingdom was already volatile on account of the

Islamic militancy that had spilled over its borders in consequence of the struggles that were occurring in the states to the north and an internal dynastic dispute between rival factions led by Majia and his cousin Jimada. Majia was unwise enough to appeal to Mallam Dendo for support, who, in turn, invoked the assistance of the Emir of Gwandu. The predictable, though unintended, result was that the jihadists, led by Dendo, who assumed the traditional Islamic role of military-religious leader, thereupon seized control of the Kingdom. There followed a series of coups and counter-coups. The situation when the Laird expedition visited Raba in 1833 was still unstable. In theory the Kingdom was divided between Majia and Jimada's son Idirisu, although they were no more than puppet governors. Effectively it was controlled by the jihadists who were at that time preparing for a major campaign against Igala. But Mallam Dendo was by then an old man and had largely relinquished his authority to his sons. He died while the expedition was still at Raba. What had happened subsequently, and who now controlled the Kingdom, were things the leaders of the present expedition were eager to find out.[21]

The country's current ruler, they learned, was Mallam Dendo's second son, Usman Zaki, who, although a pure-blooded Fulani, had seen fit to assume the regalia of chieftainship and proclaim himself Etsu. Idirisu and Majia were still alive but had latterly led shadowy existences. How much authority they exercised was unclear. The former was said to be living at Barra, not far from Egga, the latter somewhere north of Raba.[22] For the moment it appeared as though the country was internally at peace, although rumours abounded. According to one, Usman Zaki's younger half-brother, Masaba, Dendo's son by a Nupe wife, had raised an army and, with the support of Idirisu and Majia, was preparing for an assault on Raba.[23] Masaba, claiming a right to the throne on the basis of his Nupe lineage, had sought to oust his brother once before. The rumours the expedition heard related to a second attempt, then in its formative stages and being mounted from outside the Kingdom, which was later to result in the destruction of Raba and Masaba's replacing Usman Zaki as Etsu.[24]

This, however, was only one of the many stories of intrigue, war and bloodshed that the expedition gleaned on its passage northward. According to Samuel Crowther's Yoruba informants, major battles were also being fought in the neighbouring Fulani state of Ilorin. Apparently the jihadists there had suffered serious reverses with the result that hordes of their Yoruba converts had been flooding northward into Nupe. Many of these *mujaddidun*, as the Islamic revivalists were called, had so adapted themselves to Fulani ways as to be virtually indistinguishable from the Fulani themselves. There were also reports of successful military forays mounted from Nupe and of large quantities of booty being sent back to Raba.[25]

But what impressed the visitors more than any of these tales from afar was the state of abject terror in which the native Nupe lived and their constant anxiety that any action on their part might bring down on their heads the wrath of Usman Zaki and his followers. In village after village they heard stories of hostages seized and livestock taken. What provoked these attacks was not always clear. Most appeared to arise out of demands for tribute which, if they were not promptly met, would result in troops of horsemen descending on a village and taking away captives and anything else worth seizing. Those not ransomed would be sold as slaves. This was presumably what had happened to James Macaulay. According to Schön most were not sold down the river, as Macaulay had been, but marched overland through Yoruba territory and embarked at Lagos or one of the other slaving ports along the Benin coast.[26] So far as the Nupe were concerned, the Fulani were usurpers who had seized their Kingdom and were now plundering it in furtherance of a belief that they were the chosen instruments of God and Nupe a conquered province.

Like the Kakanda, the Nupe welcomed, at least in private, the news of a British settlement on the river and the prospect that, at some future date, they might just conceivably be able to claim its protection. Nevertheless, they viewed their visitors with understandable suspicion. Word of the expedition's antislavery intentions had spread well in advance and alarmed the slave-owning Nupe because of an erroneous belief that the British had been engaged in arbitrarily seizing and freeing slaves in the course of their journey northward.[27]

The basis for this rumour was an incident which had occured while the *Albert* was anchored at Gori. As it was preparing to depart it had been hailed by a canoe containing three slaves, two women and a man, whom its captain had purchased at Egga the previous day. This captain, it turned out, was the son of the headman of one of the villages they had visited earlier and was an acknowledged subject of the Attah. It appeared, therefore, that the purchase of the slaves had contravened the agreement drawn up at Idah and proclaimed seventeen days earlier. The captain professed to be unaware of the proclamation. In view of this, and after consultation with one of the Attah's sons who had travelled up-river with the expedition, Trotter agreed to treat the case leniently. The canoe and its contents were not confiscated, but the three slaves, much to their astonishment, were declared free, given quarters on board the *Albert*, and renamed Hannah Buxton, Elizabeth Fry and Albert Gori. They were ultimately resettled in Fernando Po, Albert Gori as an apprentice carpenter and the two women 'under the care of a respectable matron'.[28]

Not surprisingly, such apparent high-handedness did not commend itself to the *mujaddidun*, who regarded their right to buy and sell infidels as slaves as guaranteed by Islamic law. Those to whom Crowther spoke did not conceal their anger over what had been done, particularly since the slaves had been bought in Egga and freed on a stretch of the river over which they claimed control. Whatever the nature of the agreement with the Attah it did not extend to Nupe regardless of the origins of the parties involved. In any case the headman whose son, in the presence of Igala representatives, had seen fit to profess his allegiance to the Attah, also paid tribute to Raba and so ought more properly to have been treated as a Nupe dependant.[29]

This was a very different response from that given by Caliph Bello who, when told that there were no slaves in Britain and servants were hired for stated periods at regular wages, had observed, 'God is great! You are a beautiful people.'[30] But Clapperton had not presumed to interfere in the internal affairs of Sokoto nor had the British at that time even gone so far as to emancipate the slaves in their own colonies. It did not bode well for the expedition's reception should it ever reach Raba.

Whether it would do so, however, was becoming increasingly doubtful. Owing to shortage of fuel the *Albert* was obliged to make lengthy stops for wooding. Bird Allen had fallen ill the day after leaving the Confluence and there had been two further deaths. By the time the expedition reached Egga on 28 September all of the engineers were sick and several members of the crew in a critical condition.

To add to their disappointment the country in which they now found themselves was low-lying and swampy, possibly the least salubrious they had encountered so far. The town itself, a veritable human anthill, was set in the middle of a wide flood plain, which meant that at that moment it was surrounded by swirling brown floodwaters. It seemed to have been built according to no plan at all, being a maze of twisting streets and crooked alleys so narrow that passers-by had to squeeze past one another. The stench of upwards of 8000 people confined to what was effectively a muddy island carried across the water. Rows of vultures, dusty, bedraggled creatures, lined its walls like enormous yardfowl. Nevertheless, the place had more the appearance of a commercial centre than either Aboh or Iddah, as was evident from the number of different languages spoken and the heterogeneous crowds of Nupe, Hausa, Yoruba and Arab merchants thronging its alleyways and markets. Egga was pre-eminently a cloth town, specializing in woven cottons and silk embroidery, whose products were sold as far away as Timbuctu and Bornu.[31] As blacksmiths and glass-makers too the Nupe were much more skilled than any the expedition had met with so far.

On arrival, Trotter despatched Schön and Dr Stanger to wait on Rogang, the town's headman. It quickly turned out that, being a Nupe by birth, he was responsible only for local matters and that all larger issues needed to be referred to the authorities at Raba. While they talked, several Fulani could be observed lurking suspiciously in the background. After listening to Schön and Stanger's exposition Rogang invited them to a private audience in his apartments where he explained that he held his present position purely on sufferance. The Nupe hated the Fulani but were quite incapable of doing anything without their consent. He himself sympathized with the expedition's aims and would do what he could to further them, but, not being an independent agent, he feared it would not amount to very much. He regretted that he could neither visit the *Albert* nor forward messages to Raba. If he did so, Usman Zaki would immediately say 'Ah! Rogang has joined the White people' and make him pay for his temerity.[32]

If Rogang was in league with Masaba, Majia, Idirisu and the other conspirators, as the stories gathered by Schön indicated, he himself gave no indication of it. He certainly did not try to draw his visitors into any plot. On the contrary, his was the clearest statement they were to receive that their presence in the Kingdom was unwelcome. Others made the same point by refusing even to engage in conversation. What information was gleaned came mostly from slaves. The local Fulani, for their part, remained suspicious and aloof. Whether this was because they had heard about the three slaves, or, as was more probable, because they regarded the British as Christian intruders and potential rivals remained unclear. What is abundantly evident is that in a country divided between two Nupe and two Fulani factions, and with a civil war brewing, the visitors were totally out of their depths.

They lingered in the town for a week, hoping that the condition of the sick would improve and purchasing wood and other supplies for the intended ascent to Raba. Meanwhile Schön and Crowther busied themselves assembling a collection of cloths, daggers, spearheads, leatherware, pottery, decorated calabashes and other examples of local craftsmanship which they were later to present to the British Museum.[33] John Duncan, one of the few Europeans still fit for duty, made frequent trips to the town's markets to buy food. Casting a professional eye over the troops of Fulani horsemen he thought them 'sadly overrated. They are mounted on small horses . . . about the size of Hampshire New Forest ponies. They have no particular method of guiding their horse, and quite as little of using the sword, which is a very awkward, badly-balanced weapon . . . with no protection for the hand. In fact, were I in my old regiment, the First Life-Guards, I would not hesitate to make one of six to charge a squadron one hundred strong of Felattahs.'[34] Had the Nupe any knowledge of warfare, he concluded, they would have no difficulty in ridding themselves of this scourge. As it was they were compelled to sit

helplessly by while the Fulani swaggered through the town like conquerors. Samuel Crowther observed one casually pocket an ivory orna-
ment from a market woman who, having no alternative, readily let it go.
It was their habit, he was told, to take goats, sheep, cloths or anything
else that caught their fancy.[35]

The health of the crew had meanwhile worsened. On 3 October
Trotter fell ill. By the following morning the entire crew was laid up with
the exception of William Willie, the mate, and one seaman. Among the
other Europeans only Dr M'William, Dr Stanger, John Duncan and two
marines were capable of moving about. With the sick littering its decks
the *Albert* looked as if it had just returned from battle. To add to
everyone's alarm sandbanks had suddenly begun appearing where previously there had been just water. To press on upstream in their present
condition, and with the level of water already falling, was obviously out of
the question. Nor was there anything more to be achieved by lingering in
Egga where their presence was clearly unwelcome.

On being told that the *Albert* was departing for the coast Rogang did
not attempt to conceal his relief. He now agreed to transmit a message to
Usman Zaki to the effect that they had established a settlement near
Adda Kudu, that their intentions were peaceful, and that they hoped he
would instruct his warriors not to molest either it or any of the towns in
its vicinity. No mention was made of the expedition's antislavery aims. It
was, Rogang agreed, a tactful and conciliatory statement which would
usefully remove any suspicions there might be in Raba concerning his
own intentions.[36]

With Willie now in command, the *Albert* began its 350–mile journey
southward. As there was nobody competent to work the engines she was
at first allowed simply to drift with the stream. But by the second day Dr
Stanger, with the help of an instruction manual and verbal directions
from one of the engineers, had succeeded in getting up enough steam to
work the paddles. By the evening, however, Willie too was obliged to take
to his bunk leaving Dr M'William, as the only remaining naval officer fit
for duty, to assume command.

That night the chief clerk, William Wilmett, who had been delirious
for several days, leaped overboard. Hearing the splash, followed by a
loud cry, two of the Sierra Leone blacks promptly jumped in after him. A
boat was launched and although it was pitch dark and the current strong
the three were eventually located a mile down river and brought back.
The following morning the second engineer, Albion Lodge, also contrived
to jump into the river with less happy results. His head was seen bobbing
astern for some minutes, but by the time a boat was launched he had
sunk without trace.

The model farm, when they reached it on 9 October, was found to be in

131

a less than happy state with Alfred Carr, Ansell the plant collector, and Kingdon the schoolmaster all ill. Because all the labels had come off the bottles in the steamy atmosphere they had been afraid to take any of the medicines provided – which may, indeed, have been to their advantage. After hurried consultations with the ailing Trotter, M'William decided that all three should be taken on board. This meant that the farm would have to be left in the hands of the two Americans, Ralph Moore and John Jones. Some land had already been cleared. According to Moore, four acres had been planted with yams and corn and he hoped soon to begin planting cotton on eleven more. Much of the work had been done by Bassa and Kakanda refugees who, it turned out, were only too happy to work for hire. No sooner had the Eglinton marquee been erected than emaciated figures had begun appearing out of the bush with tales of villages burned, fields laid waste, and the *mujaddidun* riding off with troops of captives. They themselves had become dependent on the nearby Pandaiki who, since they could not pay off their debts, were now threatening to sell them into slavery. In their desperate state they were prepared to accept any terms offered.[37]

Yet in spite of what looked as if it might prove a promising source of labour it would obviously be some time before the farm became fully self-supporting. The first priority, in any case, was to experiment with commercial crops. M'William accordingly arranged that the settlers be left with enough preserved meat and other rations to tide them over the next nine months, and a supply of cowries with which to buy local produce and hire workers as necessary.

At the settlers' request he agreed to allow the *Amelia*, manned by eleven Sierra Leone volunteers, to remain behind to provide protection and, if necessary, refuge. Thomas King, the Yoruba interpreter, was given command and William Guy, one of Wilmett's rescuers, put in charge of the armaments. They were instructed to remain alert, provide frequent gun-drills and use the stores sparingly as there was no telling how long it would be before a relief expedition would reach them.[38]

The *Albert* spent less than twenty-four hours at the Confluence. While the sick were being carried on board and the last of the supplies landed, Dr M'William walked to the top of Mount Stirling to survey the scene. 'While looking upon these great highways for the advance of civilization into the interior of Africa,' he later wrote, 'the Niger with its rich tropical vegetation, and the more open and broad expanse of the [Benue], flowing smoothly from the eastward . . . I could not but grieve that such a country was about to be abandoned . . . and that an enterprise which had originated in the most noble of human motives, with all appliances that human ingenuity and human foresight could devise . . . was now, alas, doomed to so melancholy a termination.'[39]

The remainder of the descent was completed without mishap. At Idah they paused only long enough to exchange messages of goodwill and confirm the correctness of their behaviour with regard to the three slaves. At Aboh they remained rather longer, taking on board supplies of wood and burying Kingdon who had died in the night. After disposing of his remains, Schön and M'William returned to find the Obi, in full regalia, knife and fork in hand, tucking into a hearty breakfast which Stanger had provided for him. Simon Jonas, who now rejoined the *Albert*, spoke warmly of the kindness with which he had been treated during his stay in Aboh. It emerged, however, that he had had little opportunity for missionary work as the Obi, learning of his training as a tailor in Sierra Leone, had kept him busy making up the length of cloth presented by the commissioners. After breakfast, the Obi visited Trotter and Bird Allen in their cabins and wished them both a speedy recovery. He had, he said, picked out a good spot for the building of a mission house and was eagerly awaiting the visit of a trading ship.[40]

In their anxiety to press ahead, they weighed anchor with the Obi's chief judge on board. As there was no hope of turning the vessel around he was obliged to leap into the river, where he floated, his robes billowing around him, until one of the Obi's canoes picked him up. Much to their surprise, the river here, presumably because of the recent rains, was still in full flood so that, borne along by the current, with M'William and Brown navigating and Stanger working the engines, they were able to proceed downstream at a good ten knots.

They were thus within eighty miles of the sea when, later that same day, they met Captain Beecroft in the *Ethiope* hastening to their assistance. It turned out that William Allen, immediately upon arriving at Fernando Po, assuming that the *Albert* would be in trouble, had sent Beecroft to her rescue. The tidings he brought with him were mostly melancholy. The *Soudan* had lost both of her doctors and her purser; the *Wilberforce* had also lost her purser and there had been deaths among the crew. What had happened to the sick aboard the *Dolphin* he did not know.[41]

Beecroft at once took charge. With his help they made their way through Louis Creek and by the following afternoon had begun taking on wood for the final leg of the voyage to Fernando Po. It was, John Duncan noted, the very spot where they had buried John William Bach on the day they entered the river. Since then the water had risen and the grave was covered.[42]

CHAPTER SEVEN
Picking Up the Pieces

Important events had meanwhile been occurring in England. On 11 May, the day before the expedition sailed, the Melbourne Government had introduced a motion to lower the duties on foreign-grown sugar sufficiently to make it available to British consumers. That there was a case for such a measure was plain enough as the price of West Indian sugar, following the ending of apprenticeship, had doubled. What had happened was that the freedmen, or at all events their wives and children, had withdrawn their labour, which, in turn, had led to a shortfall in production. The British, in other words, found themselves paying for their philanthropy in ways they had not anticipated and did not like. Free traders naturally supported the measure on ideological grounds. On the other hand, to accept foreign sugar – 'bloodstained produce' as it was called – would not only harm Britain's colonial producers, planters and freedmen alike, but would give a great boost to their slave-importing rivals and thus to the Atlantic slave trade.[1]

If the Government's support of the Niger expedition was supposed to win over the humanitarians, its proposal to admit cheap slave-grown sugar into Britain was a sure way of alienating them. One of the immediate results was to unite the Buxton and Sturge antislavery factions in opposition to the Government. As before, it was the Buxtonites, led now by Stephen Lushington, who spearheaded the attack within Parliament, leaving Sturge's organization to bring pressure to bear on MPs from outside. But what in the end made the Government's position untenable was a bizarre alliance that was now formed between abolitionists, West Indian planters and diehard Tory protectionists who believed that if the preferential rates accorded colonial sugar were scrapped the corn laws would surely follow. After an eleven-day debate the Whigs were roundly defeated by a margin of thirty-six votes. Three weeks later, defeated again, this time on a motion of no confidence, Lord John Russell announced the dissolution of Parliament.

There was little doubt that in the forthcoming General Election the

Whigs would be swept from office. Buxton felt few regrets at the prospect. He was only sorry that ill health had prevented him from taking a more active part in attacking their proposals regarding the sugar duties, although he was happy at the way his son Edward and Lushington had spoken out against them on his behalf.[2] His doctors diagnosed his troubles as stemming from a 'disorganized stomach' caused by 'mental excitement' and prescribed a diet 'confined to poultry, mutton and game'. He was also warned not to drink more than one cup of tea a day, although he was allowed four glasses of wine. By late July he was sufficiently recovered to accompany his sons on a shooting expedition to Scotland where, to his and everyone else's astonishment, he found himself striding up and down mountains with greater alacrity and sleeping more soundly than for many years past. Together they shot over 500 grouse, 70 blackcock and 5 stags. So successful had they been, he wrote, that the whole area was practically cleared of birds.[3]

He was still in Scotland when news arrived that the Melbourne cabinet had resigned and been replaced by a Tory ministry under Sir Robert Peel with a parliamentary majority of eighty. Whether or not such a government would have agreed to launch the Niger expedition was now a purely academic question. The fact was that the expedition was fairly launched. It was remembered, moreover, that Sir Robert Peel himself had been one of those who had attended the Exeter Hall meeting and in his speech had drawn attention to the sense of common purpose that had united the gathering. According to Buxton there were grounds for supposing that the new Colonial Secretary, Lord Stanley, might actually prove more supportive in his attitude towards some aspects of their cause than Russell had been.[4]

This was wishful thinking. To those more directly in touch with colonial affairs it soon became evident that Stanley did not like what he saw as Russell's expansionist policies. This was revealed when, shortly after assuming office, he received a set of treaties which John Carr, continuing the work begun by Sir John Jeremie, had negotiated with the tribes around Sierra Leone. Carr's treaties, however, went considerably further than Jeremie's, involving obligations to provide rulers sympathetic to British policies with armed protection and the building of forts and stockades. In short, he was proposing a new antislavery policy that would oblige Sierra Leone to expand her area of authority well beyond her present boundaries. Aware of Sierra Leone's unhappy history, Stanley sent these to the Prime Minister with covering notes expressing his own and Stephen's reservations. Peel replied that he certainly did not want forts or stockades, or any further land acquired. Above all, he did not want any undertakings that would require using troops. Carr had shown more zeal than judgement and should be recalled as soon as someone more sensible could be found. Stanley duly passed on the word to Carr that his treaties had been disallowed and that he should suspend all such proceedings.[5]

In the same vein, Stanley's first despatch to the Niger commissioners warned them not to enter into agreements which would entail 'any right of sovereignty or of protection over any portion of the soil or waters of Africa'. The most that they could do, and that only in exceptional circumstances, was to forward any requests they might receive for protection from African rulers to the Colonial Office where they would receive appropriate consideration.[6]

News of the expedition had meanwhile been trickling slowly back to England. Letters addressed to wives and relatives were passed from family to family. Some were reprinted in the *Friend of Africa*. All were optimistic. William Kwantabisa assured the Reverend Pyne that the days were not far off when all Africans would 'unite together with the European Christians to praise the Lord and Saviour Jesus Christ'.[7] The last letter written before the steamers disappeared into the interior was one from Trotter to his wife, dated 20 August, informing her that with a few minor exceptions 'we are all, thank God, in the enjoyment of good health and excellent spirits, everything going on prosperously. The season is decidedly a healthy one so far as we can judge.'[8] For those left behind, Buxton reflected, there was only one thing left that they could do for Africa: 'we must most heartily pray for her.'[9]

The first intimations of the disaster that had overtaken the expedition arrived at the Colonial Office on 1 December in the form of a batch of letters describing the *Soudan*'s descent from the Confluence and the transfer of her sick to HMS *Dolphin*.[10] 'I wish thee could have heard Fowell's cry for mercy upon Africa and the Expedition this evening at our prayers in the family', Buxton's wife wrote to Anna Gurney on receipt of the news.[11] In public, however, Buxton put on a brave face. It had been known from the first that a degree of risk was involved. In a war casualties were readily accepted. Why should they not also be borne in pursuit of a far nobler cause? To close friends like Trew, however, he was prepared to confess that 'the blow is a terrible one'.[12] But what, in his inmost heart, he could not understand was how God could have allowed it to happen. No enterprise was ever launched with purer motives or in a better cause.

It was a problem with which he went on wrestling during succeeding months as, like hammer blows, one set of disastrous tidings succeeded another. Yet of one thing there could be no doubt. 'It is the doing of our merciful Lord, and therefore is not only intended to be, but is, done in mercy and in love.' The problem was to know why God had done it. Was He testing their faith? Had He provided an initial check in order that they would be obliged to redouble their efforts? Or did He have quite other plans for Africa? After months of brooding and prayer Buxton was no nearer to a solution than he had been when he wrote to Trew, on hearing the first bad tidings, 'it may be mysterious, it may be disappointing, it may be painful, but it must be right.'[13]

No such soul-searching was evident in the columns of *The Times*. On 6 December it printed a largely factual account of the ascent of the river, describing how the commissioners had met the Obi, 'dressed like a mountebank', and the Attah, and how the model farm had been established before fever forced them to send the *Soudan* back to the coast. This was followed on 9 December by a lengthy editorial attacking 'the wretched charlatans', who, 'by dint of combined pressure which the Whigs were not in a condition to resist [had sent] the glorious expedition to the Niger for the purpose of cultivating fancy farms, raising supernatural crops . . . and eventually causing the Ethiopian to change his skin'. The latest news merely confirmed what the paper had prophesied from the first, namely that the originators of the enterprise, who contrived to remain safely at home, were quite happy to bolster their sense of self-importance by sending others to their deaths. It was 'sufficient to consign African philanthropy to everlasting ridicule and scorn'.

News of the *Soudan*'s descent elicited no immediate response from the Colonial Office. On 21 December, however, upon receiving a Treasury estimate of the cost of the expedition in the coming year, Stephen expressed doubts as to whether there would be much in the way of expenses to meet: 'I confess my own impression to be that the best that can be done will be to instruct the survivors to return home as soon as possible.' From what he had learned, the Niger was navigable only for about ten weeks in the year, and at the most unhealthy season, a fact which, in his view, rendered the whole project impractical.[14]

A report of the *Wilberforce*'s arrival at Fernando Po, together with an account of further deaths among the sick taken by HMS *Dolphin* to Ascension, reached the Admiralty on 6 January. A copy was immediately forwarded to G.W. Hope, Stanley's junior minister, asking him to 'call his Lordship's attention to the great mortality involved in this report'. Stanley responded by asking Stephen to prepare a brief summary to lay before the Cabinet.[15]

As before, Buxton attempted to put a favourable gloss on events. It was a great pity, he told George Anson, Prince Albert's aide-de-camp, that he was not well enough to come to London as he would have liked to give the Prince a full briefing on the latest developments. Alas, he was quite laid up. However, he hoped that Anson would point out to the Prince that the accounts appearing in the papers were very prejudiced. He was forwarding a batch of personal letters from members of the expedition which showed that treaties had been made and land purchased – in fact that, apart from the fever, 'their success exceeded their most sanguine anticipations'.[16] Trotter and Bird Allen were now on their way to Raba. To Bird Allen he wrote, 'May we soon be favoured with good tidings of the *Albert*! . . . With deep interest we look forward to your next assault on the regions of darkness.'[17]

The arrival, on 20 January, of a third batch of letters describing the *Albert*'s return and Bird Allen's death was the heaviest blow of all. 'We are afflicted indeed,' Priscilla informed Anna. 'All the accounts are most bad. . . . Alas for my Father.'[18] Buxton himself was for the moment at a loss for words. 'What can I say?' he wrote to Trew. 'It has pleased God to send us *a deep disappointment*, a personal as well as a public calamity of no common kind. That dear Bird Allen! . . . And at present we know of no balancing circumstances of good, I mean in these last accounts.'[19] It looked like an unmitigated catastrophe.

The Times, joined now by other newspapers, renewed its attack on 'smooth gentlemen, borne luxuriantly along on the easy gale of popular enthusiasm, taking full advantage of the opportunities given them to display in full dress their costly sensibilities'.[20] It was ironical that this expedition, equipped with every gadget known to modern science and mounted at exorbitant public expense, had in the end been rescued by a vessel belonging to a private merchant who, from the first, had publicly warned against the enterprise. Another irony, to which the *Morning Herald* drew particular attention, was the fact that it had all happened before. Anyone who had read the Laird–Oldfield account would have known what would happen. Had the Government listened to Jamieson and others, so shamefully calumniated by Sir George Stephen, instead of being swayed by 'the schemes of dreamers' this whole melancholy episode would have been avoided.[21]

Friends, meanwhile, hastened to offer their sympathy. God would not fail to note, J.J. Gurney assured Buxton, that those who perished had done so in pursuit of worthy goals. They were, his business partner Robert Hanbury had no doubt, 'martyrs in a holy cause – and the crown of martyrs would be theirs'. The same, he added, also applied 'with respect to those who have been instrumental in sending them'. It was, Elizabeth Fry noted, a 'close exercise of faith and patience. . . . We must leave it to Him who does all things well.' Similar condolences were expressed by the Bishop of Calcutta, Daniel Wilson: 'Be not cast down my dearest friend. . . . Soon, soon, the tempest will be calmed – your life will be past – soon the Heavenly Port will open . . .' One of the few correspondents to take a different line was Stephen Lushington, who confessed, quite frankly, that he thought he had been at least partly responsible for causing unnecessary deaths by urging the expedition forward without first informing himself about the state of Africa, although he absolved Buxton from similar blame as he had spared no pains to master the subject. Nevertheless, the time had come for Buxton to 'look the evil in the face' and accept that the enterprise was now at an end.[22]

Similar thoughts prevailed at the Admiralty and Colonial Office. Writing from Fernando Po, Trotter described in detail what had befallen the *Albert* and its crew since leaving the Confluence – the ascent to Egga, the progress of the fever, the voyage downstream, the meeting with the *Ethiope* and the way even those who, like M'William and Duncan, had escaped the fever on the river had subsequently come down with it. Some of these later cases were proving among the most severe. Besides Bird Allen, Willie the mate was dead; so too was Wilmett, the clerk whom the Krumen had rescued when he jumped overboard. Of the 150 whites who entered the Nun, only 9 had escaped the fever and 24 had died. This last figure did not include any (in fact 8) who had perished on their way to Ascension. At the time of writing many of the sick were still in a critical condition. His present plan was to leave the *Soudan* at Fernando Po and follow the *Wilberforce* to Ascension. He would then return to England for consultations, which would still allow him ample time to rejoin the expedition should the Government decide to renew the attempt.[23]

'This is,' Stanley wrote, 'a frightful statement. I have little doubt of the course which ought to be pursued, but I wish to bring the whole case before the Cabinet.'[24]

Within days Trotter himself, accompanied by William Stanger, arrived bearing tidings of yet more casualties. He had not gone to Ascension but at the command of his doctor had returned directly home. He reported that some of those who had survived the fever, among them Theodor Vogel, had since succumbed to dysentery. Trotter's appearance, everyone agreed, was greatly altered. Shavenheaded, emaciated, he was a shadow of his former self. 'When I knew the fact of its being he,' Lady Parry wrote to Richenda Buxton, 'I could not detect the likeness.'[25] Buxton, who had hastened to London, was shocked at the sight of the gaunt figure that greeted him. He was also disappointed that neither Trotter nor Stanger was able to provide him with any 'balancing circumstances' of the kind for which he had been hoping. Indeed, Stanger's account was even bleaker than Trotter's: poor soil, a wretched climate, badly designed vessels, terrorized villagers, no high ground, delirious patients – the only good news was that no shots had been fired in anger.[26]

Having been carried along by their father's enthusiasm, the Buxton children were appalled at what had happened. Their mother hoped that none of them would choose to devote their lives to such concerns. 'Certainly,' Edward wrote to Priscilla, 'the climate seems like a wall of fire round the land and it is a hindrance which no time or perseverance can overcome.' It was 'a great relief', Richenda observed, that the Government had decided to call the whole thing off, otherwise 'to have had it possible and necessary to have sent more people up might have made it a duty . . .'[27]

Little by little, however, it began to dawn on them that this was far from being their father's attitude and that his appetite for African ventures was still far from assuaged. Having recovered from his initial dismay he was now looking around for alternative approaches. Granted that the climate had proved lethal to whites, it had been equally clearly demonstrated that the same did not apply to blacks, or not, at all events, to African blacks. Perhaps Africa could be redeemed by black agents trained up in the West Indies and Sierra Leone. It had earlier been agreed that John Trew would go on a recruiting mission to Jamaica. That was now more important than ever. Above all Buxton pinned his reviving hopes on the model farm. Perhaps it was flourishing. Carr and Moore's reports on its first month's operations contained much that was encouraging. Surely it could not simply be abandoned. At the very least the settlers would need to be told of the Government's plans. Someone would have to go back. Who knows – victory might yet be snatched from the jaws of defeat.[28]

Trotter remained studiously noncommittal about the advice he intended to give his superiors. It turned out, however, that before leaving Fernando Po he had written to Thomas King of the *Amelia* indicating that a relief expedition might be expected sometime the following summer. He had given the letter to Alfred Carr who, having recovered from his fever, had set out for the farm by canoe. Both Trotter and Stanger regarded this as a foolhardy undertaking. Like his brother John, Alfred was deemed to have shown more zeal than judgement. He was altogether too anxious to please. Trotter had written to Buxton expressing doubts as to his competence. From their comments it appeared that Trotter and Stanger had grounds for doubting whether he had got any further than Brass Creek. Nevertheless, Trotter's letter and the instructions left behind by M'William could be seen as implying some sort of official commitment not to abandon the expedition.[29]

Whether Lord Stanley would regard them as such was another matter. In view of the outcry in the press there was a distinct possibility that he would not. Buxton was not on the same easy terms with the Tories that he had been with their predecessors. His great fear was that they would simply announce their determination to wash their hands of the whole business without even bothering to consult him.[30]

To forestall any such action, he told his sceptical colleagues on the ACS Committee, they would need to act promptly and boldly. Defeated though they were, they must not appear downhearted; indeed, they must not even admit to defeat. Wringing any concessions from the Government would depend on their being affirmative. 'I vowed,' he told Priscilla, 'that I would not hear of the abandonment of Africa or surrender any part of the vitals of my plan – that we were *not* defeated but almost completely triumphant.' Except that they would now use black agents instead of white the whole plan could go ahead as originally planned.[31]

On 22 February Buxton, Lushington, Sir Robert Inglis and Sir Thomas Ackland waited on the Colonial Secretary. 'To tell you the truth,' he later told Priscilla, 'I was terribly afraid of my companions – there seemed no fight in them.' In the event, however, they proved more supportive than he had expected. His own contribution was a 'chant of victory contending that, making allowance for our deep regret for the loss of so many good men, we had succeeded beyond expectations and that it would be a most wicked scheme to abandon Africa in consequence of anything that had occurred'. Stanley listened patiently to their exposition. The issue, he told them, was still before Cabinet. He had submitted a paper recommending the abandonment of the entire enterprise, including the farm. But if the Society would let him have a memorandum outlining its views he would gladly circulate it among his colleagues.[32]

This was little more than a polite gesture. As Lushington and the other members of the ACS Committee were well aware, they were, politically speaking, a spent force. Whatever influence they had formally exercised over the public or with the Government had gone. The one person who seemed unaware of this was the ailing Buxton whose views, as his embarrassed colleagues and family began to realize, were quite out of touch with reality. Rather than diminishing, his ambitions seemed to have grown. This was not, as they had at first supposed, a matter of political tactics but of genuine aspiration. A relief expedition was the least of his requirements. He also wanted the Government to provide a regular steamer service, assume sovereignty over the land already acquired, and supply a black police force to guard it. His great fear, he told Lushington, was of 'our Model Farm manager and missionary being swept away some fine morning by the crew of a Slave Trader'.[33] (How a slave trader was to get that far up-river he did not explain. The advent of a steam-powered slave trade was still many years in the future.) He drafted a letter to Stanley pointing out that in former times the Government had been willing to support black garrisons in the Gold Coast forts. In those days the object was to promote the slave trade. Could it, in all conscience, bring itself to do less now? Quite knocked out by his exertions, Buxton retired to Norfolk. From there he even began writing letters that cast doubt on the validity of the expedition's findings as 'directly at variance with the Reports of every preceding Traveller'.[34]

In spite of their doubts, the ACS Committee presented Buxton's requests to Stanley. After all, what had they to lose? In their own submission they mentioned the possibility of employing black police but otherwise strove to make their requirements appear modest – a treaty with Rabba, an occasional showing of the flag by a steamer manned principally by native-born Africans; they did not want to put more white lives at risk or even press the Government to take permanent possession of the land acquired in its name.[35]

Trotter had meanwhile submitted reports to the Admiralty and Colonial Office setting out, clearly and concisely, the present situation and the available options.[36] The *Wilberforce* and *Albert* were at Ascension with orders to remain there until June; the *Soudan* was laid up at Fernando Po. It was now known that 39 out of the 145 whites who set out from Devonport, more than a quarter of the total number, had died of fever. There had also been deaths from other causes. Many of the survivors were not yet fully recovered. However, the *Wilberforce*, and very probably by now the *Albert* too, had made up for these losses by recruiting seamen from merchant ships touching at Ascension. If required, all three vessels could reascend the river. Should it be decided that only one should go, it would be better to employ one of the larger vessels, as it would be faster and able to carry more fuel. In that event it should be possible to get to the model farm and back to the coast in under two weeks. He doubted if Captain Allen's health would permit his going up the river a third time, but Mr Cook was one of those who had escaped the fever and was quite willing to go. Apart from this Trotter did not express any personal views. The choice was wide. It was up to ministers to decide the best course to take.

The course eventually chosen proved to be a fudge of the kind James Stephen particularly disliked. Everyone concerned must understand, Stanley ruled, that the expedition was now at an end, that all the personnel must immediately return home, and that the Admiralty should dispose of the vessels and their equipment in whatever way it thought fit. However, a single vessel, manned as far as possible by Africans, would return to the Confluence so as to allow the settlers the opportunity of leaving should they so wish. If the farm was found to be in a prosperous state and the settlers wished to stay, then the commissioner in charge of the expedition could authorize the *Amelia* to remain as a means of defence and possible source of refuge. On the way to the Confluence he was to tell the Obi and the Attah that the treaties signed the previous year had been formally ratified. In exceptionally favourable circumstances, which was to say supposing no fever to have broken out or other misadventures occurred, he could proceed as far as Raba, but no further. Which of the commissioners on the Coast, Commander Allen or Mr Cook, would lead the expedition, and in which vessel, were matters they themselves must decide.[37]

The enterprise was to be called off, and yet it was not. The Government had declined any responsibility for the land acquired, but was prepared to leave a naval vessel standing guard ready to repel invaders. It had agreed to enter into treaty arrangements and now proposed leaving the parties concerned to their own devices. As Stephen pointed out, it was all a muddle.[38] But what else could the Government do? Far removed as it was, ignorant of local circumstances and what might have happened to the model farm, there simply was no alternative but to rely on the judgement of the agents they had sent out. In spite of Stephen's misgivings, not all British officials in remote places were rogues or fools. Allen and Cook were men of wide experience. There was no reason to doubt their competence. Whichever of them led the new expedition would certainly be in a much better position than the Colonial Secretary to choose the most appropriate course of action.

The matter acquired a new urgency when a letter arrived from Ascension indicating that, contrary to Trotter's instructions, Allen was intending to renew the attempt as soon as the Niger became navigable, probably in early June.[39] The steamship *Kite* had been standing by at Woolwich. On 21 April she was despatched with instructions to hasten to the Nun, where, with luck, she might still be able to intercept the expedition before it vanished once more into the interior.

Compared to the other vessels the *Wilberforce* had escaped lightly. She had lost only four crew members and two passengers, a total of six as compared with twenty-three aboard the *Albert* and ten out of the significantly smaller ship's complement of the *Soudan*.[40] William Allen's illness proved transitory and William Cook, a seasoned visitor to tropical parts, had escaped entirely. So also had all three ship's doctors, in their case almost certainly because they had been taking regular doses of quinine (about which more in due course).

Allen attributed his crew's relative good fortune to his own promptitude in removing them from the deleterious atmosphere of Africa and to the restorative effects of sea breezes.[41] After sending the *Ethiope* and the *Soudan* to the *Albert*'s rescue he had lost no time in putting to sea, so that by the time the *Albert* and its two escorts reached Clarence Cove the *Wilberforce* was already well out into the Atlantic.

Arriving at Ascension on 17 November, they learned that eight of the sick transferred from the *Soudan* to the *Dolphin* had died on the passage out and that most of the rest had been invalided and would shortly be returning to England.[42] The *Wilberforce*'s own crew, however, was now pretty much recovered. They were thus able to begin work immediately on repairing the damage to the ship's superstructure caused by her collision with the tree-stump and making various alterations to the vessel itself. One of the problems most complained of up the river had been the suffocating atmosphere below decks caused by the dividing bulkheads and the inadequacy of Dr Reid's ventilating apparatus. Holes were accordingly made in the upper sections of the bulkheads so that air, still driven by the fans, could circulate more freely. The purificator, having totally failed to serve the purpose its inventor had intended, was jettisoned. As there was no boat large enough to take it, it was floated ashore looking 'like a floating omnibus' and there put to use as a water tank.[43]

A volcanic island, part of the mid-Atlantic ridge, Ascension was one of the loneliest outposts of empire. The navy had long used it to provision ships bound to and from the South Atlantic. Apart from the company of marines, whose sole duty it was to guard the stores and arsenal, it had no inhabitants at all. Allen compared it to a giant cinder. Tiny, arid, remote, without seasons, each day was indistinguishable from the last. The sun rose in the east, passed directly overhead and set in the west; between times the island baked. In short, it was the sort of place where normally sensible men, isolated from the rest of the world, begin to object to one another's views, appearances and habits, fail to take account of their own irritating traits, brood over trifles, detect slights to their honour and wind up having bitter quarrels.

The Commandant of Marines, a genial captain, died of a stroke within days of the *Wilberforce*'s arrival. His successor, a junior lieutenant, did not relish being outranked by his visitors or having his tiny outpost overrun by bored sailors. He objected to their getting drunk, stealing bananas and interfering with the turtles that came on shore to lay their eggs; he also refused to provide fodder for the *Wilberforce*'s livestock and would not allow Allen to send sailors to the peak in search of alternative supplies. Angry letters passed back and forth with copies to the Admiralty.[44]

Altogether more worrying, however, was the gradually developing rift between the two commissioners. Their original plan had been to remain at Ascension until early January and then return to the Coast where they would join up with Trotter and Bird Allen in time for a second ascent of the river, possibly in March. That, at least, was how they construed the instructions given them at the Confluence. But, just as they were preparing to sail, HMS *Buzzard* arrived with news of the *Albert*'s arrival at Clarence Cove, Bird Allen's death and Trotter's departure for England. The *Buzzard*'s commander, Lieutenant Levinge, also brought letters from Trotter explaining that he had arranged for the *Soudan* to be laid up in Fernando Po under the care of ship-minders and for Lieutenant Fishbourne to bring the survivors, as soon as they were sufficiently recovered, to Ascension in the *Albert*, where they were to await further instructions. Should none have arrived by June, both vessels were to return to Clarence Cove and prepare to reascend the river as soon as its waters began to rise.[45]

The instructions were admirably clear and concise. Whether they should be obeyed was another matter as Levinge also brought tidings which raised doubts concerning the fates of Alfred Carr and the model farm. According to Levinge, a rumour was circulating along the Coast that Carr had been murdered shortly after entering Brass Creek and that the farm had been attacked, presumably by the *mujaddidun*, and its settlers either killed or made slaves.[46]

These were the same rumours Trotter and Stanger had carried back to England. So far as the farm was concerned, the stories had struck them as improbable. As for Carr, if he was foolish enough to attempt to traverse the Delta in an open boat, his fate was his own responsibility. Whatever it was, it did not warrant any change in the expedition's plans.

This was not the view taken in Ascension. Commissioner Cook's response, in particular, was of a kind with which James Stephen's long experience of the behaviour of British officials in remote places had made him all too familiar. According to Lieutenant Levinge, a British settlement had been attacked and a British subject murdered. The honour of Great Britain was thus at stake. At the very least these were matters calling for immediate investigation. If the farm personnel had not been killed, they were in all probability being held captive, which made action even more urgent. In such circumstances it ill befitted Her Majesty's Commissioners to idle away their time in mid-Atlantic. Allen agreed that the news was worrying but thought it advisable to await confirmation that some disaster had, indeed, occurred.

Suspicion that some misfortune had befallen Carr was strengthened when, on 28 January, the *Albert* arrived bringing Allen's old friend Brown, the coloured clerk from Cape Coast, who, on Trotter's instructions, had accompanied Carr on the first leg of his journey. According to Brown,[47] they had arrived off the Rio Bento aboard the steamship *Pluto* early on the morning of 7 November. It was a stormy day with frequent tornadoes. They took the longboat over the sandbar and had rowed some way in what they took to be the direction of Brass Creek when they were hailed by a large, heavy-laden canoe whose crew said they were on their way to Aboh. On hearing that Carr was intending to go there they offered to take him with them. Brown was suspicious, not least because they failed to mention payment, which was all the more remarkable because to accommodate Carr and his servant required their jettisoning various possessions of their own. He urged Carr not to go. Carr, however, would listen to no such arguments and, having settled himself and his companion aboard the canoe, vanished into the rain.

Not long afterwards the longboat encountered a Brass canoe coming in the opposite direction, whose commander assured them that the canoe in which Carr was travelling was not bound for Aboh and that its crew had murdered two white men in similar circumstances on an earlier occasion. Alarmed, Brown turned the longboat around, and, accompanied by the Brass canoe, set off in pursuit. But after rowing for half an hour and seeing no sign of their quarry they pulled into the bank and began cooking a meal. The Brass crew, meanwhile, went on to a nearby village, gathered armed reinforcements, and creeping up on the sailors, suddenly leapt out from the surrounding mangroves. With commendable nimbleness the British managed to get into their longboat and cast off leaving their arms and various other possessions behind.

In view of what happened later it seems likely that the story of the murder of the two white men was a subterfuge. All the same, white men had vanished thereabouts, among them several Rhode Islanders from the brig *Anegoria*, whose probable murder by the Delta people is mentioned by Oldfield.[48] Although the slave trade had largely vanished from the Nun it was still being carried on by way of Brass Creek and the Rio Bento. According to various informants to whom Brown had spoken, King Boy had told his people to attack any British man-of-war boat approaching Brass Town. Brown was in no doubt that Carr had been murdered.

This was also Cook's view. Carr was a British subject. If he had not been killed, he was presumably being held hostage, which made the argument for action all the more compelling. What was clear, beyond any shadow of doubt, was that a vessel belonging to Her Majesty had been attacked and robbed. Retribution was called for. Such a slight to Britain's dignity could not be allowed to pass unnoticed.[49]

Allen was less sure. There was no proof that Carr had been murdered. Even if he had been it was not clear what, after so long an elapse of time, would now be achieved by rushing to the scene. It was doubtful, moreover, whether the *Wilberforce* could even cross the Rio Bento sandbar. To send a longboat would, as events had shown, involve putting the lives of her crew at risk. In any case, as he later explained, 'The idea of sending a boat up the river with one flood, to enquire among the mangrove swamps, where not a hut is to be seen for many miles, is manifestly absurd.' The fact was that Carr, with a quantity of valuable goods, his constitution already weakened by fever, had trusted himself to the first canoe he met, intending to travel 270 miles through hostile territory at the unhealthiest time of the year. If the natives had not killed him the climate almost certainly would have done. His chances of getting to the farm were remote. As for the stories about the farm being attacked, they were unreliable, and in any event there was really nothing that could be done until the river next rose.[50]

Cook had not failed to note the almost unseemly haste with which Allen had departed, first from the Confluence and then from Fernando Po. His refusal now to take what Cook regarded as the only honourable course open and return immediately to the Coast strengthened a suspicion that had already begun to form in his mind, namely that Allen was a coward. Quite simply, he was afraid to go back to Africa. Everything else – his scepticism regarding Brown's account, his anxiety not to deviate from Trotter's instructions, the letters he sent to the Admiralty about preparing another expedition to ascend the river – were now revealed to Cook as pure sham. Suddenly everything was clear. Overwhelmed by the truth of his discovery, of which he made no secret, Cook also succeeded in persuading himself, contrary to all the available evidence, that March was the very best time for ascending the river as 'the quicksands which compose the greatest part of its bed will become so drained and consolidated as to throw the stream into one channel, it will be found deeper and more rapid at that time . . .' The less water there was, apparently, the more readily navigable the river would become.[51]

Allen regarded this as total nonsense. There were, in fact, no compelling operational reasons for leaving Ascension before June. Yet to remain there in idleness, month after month, quarrelling with its acting commandant and being taunted by Cook, was not an agreeable prospect. The *Wilberforce* was now repaired and its crew ready for duty. In his original instructions, issued at the time the *Wilberforce* was preparing to leave the Confluence, Trotter had referred to Lord John Russell's instructions about the desirability of making antislavery treaties with the coastal chiefs. By busying themselves in that way the commissioners would at least be doing something useful while they awaited further orders.

Whatever may or may not have been Allen's private feelings, the plan was eminently sensible. In order to mollify Cook, however, he inserted into the official minutes of their commissioners' meeting held in Ascension on 3 February the words 'It was ultimately agreed, that it is expedient an attempt be made to enter the river as early as possible in order to carry out the commands of Her Majesty's Government.' This was a purely verbal concession. As the senior commissioner it was up to him to decide what was possible. But to those in England, eager for news and unaware of the widening rift between the two commissioners, his meaning was unclear. Was he going back or wasn't he? The Government feared he was, although from his despatches it was impossible to tell quite what his intentions were.

Clarence Cove, Fernando Po.

The *Wilberforce* left Ascension on 10 March for Cape Coast Castle, where her crew again enjoyed the hospitality of Captain Maclean. From him they learned that all had not gone well with the Asante princes on their return to Kumase. The elder of the two, Kwantabisa, had been caught committing adultery with a wife of the Asantahene's principal adviser. In the event he had been treated leniently 'because of his education' and his British connections, but the woman, whom he claimed had seduced him, had been beheaded in front of the missionaries' residence. For a time it even seemed as if the whole mission might have to be abandoned. Maclean was very angry and stopped Kwantabisa's pension. Far from the princes helping the mission, it was proving quite the other way round.[52]

From Cape Coast the *Wilberforce* proceeded to Fernando Po. Apart from Stanley's despatch of 11 November warning them not to offer protection to African rulers, they found no instructions awaiting them in either place. This was disappointing. The day after their arrival, Allen and Cook formally convened to consider future plans. Having just sailed past the Nun without pausing to enquire if the people at Akassa had any news of either Carr or the farm had persuaded Cook more than ever that so long as Allen remained in charge the Niger expedition would remain a mere charade.[53] Allen, he believed, was simply playing for time in the hope that word would arrive calling them all back to England. This may well have been the case. If so, it was an excusable attitude, shared, according to William Simpson, by most of the seamen who were praying daily for just such a summons. On the way south from Cape Coast they had been heard referring to Cape Nun as 'the gateway to the cemetery'. They plainly did not want to go back. These were not, however, sentiments that could be expressed in despatches. They were not even sentiments which a naval officer was supposed to entertain. In his letters to the Admiralty Allen continued to give quite the opposite impression – that he and his crew were positively impatient to return to the river. Naval etiquette required a measure of make-believe.[54]

Less easy to explain is Cook's personal animosity towards Allen. Perhaps, as a mere merchant captain, he had had more than enough of Royal Navy etiquette and make-believe. Subsequent events suggest that his assessment of Allen's intentions may, indeed, have had some basis. What is plain is that he had convinced himself that anything short of an immediate return to the river was evidence of Allen's personal pusillanimity. At his sarcastic insistence 'as soon as possible' was changed to 'as soon as the Naval Commander ... deems it safe'. He vetoed a proposal that they appoint Lieutenant Ellis, who had now taken over command of the *Soudan*, as a fourth commissioner in place of Bird Allen on the grounds that he was insufficiently imbued with antislavery principles. The meeting adjourned with the two commissioners deadlocked.[55]

The final break came a week later. HMS *Driver*, a gunboat en route to China, arrived bearing newspapers of 5 March containing reports of a parliamentary statement by Lord Stanley to the effect that it was not the Government's intention to continue the expedition in its original form.[56] Allen summoned Cook to a meeting to discuss the implications of this. Cook replied that he would be having dinner on shore at the time indicated. After further exchanges of notes Allen ordered Cook to appear. At the appointed hour, according to Allen, 'Mr Cook ... came on board in very great excitement and taking off his hat, and bowing very low, he said with the most outrageous mockery of respect on the Quarter deck of the vessel which I commanded "I am come on board Captain Allen in obedience to your *Mandate* and the *Khan of Tartary* never issued a more imperious one."' This was done in full view of the ship's crew. When asked what he meant by such behaviour he repeated the whole performance.[57]

At the meeting that followed he charged Allen with cowardice and with trying to fill up the commission with his friends. Why had Allen not sent a vessel up the river long since? After much shouting and gesturing he said he had had enough, pleaded illness and left. Allen sent the minutes to Stanley in a sealed envelope with a note saying that it would be inappropriate to show them either to Parliament or the public. He also ordered Cook to remove himself and his effects to the *Soudan* forthwith.[58]

Rather than obey this instruction Cook chose to take up quarters on shore. For the next two months Her Majesty's Niger commissioners conducted a correspondence of icy formality.[59] From time to time the *Wilberforce* and *Soudan* cruised around the Bay of Biafra. Cook declined to take part, begging to inform Captain Allen 'that it is not my intention to embark on board any of the vessels of the Expedition until they are ready to ascend the Niger'. Allen, in turn, wished to inform Mr Cook that he had learned that the stories concerning Carr and the farm were false and therefore that he intended waiting for instructions from London. Cook asked Beecroft to take him up the river in the *Ethiope*. Beecroft refused. He had, he said, other things to do.

Meanwhile time was slipping away so rapidly that even Allen was becoming anxious. During the latter part of May he led an expedition which took a forty-foot galley into the interior of the Cameroons where he concluded treaties with two local chiefs similar to those made with the Obi and Attah. The political situation there, it turned out, was much the same as on the Niger, the coastal rulers being equally hostile to the notion of Europeans having direct intercourse with the hinterland. One consequence of this expedition was an outbreak of fever, from which the crews had been largely free since their return to the Coast.[60]

By mid-June, with the rainy season already begun and the river rising, Allen set about loading both steamers with coal ready for a renewed attempt. He had written several times to the Admiralty saying that he was planning to go back as soon as the river became navigable. As they had not replied, and having recently seen in a newspaper the announcement of his own promotion to captain, he could only assume that they approved of his intentions regarding a second ascent. According to his later account his plan was to take both steamers to the Confluence, leave the *Soudan* there and go on to Raba in the *Wilberforce*, possibly exploring the Benue on the way back.

The expedition was within a day of sailing when, in the early hours of 24 June, the crews were brought from their beds by the sound of a heavy steamer making its way into Clarence Cove. A longboat was promptly lowered and within minutes Lieutenant Gooch of the *Kite* was on board the *Wilberforce* with Stanley's instructions. Among the crews, according to Simpson, long 'on the tip-toe of expectation to ascertain whether we are on the eve of proceeding homeward or to direct our steps again to the ill-fated Niger', there was general jubilation at this last-minute reprieve.[61]

Allen sent a copy of Stanley's memorandum to Cook. There followed an unseemly wrangle out of which it emerged that *neither* commissioner was prepared to go back up the river. Allen claimed that as the main object now was to ascertain the state of the model farm, and possibly to wind up its affairs, responsibility naturally lay with the civilian commissioner. On the other hand, having decided not to go himself, he was determined to put obstacles in the way of his rival's going. He therefore refused to show Cook the orders he had given to Lieutenant William Henry Webb, the *Wilberforce*'s second-in-command and former mate of the *Soudan*, who had volunteered to take charge of the relief vessel, supposedly because they were a strictly naval matter. This was patently untrue. There was no technical reason for refusing to let a fellow commissioner know under what orders he would be travelling, although it was difficult to conceive that they would differ much from the very specific directions given in Lord Stanley's memorandum, a copy of which Cook already had. Nevertheless, this rebuff did provide Cook, whose much-proclaimed eagerness to return had suddenly evaporated, with a convenient excuse for withdrawing on the grounds that he was not prepared to 'be a mere cipher on board without power or authority either as regards Lord Stanley's instructions or of benefiting the cause of Africa'. In view of Allen's refusal he had, he said, made up his mind to return at once to England.[62]

In company with William Simpson, he embarked on the *Golden Spring*, a palm-oiler belonging to the West African Company, the following day. They landed in Plymouth in the early hours of 19 September. The customs house was already closed when they docked, but upon its becoming known that they were survivors of the Niger expedition they were allowed through in time to catch the morning train, and thus, 'propelled with great velocity', were in London in time for breakfast.[63]

William Allen and the naval personnel returned home in HMS *Kite*. Before departing on her return journey the *Kite* towed the *Wilberforce* to the mouth of the Nun. The weather was as stormy as it had been the previous year with leaden skies and driving rain. As the two vessels parted the crew of the *Kite* gave three cheers. They watched the *Wilberforce* enter the breakers, pass the gallows tree, and then hoist her ensign as a signal that she had crossed the bar in safety, whereupon she was lost to sight in a squall of rain.[64]

CHAPTER EIGHT
Return to the Model Farm

In accordance with Lord Stanley's instructions the *Wilberforce*'s complement of Europeans had been cut to an absolute minimum. Besides Lieutenant Webb himself, it consisted of a surgeon, a clerk, a boatswain, a carpenter, and three engineers, all volunteers. Apart from Hinsman the surgeon, who had previously served in that capacity in Fernando Po, and Cameron the second engineer, a new recruit who had joined the *Wilberforce* in Ascension, all had ascended the river the previous year and suffered in varying degrees from fever. The remainder of the crew was made up of 40 of the best Krumen, among them William Allen's former servant Jack Smoke.[1]

Webb's orders, about which Cook had harboured such suspicions, were little more than a gloss on Stanley's minute of 13 April. The *Wilberforce* was to proceed with all speed to the Confluence to determine the condition of the model farm. What became of the settlement was a matter for Webb to decide when he got there. Should the settlers wish to remain, they were to be told that they would be living under the laws of Igala, not those of Britain. How much territory they would have, and on what terms, were questions they would need to discuss with the Attah. Should there be no fever, Webb was empowered to go as far as Raba but no further. Otherwise he was to return to the coast with all possible speed. Allen's only significant addition was to warn him not to go out of his way to seize slaves, destroy canoes or otherwise attempt to enforce the articles of the previous year's treaties. Those agreements had been drafted on the assumption that Britain would be maintaining a permanent presence on the river. It was now plain that this was not going to be the case. If there was no prospect of enforcing the treaties, at least not on any continuing basis, it would be foolish to make enemies. Slavery, as Allen well knew, was endemic throughout the region. If Britain were to begin seizing slaves, many would simply assume that she was intending to use them for her own purposes. Thus to invoke the treaties in the present instance would be merely irritating, provocative and likely to cause mischief when, as would presumably prove the case, attempts were subsequently made to establish purely commercial relations.[2]

As had happened the previous year, it was found on crossing the bar that the tail fin of the rudder had been lost in the heavy seas, so once again the *Wilberforce* had to be beached and repaired. The estuary looked much as it had done before. There were the same mudbanks and mangroves, the same flights of pelicans. But once above the reaches subject to the influence of the tide the appearance of the river was much altered. The bed of the Niger was wide and shallow. Passing through Louis Creek on 3 July they discovered, instead of the sheet of water that had greeted them the previous August, a broad expanse of mudflats through which the river, shrunk to a fraction of its former self, meandered its way in a leisurely fashion. Here and there the branches of uprooted trees protruded from the mud. Further on, the entrance to the creek where the *Wilberforce* had made its lengthy diversion was now quite silted up, and Aboh Creek, when they eventually reached it, instead of being quarter of a mile across, was scarcely broad enough to accommodate galley's oars. Although the relative slackness of the current reduced the amount of fuel consumed and allowed the vessel to proceed faster than before, much time was lost seeking out navigable channels and winching her off when, as frequently happened, she ran aground.[3]

Another striking difference noted was the lack of curiosity displayed by the villagers, working in their fields or navigating their canoes, who allowed the vessel to pass almost unnoticed. At first this was put down to familiarity but it seemed almost too studied for that. Could it be, Webb began to wonder, that they had heard what had happened to Carr and saw the *Wilberforce*'s return as being in the nature of a punitive expedition? They impressed him as behaving with the air of people anxious not to draw attention to themselves.

His suspicions were strengthened when, on the morning of 6 July, they arrived at Aboh to find the Obi less than his usual ebullient self. He appeared, in fact, notably subdued. He was dressed in the garments made up for him by Simon Jonas and enquired when the promised trading vessels would be arriving. That much was in character. But only when pressed did he produce, and even then with evident reluctance, a box of letters from the farm, dated the previous October. He confessed to having received them six months previously but had failed to forward them either to Brass or Bonny for lack of opportunity. This was patently nonsense. The Obi's canoes were plying back and forth all the time. The *Wilberforce* had met some of them. He also denied any knowledge of a white man entering the river, but with his eyes averted in a manner that persuaded Webb that he knew more than he was prepared to disclose. He subsequently failed to turn up to receive his presents, which was not like him at all. After a fruitless wait, these were given to one of his sons who promised to take them to his father.

As Webb was returning to the *Wilberforce* his eye was caught by a large flotilla of canoes moving about in Aboh Creek. On enquiring of the Ibo pilot he was told that they contained King Boy of Brass and his entourage. This struck him as strange because in his discussions with the Obi Boy's name had been frequently invoked without any mention of his being in Aboh. Webb immediately sought him out only to find that Boy's responses were even more evasive than those of the Obi. He admitted to having heard that Brown and a party of British sailors had entered Brass Creek and spoken to some of his people but professed not to have heard of Carr or to know why Brown was in the vicinity of Brass. How he could have learned some things and not others was not at all clear. 'Boy's fawning and abject behaviour greatly disgusted me,' Webb later reported, 'and confirmed my fears as to Carr's fate. I fully resolved, should I be spared, to make him account on my return for Mr Carr, or to carry him a prisoner to Fernando Po.' Neither Stanley's minute nor Allen's instructions had mentioned Carr. Solving the mystery of his disappearance – if, indeed, that was what had happened – and punishing the culprits – if such there proved to be – was just the sort of task to appeal to the imagination of a 29-year-old naval lieutenant. Other naval officers had lately gained fame and promotion by their daring exploits. It was under the pretext of rescuing a British subject, Mrs Troy Norman, a black washerwoman from Sierra Leone, that Commander Joseph Denman had initiated Palmerston's new, aggressive policy against the slave traders by crossing the bar of the Gallinas river and burning the barracoons there. Since then other settlements had been attacked and destroyed.[4] Such stirring events appealed to the popular imagination and received wide coverage in the British press. Alfred Carr, supervisor of the model farm and brother to the acting governor of a British colony, was a much more important figure than Mrs Norman. Even though it might not be quite what Buxton, or for that matter Webb's superiors, had in mind, it was a way to make his mark. After all, fighting enemies, punishing wrongdoers, that was what naval officers were supposed to do.

For the moment, however, there was nothing to be done and the *Wilberforce* proceeded upstream. Above Aboh the villagers were just as friendly and curious as on the vessel's last ascent. Whatever guilty secrets plagued the Delta, they had not spread this far. But the crew found the going difficult. Everywhere there were sandbanks. Time and again they were compelled to turn back and try another channel.

Along the way they were hailed by an Aboh canoe carrying provisions. While the crew were making their purchases they noticed a slave bearing Hausa marks chained to the bottom of the boat. Much against his inclination Webb obeyed Allen's instructions about not enforcing the treaty, by which he would have been entitled to liberate the slave and seize the canoe and its cargo. But he felt impelled to point this out to the canoe's headman, who lost no time in casting off and disappearing downstream.

Anchoring off Idah on the afternoon of 8 July, Henry Davey, the carpenter, was despatched to inform the Attah of their arrival. He returned with the news that the Attah would not see them until the following day. From what he could gather, the settlers were safe, although nothing had been heard of Alfred Carr.

Being unwilling to delay on account of what he took to be the caprice of an African chief, Webb ordered the *Wilberforce* to resume its ascent only to find that they had taken the wrong channel. Returning downstream the vessel ran onto a shoal where she remained ignominiously stranded until the following afternoon. To add to their humiliation they were visited by the Attah's head mallam who enquired, with some puzzlement, why they had departed so abruptly. He brought with him a packet of letters from the settlers, dated the previous January, expressing their fear of being attacked by the *mujaddidun* and enquiring when a relief expedition might be expected.

Having finally managed to haul the *Wilberforce* off they resumed their ascent, this time by a channel which the mallam pointed out to them. Even so, the way was slow and became progressively more so as they entered the boulder-strewn gorge below the Confluence. From marks on the rocks they could see that the river was a good thirty feet below the level of the previous September.

It was here that the *Wilberforce* suffered her worst misfortune. At noon on 12 July, threading her way through a cluster of rocks, she struck a reef with such force that water began pouring into the second compartment through a hole in the hull. The paddles were immediately put into reverse but to no effect and the vessel began slowly settling. Within minutes the water had risen to the level of the lower deck. The ventilation holes which Allen had ordered cut in the bulkheads were sufficiently high to prevent it flooding the other compartments, but some did begin to seep into the adjoining engine room as a result of sprung rivets.

The expedition was now only sixteen miles short of the Confluence. A galley was despatched early the next morning to get help from the settlers. It returned that evening accompanied by the *Amelia*'s galley, followed the next day by the *Amelia* herself. Relays of Krumen, settlers and Bassa tribesmen, these last being refugees who had fled to the farm for asylum, worked around the clock transferring the *Wilberforce*'s stores and provisions to the *Amelia* in the hope that she could be lightened sufficiently to be winched free.

While this was being done an Igala deputation arrived, led by Amanda Bue, bringing the Attah's good wishes and gifts of provisions. She also brought with her one of the Attah's mallams with whom they were supposed to negotiate changes affecting the farm's status. After her departure the mallam came over from the island where he had encamped in a canoe which he had commandeered from some passing Igala traders and which, on examination, turned out to contain two Kakanda slaves recently purchased up-river. Finding the Igala as neglectful of their treaty obligations as the people of Aboh, Webb berated the mallam, who took his leave and was not seen again.

After five days of strenuous effort involving the removal of her entire cargo and much pumping and baling the *Wilberforce* finally hove off on the morning of 17 July. Taking the *Amelia* in tow she headed at full speed for the model farm.

On arrival, it was found to consist of twelve mud huts and a wooden farmhouse not yet completed. Between twenty and thirty acres had been cleared and planted, mostly with cotton but with some yams and maize. The first cotton crop had failed entirely, possibly because the seed had been damaged on the way out from England or because it was unsuited to African conditions. There had been a second sowing in April, for which locally acquired seed had been used, and that seemed to have taken well, although it would be some months before the first crop could be picked. The threatened *mujaddidun* attack had not materialized. However, parties of them had been active in the neighbourhood. A common tactic was to send a troop of about ten horsemen together with some foot soldiers to lie in wait in the bush near a village and at daylight seize the villagers on their way to the fields. There had been many such incidents in the surrounding countryside but none that affected the farm or its workers, from which it was inferred that the messages and presents sent to Raba had had their desired effect.[5]

So at least the farm had survived. Things could be worse. On the other hand, there was no word of Alfred Carr. Nor, it had to be admitted, was there much to show for all the expense and effort that had gone into establishing the settlement – a few huts, a partfinished farmhouse, some acres planted with local seed – it hardly amounted to a showpiece. It certainly would not revolutionize the economic life of the area. Any one of the refugee villages around had as much, or more, to show for itself.

Moreover, it turned out that virtually none of the actual labour had been performed by the settlers themselves. Observing the Eglinton marquee and the activities of the steamers the previous summer, groups of refugees, Kakanda mostly but some Bassa too, had begun venturing down from the hills where they had fled for fear of the horsemen. They had been employed initially at a rate of 100 cowries (about 3d) a day, later reduced to 50 as the stock of cowries declined. This reduction was apparently accepted without protest. In fact, the fugitives' main concern appeared to be the desire for protection, which allowed them to establish nearby settlements where they could cultivate crops of their own, although they were pleased to have an opportunity to earn wages, which enabled them to pay off debts to the local tribes on which they had previously been dependent. They were said to be looking notably healthier than when they had first arrived. On an average day 100 were employed, although on one occasion the number had risen as high as 237. By all accounts they were willing workers, anxious to do what they were told and remarkably long-suffering.[6]

The same could not be said of the settlers. No sooner had the *Albert* departed, according to Thomas King, commander of the *Amelia*, than the crew began refusing to obey his orders. Ralph Moore encountered similar problems with the farm personnel. Not only did both groups strip off their European clothes and decline to work but they also began molesting the refugee women. Exactly what happened we are not told but evidently it involved a good deal more than what Trew, with Victorian reticence, termed 'habits of gross immorality'.[7] King refers to his crew's insubordinate behaviour as having been 'marked by every crime, short of murder, which was several times with difficulty prevented'. On one occasion they almost provoked their Kakanda workers into staging an uprising. This was prevented when King and Moore agreed to pay compensation of 10 000 cowries to Kulema, the Kakanda leader, out of the settlement's reserves. No mention is made of the offenders having been punished. It also emerged that the clerk in charge of the farm's stores had been busier trading on his own behalf than on behalf of his fellow settlers.

Webb's observations convinced him that the settlers' conduct had sunk too low for there to be any prospect of significant improvement. 'I found them indolent and lazy, not one . . . willing or even disposed to manual labour, but ready enough to exercise authority over the negroes they hired, and whom they employed on the most trifling occasions rather than exert themselves.' Most shocking of all was the sight of two of them armed with whips 'apparently for the purpose of urging the natives to greater exertion'. Everything he saw persuaded him that the settlers, far from setting a good example, were infatuated with their own power and had unscrupulously set about exploiting those who had sought their protection.

It also turned out that only seven of the eighteen settlers and two of the *Amelia*'s crew were willing to remain at the Confluence and then only on condition that they were given higher wages and the additional protection of having a European supervisor. Hinsman, the surgeon, had tentatively offered to serve in that capacity, but with Davey the carpenter and Johnstone the chief engineer already down with fever, and given the obvious demoralization of the settlers, Webb decided that the farm would have to be abandoned. He divided what was left of its possessions among the refugee workers, the Kakanda being given the farm buildings and growing crops and the smaller Bassa group the livestock and moveables.

Meanwhile, the *Wilberforce* had been beached, revealing a five-foot tear in the hull requiring the fixing of an iron plate from the inside. No sooner had this been done than it was discovered that water had leaked through the bilge system, flooding the storerooms at the stern of the vessel, so that their contents, only just reloaded from the *Amelia*, had to be taken on shore and dried.

While this was being done word arrived of a *mujaddidun* attack on one of the Mount Patti villages. Webb hastened to the spot hoping to make contact with the local *mujaddidun* leaders only to find the villagers celebrating their victory at having driven off their assailants empty-handed. Evidently the attack had been more in the nature of a kid-napping raid than a serious attempt to take the village. According to the chief, who proudly displayed arrows fired by his opponents as tokens of his triumph, he and his people had successfully resisted similar attacks for a number of years without having either to flee across the river or into the mountains, but his enemies were becoming more numerous and he worried about the future. Webb presented him with two muskets and wished him well.

In the hope that it might do some good, Webb also wrote to Usman Zaki requesting him 'to afford every protection and indulgence to the natives surrounding the colony we established, who always proved good neighbours to our settlers, and therefore have become friends of Her Britannic Majesty'.[8] He entrusted the letter, along with various gifts intended for the Etsu and the Sultan of Sokoto, to Finlay, a liberated African and the expedition's Arabic interpreter, a native of Raba, who had asked to be discharged at the Confluence so that he could return home.

With her hull finally repaired and the *Amelia* in tow the *Wilberforce* began her descent of the river on the morning of 23 July. At Idah, where they arrived later that day, the Attah claimed once again that etiquette prevented his receiving them at such short notice. As usual, however, Amanda Bue was on hand to act as intermediary. Being anxious to part on good terms, Webb did not mention the mallam and the slaves or Thomas King's account of the many Igala canoes carrying captives that he had seen going down-river during the year he had spent at the Confluence. He explained, however, the circumstances in which the farm had been left and presented her with various pistols, robes, lengths of cloth and other gifts for the Attah. Word came back from the Attah himself to the effect that he regretted their going and hoped they would soon return.

By the time the expedition reached Aboh on 25 July all the Europeans with the exception of Webb himself, Hinsman the surgeon and J.H.R. Webb the Chief Clerk were ailing. Here a tricky situation developed. No sooner had they dropped anchor and sent word of their arrival to the Obi than two messengers arrived with word that King Boy, who was encamped on a sandbank in mid-river opposite the entrance to Aboh Creek, wished to talk to them. Hinsman volunteered to collect him in the galley. Boy, however, refused to leave his encampment. On Webb's arriving he repeated what he had already told Hinsman, namely that Alfred Carr's clothes and other possessions were now at Brass Town having been taken from two Bassa captives at about the time Carr had disappeared. Webb asked why he had kept the information to himself until now, to which Boy failed to give any satisfactory answer.

At that point, according to Webb, he would have seized Boy had his own small party not been greatly outnumbered. Seeing three swivel-guns, mounted on the prows of Boy's canoes now pointed menacingly in their direction, they rowed back to the *Wilberforce* intending to force Boy into surrendering by bringing their twelve-pounders to bear on him. On arrival, however, they found the vessel surrounded by canoes and the Obi, who had received their earlier message, on deck patiently awaiting their return. Ignoring his guest, Webb ordered the two Brass messengers, who had remained on board, to be put in irons and the engineers to get up steam so as to cut off Boy's line of retreat. In the ensuing confusion the Obi hastily decamped and Boy's canoes managed to slip into Aboh Creek where, the river still being low, the *Wilberforce* was incapable of following.

Having badly mishandled the situation, Webb sent word to the Obi that no rudeness towards himself had been intended and inviting him to return to the *Wilberforce*. The messenger returned with the information that the Obi would gladly come if the young lieutenant would be so good as to collect him. But, on taking the galley into Aboh Creek, Webb found war canoes gathering and armed men concealed in the bushes along the bank. Suspecting a trap and brandishing his pistols at any canoe that did not immediately give way, he had himself rowed back to the *Wilberforce*. Seeing what was happening, and mindful of what had happened to their Brass counterparts, the Obi's messengers, who had remained on board the *Wilberforce*, leaped over the gunwales and began swimming towards the bank; but the Krumen aboard the galley, coming up at that moment, managed to catch hold of one of them and carry him back on board.

On being questioned the following morning, King Boy's messengers claimed that the canoe Carr had taken had belonged to Bassa men who had tied him and his companion to a tree and shot them. They were able to describe in sufficient detail the clothes, books and other articles now in Brass Town to establish beyond doubt that they were Carr's belongings. But how they came to be in Boy's possession, and what Bassa men were doing in Brass Creek, remained a mystery. Apparently the Bassa men now in Boy's custody denied responsibility for the murder. It all sounded highly implausible. The Aboh messenger denied all knowledge of the affair; also of the Obi's motive for quitting the *Wilberforce* and then inviting Webb into Aboh Creek beyond the fact that the white men's behaviour was alarming.

Having successfully alienated the two principal rulers of the middle Delta, Webb now determined to find out from the Bassa people themselves if there was any truth in Boy's story. These Bassa, according to Boy's emissaries, were a quite separate group from those of the Confluence. They lived at the opposite end of the Delta from Brass, somewhere in the direction of Benin. After wasting the better part of a day on this fool's errand, running aground frequently in the process, they were obliged to turn back. All the Europeans were now confined to their bunks with the exception of Webb and the clerk, both of whom were thoroughly unnerved. They fired the brass swivel guns over the heads of some canoeists they saw approaching, who leaped overboard and disappeared into the bush. Further on, they themselves came under fire from the shore, but from such a range that the bullets failed to carry so that no harm was done.

Other misadventures followed. While attempting to come up alongside the *Amelia*, which had been left behind, the *Wilberforce* lost her bowsprit. After crossing the bar the *Amelia* sprang a leak and the *Wilberforce*'s forty-foot galley, which was being towed, collided with the *Amelia*, turned turtle and had to be abandoned. It was a forlorn and much shaken ship's company that anchored in Clarence Cove on 29 July.

During the months the *Wilberforce* spent refitting for her journey back to England both Webb and the clerk, J.H.R. Webb, came down with fever. John Waddington, the boatswain, died on 12 September and was buried alongside Bird Allen, Theodor Vogel and the other casualties of the previous year's expedition under the large cottonwood tree in Clarence cemetery. On being questioned by Beecroft, the two Brass captives changed their story and claimed to have no knowledge of Carr's having been killed. The African Civilization Society subsequently offered a reward for information but none was received. Webb's conclusion was that he had been murdered by Brass people and that King Boy, who might well have instigated the deed, subsequently tried to escape retribution by pinning the blame on others.[9]

With its hull and bowsprit repaired, the *Wilberforce* departed for

The burial place of the expedition and of Lander, Fernando Po.

England on 18 September. J.H.R. Webb, the last of the expedition's members to succumb to fever, was buried at sea off Cape Coast Castle, bringing the final death toll from fever to 44 and from all causes combined to 53.[10] Some of the Krumen and most of the model farm personnel were paid off along the Coast. Nevertheless, it was still a largely black crew that, after a stormy crossing of the Bay of Biscay, brought the vessel into Plymouth on 17 November.

The Times, hearing of the model farm's refugee labour force and the settlers' use of whips, could not contain its glee.[11] A slave plantation! In the middle of Africa! It was too good to be true. 'Looking back at this whole transaction,' it declared, 'the facts appear so marvellous that we doubt if a more incredible narrative is to be found in the pages of Gulliver of Munchausen.' As in one of those tales, the great and the good had assembled in all their dignity to witness the launching of the enterprise: dukes and Quakers, bishops and dissenting ministers, committee ladies and members of Parliament, Sir Robert Peel and Daniel O'Connell, they had all been there that June morning, not one of them daring to say what was obvious from the first, namely that the whole thing was patently ridiculous. Yet there they had sat in Exeter Hall on that memorable day three years before imagining 'that no more was necessary than to steam up that river, as a Margate steamer might steam up the Thames', for Africa to be civilized.

Well, steamers had now ascended the Niger and what was the result? It was 'that the Niger ANTI-Slavery Expedition has . . . planted a *very* "model" of the most cruel and iniquitous SLAVERY, and that in a spot where such, or at least such systematic scourge-bearing slavery, was probably unknown before'. Coolly and deliberately, slave-whip in hand, the former objects of Britain's philanthropy, the liberated blacks of Sierra Leone, had set about civilizing Africa in their own inimitable fashion. So much for Exeter Hall and its humbug!

John Trew hastened down to Woolwich, where the *Wilberforce* was now docked, and was able to assure Buxton that *The Times*'s story was quite without foundation. He had spoken to Moore and Jones, who had assured him that there had been no flogging of workers by settlers and certainly no dealing in slaves. Every offer to sell slaves had been punctiliously refused. Workers had been paid individually for their labour. The only occasions when beatings were administered on the farm were when workers were punished, mostly for theft, by their own headmen. Regrettably there had been a reversion to uncivilized behaviour on the part of the settlers and a degree of sexual indulgence, but apart from that there was absolutely nothing to be ashamed of. Official denials of *The Times*'s charges were duly published.[12]

But by that time the public had grown weary of what was seen as a lost cause. Much grander events now occupied the nation's attention. British gunboats had ascended the Yangtse and bombarded Nanking; Boer settlers were besieging a British force in Port Natal; a whole Anglo-Indian army of 16 500 had disappeared in the snows of Afghanistan. Who cared whether or not black settlers had armed themselves with whips? Who now cared about West Africa at all?

This was also the accepted view at the Colonial Office. 'I presume,' Stephen minuted on receipt of Allen's account, 'that the only Instruction to be given is that the Report be laid aside for future reference. I suppose that the subject to which it refers is entirely obsolete and that we shall have no more Niger Expeditions.'[13] The references to whips, the demoralization of the settlers and the continuation of the slave trade in Webb's report were duly underlined and asterisked.[14] 'Our friend King Obi,' Hope noted, 'who acceded and drank port wine for joy at signing the treaty for abolishing the Slave Trade, does not show very well in the affair.'[15] Webb's conduct, however, was thought deserving of commendation and he was duly granted a commissioner's salary, in addition to his naval pay, from the time of his entering the river.[16] The Treasury also agreed to make an *ex gratia* payment of £500 to William Stanger for his exceptional services in helping to bring the *Albert* to safety.[17]

The most troublesome item remaining was William Cook's report charging Captain Maclean with trading in slaves and William Allen with cowardice and incompetence. He had already taken it upon himself to denounce Allen at a meeting of the African Civilization Society. This led Allen to appeal to Stanley for an official enquiry. But Stanley ruled that he could not authorize an investigation simply on the basis of charges made at a meeting of a private society.[18] Cook's official report was another matter. If it were presented to Parliament, as by the spring of 1843 it had been decided all the reports should be, Allen would have to be court-martialled. It was hard to see, Stephen observed, what good that would do, particularly as Allen had announced that he was retiring from active service. Stanley, who found 'the tone of Mr Cook's correspondence . . . very embarrassing', resolved the issue by scoring out the offending passages with his own hand.[19] Allen's record of the commissioners' meetings at Fernando Po was also dropped from the published version.[20]

Buxton accepted it all with weary resignation. 'We have to be satisfied, though astonished,' he wrote to Andrew Johnston, 'with the event of the Expedition and to feel, and to be able to say, "God's will be done, though it be in the teeth of our fondest wishes."' He could now scarcely bring himself to speak of Africa. However, he agreed with Lushington that the African Civilization Society would have to be wound up. He was, he told Samuel Gurney, pleased that the model farm settlers had accomplished all they had and only sorry that, with fever striking the expedition and no European supervisor being available, the farm had had to be abandoned in the way it was. He took it upon himself to report these matters to Prince Albert. He, Hannah and Edward travelled to Slough on the new rail line and there hired a fly to take them to Windsor. It was a raw January day. The Prince received them with great kindness. The only hope now, Buxton told him, was that Africa would be redeemed by Africans themselves, in particular by those now being trained up in Sierra Leone and the West Indies. They ended the meeting by discussing the recent shooting season.[21]

This was Buxton's last official engagement. Since the news of the expedition's collapse and Bird Allen's death his health, long subject to sudden change, had taken a decided turn for the worse. Friends and relatives did their best to shield him from public attack but there was no way of assuaging his private grief. On one occasion he was heard to exclaim with great fervour, 'O Lord, with my whole soul I thank thee, that, instead of ease and prosperity and the best things of this world, Thou hast sent this illness.' He died at Northrepps on 19 February 1845, surrounded by his adoring relatives, still only in his fifty-ninth year, and was buried in the chancel of the nearby church at Overstrand.[22]

The obituaries, while paying tribute to his early achievements, tended to skate over his later years. Sturge's *British and Foreign Anti-Slavery Reporter*, pleading lack of space, ended its account of his life abruptly in 1833.[23] Nevertheless, *The Times*, pursuing implacably its crusade against philanthropic humbug and benevolent vanity, saw fit to refer to more recent events:

> We shall not pursue the subject of this memoir beyond the grave, neither is it necessary to review those painful discussions with regard to the disastrous Niger expedition, on which public opinion has long since been unequivocally expressed and the judgment of society put forth in a manner but little advantageous to the character for foresight or sound information of Sir Fowell Buxton. He was the mainspring of that lamentable undertaking; those who usually differed from him censored it without reserve, and even those with whom he was accustomed to act withdrew from him that confidence of which he had for so long been the depository. Ill health supervened, and his maladies were grievously aggravated by the regrets and disappointments which attended his later labours; thus probably his life was shortened by the erroneous estimate which he formed of his own qualifications as a statesman and a reformer. He has quitted this life long before old age could be said to have made any inroads on his strength, leaving behind him a name not very remarkable for wisdom or ability.[24]

Epilogue: *From Antislavery to Imperialism*

Given that most people believed that the Niger expedition had been a disaster, it was hardly surprising that they laid the blame at Buxton's door. The scheme, after all, was his brainchild. His belief in himself as God's agent and his capacity for moulding the external world to make it appear to correspond to his inner vision made him an obvious choice as scapegoat.

But although Buxton was the originator, and for a time the prime mover, the expedition that resulted was the product of more than one man's driving obsession. After all, it was not the first African project to receive official Government support, nor would it be the last. It was, however, remarkably ambitious. Given Melbourne's own views on public philanthropy and the very considerable costs, it is plain that the Government would not have supported it but for an unusual set of circumstances, among which must be included its own weak position in Parliament, the wish to placate what ministers perceived as an influential minority and the apparent failure of Britain's blockade policy. To this list must be added the recent triumph of the British antislavery movement in putting an end to slavery in the British Empire and a new awareness of Britain's growing economic and political strength. If responsibility is to be assigned it belongs at least as much to Melbourne, Russell, Palmerston and their colleagues who agreed to put up the money for the venture, and the British public whose enthusiasm persuaded them to do so.

So far as Buxton himself was concerned, not everyone agreed with *The Times*'s assessment. Old friends remained loyal. Within weeks of his death a group of them got up a committee to erect a memorial. Prince Albert, Sir Robert Peel, Lord John Russell, James Stephen and Captain Henry Trotter were among the many who gave the project their support.[1] Contributions came in from the freedmen of Sierra Leone and the West Indies. With the £1500 collected a full-length statue by Frederick Thrupp was commissioned. This was exhibited at the Royal Academy in 1848 and subsequently placed in the north transept of Westminster Abbey. Thomas Binney's *Sir T.F. Buxton: A Study for Young Men* appeared in 1845 and Charles Buxton's notably filiopietistic *Memoirs of Sir Thomas Fowell Buxton* in 1848. Both ran through many editions. The process of transmogrification into Victorian saint had begun.[2]

But, exemplary though Buxton's life might appear – and who could deny that he was a model of evangelical highmindedness? – few had kind words to say about the cause to which that highmindedness had led and which he had hoped would prove the crowning achievement of his career. In the popular imagination no less than in Whitehall and Westminster the Niger expedition was seen as a cautionary tale. Its impact on attitudes towards Africa was, in fact, precisely as Thomas Stirling had predicted. Hope gave way to disillusion, enthusiasm to apathy. Africa was an awful place. Why should the British take it upon themselves to redeem her? The history of all their efforts to date was one of repeated and humiliating failure. Moreover, as the high tide of enthusiasm which had lapped around the platform of Exeter Hall in the summer of 1840 began to recede, doubts were voiced with increasing frequency about recent British attitudes towards blacks in general. Had they been too idealistic? Was it not true that West Indian freedmen were refusing to work on the plantations? Had not this resulted in a doubling of sugar prices? Perhaps the Emancipation Act of 1833 had not been the great humanitarian triumph that had been claimed. Little by little the racial prejudices that had characterized popular thinking in the eighteenth century, and which the abolition movement had driven into abeyance, began to reassert themselves. Thomas Carlyle imagined the blacks of the West Indies 'sitting yonder with their beautiful muzzles up to the ears in pumpkins, imbibing sweet pulps and juices . . . while the sugar crops rot round them uncut'.[3] Even if it were allowed, as the Sturgeites in their struggle to prevent the admission of Cuban and Brazilian sugar into Britain were forever arguing, that Britain had a special obligation towards the West Indies, the same could hardly be said of Africa. In the new mood of disenchantment it became permissible to wonder whether all the efforts made to assist Africans, from the 1780s onwards, amounted to anything more than a catalogue of hopes disappointed, resources squandered and lives sacrificed.

Charles Dickens, reviewing Allen and Thomson's two-volume *Narrative of the Expedition to the River Niger* (1848), caught the popular mood. 'It might,' he began, 'be laid down as a very good general rule of social and political guidance, that whatever Exeter Hall champions, is the thing by no means to be done.' To admit of this truth was no reflection on the many brave men who had sacrificed their lives in what should have been seen from the first as a hopeless cause. Their courage and devotion

166

deserved the warmest admiration. They had, nevertheless, been the victims of a cruel deceit practised on a credulous British public by pious charlatans. Indeed, the only participants in the whole affair with a firm grip on reality, which they combined with a shrewd notion of where their interests lay, were the savage potentates of Africa. There was the Attah, with his ultra-orthodox notions of Divine Right, receiving the obeisance of Her Majesty's Commissioners while his 'feet, enclosed in very large red leather boots, surrounded with little bells, dangled carelessly over the side of the throne'. But it is Dickens's description of the negotiations at Aboh that best captures what he regarded as the absurdity of the whole affair:

> Obi, sitting on the quarter-deck of the Albert, looking slyly out from under his savage forehead and his conical cap, sees before him her Majesty's white Commissioners from the distant blockade-country gravely pro- pounding, at one sitting, a change in the character of his people ... the substitution of a religion it is utterly impossible he can appreciate or understand ... for that in which he has been bred, and with which his priest and jugglers subdue his subjects, the entire subversion of his whole barbarous system of trade and revenue – and the uprooting, in a word, of all his, and his nation's, preconceived ideas, methods, and customs. In return for this, the white men are to trade with him by means of ships that are to come there one day or other; and are to quell infractions of the treaty by means of other white men, who are to learn how to draw the breath of life there, by some strong charm they certainly have not discovered yet. Can it be supposed that on this earth there lives a man who better knows than Obi, leering round upon the river's banks, the dull dead mangrove trees, the slimy and decaying earth, the rotting vegetation, that these are shadowy promises and shadowy threats, which he may give to the hot winds? ... 'Too much palaver,' says Obi, with good reason. 'Give me the presents and let me go home, and beat my tom-toms all night long, for joy!'[4]

Dickens later made use of some of this material in *Bleak House* (1853), in which the ridiculous Mrs Jellyby, a caricature Buxton figure, neglects her husband and children because her whole life is taken up with organizing a mission to Borrioboola-Gha, on the left bank of the Niger, where, so she claims, the climate is the finest in the world. As one of Dickens's characters observes, her eyes had 'a curious habit of seeming to look a long way off. As if ... they could see nothing nearer than Africa.' Mean- while all kinds of disasters are occurring around her to which she is oblivious. The resentment this arouses is expressed by her daughter Caddy, a pale, ink-stained creature whose task it is to copy out her letters, who confides in the narrator, 'I wish Africa was dead! . . . I do! I hate it and detest it. It's a beast!'[5]

And yet, for all his scorn, Dickens was too much of a Victorian optimist to doubt that Africa would one day be changed for the better. It would not, however, be as a result of overambitious schemes like the Niger expedition which sought to bring about major changes at one stroke. Rather it would be by a gradual, incremental process beginning, as *The Times* had all along argued, in Britain itself.

> The stone that is dropped into the ocean of ignorance at Exeter Hall, must make its widening circles, one beyond another, until they reach the negro's country in their natural expansion. There is a broad, dark sea between the Strand in London, and the Niger, where those rings are not yet shining; and through all that space they must appear, before the last one breaks upon the shore of Africa. Gently and imperceptibly the widening circle of enlightenment must stretch and stretch, from man to man, from people on to people, until there is a girdle round the earth; but no convulsive effort, or far-off aim, can make the last great outer circle first, and then come home at leisure to trace out the inner one. Believe it, African Civilisation, Church of England Missionary, and all other Missionary Societies! The work at home must be completed thoroughly, or there is no hope abroad.[6]

It was a fine vision. Yet what it reveals is that beliefs that a decade earlier had seemed narrow and carping could now be made to seem not merely commonsensical but positively progressive.

Nevertheless, causes that appear discredited have a way of coming back into fashion. Even while Dickens was writing, Dr David Livingstone, penning a letter in the bush south of Lake Nyasa, was explaining to a friend, 'I feel assured if our merchants could establish a legitimate commerce on the Zambesi, they would soon drive out the slave dealer from the market and be besides great gainers in the end.'[7] In 1857, on his triumphal return to England, he addressed audiences in terms almost indistinguishable from those used by Buxton in Exeter Hall seventeen years before. Wherever he lectured, crowds turned out to hear him. He was going back to Africa, he told a massed audience in Cambridge, to persuade the chiefs of the Zambesi to give up the slave trade and cultivate cotton instead. Only by opening up its dark interior to traders and missionaries could Africa be redeemed.[8]

The effect of Livingstone's speeches, particularly his revelation that while the European slave trade was diminishing the Arab slave trade was growing, was to give a new impetus to the abolitionist cause.[9] At the same time other changes were occurring, some of which can be traced back to the events of 1841, that were destined to transform British attitudes and policies towards Africa.

What had made the 1841 expedition a failure was, of course, the fever, but because of the high expectations that had been aroused and the subsequent sense of let-down this was often forgotten. As in Dickens's account, it was only too easy to present the whole episode as absurd. Who could take seriously Buxton's claim, well founded though it might be, that apart from the fever the expedition had succeeded far beyond expectation? By the same token the charge of the Light Brigade was a military triumph. Even granting that what Buxton said was true, what was the point of steamers, treaties, a willingness to trade, model farms, if Europeans could not breathe the air of Africa without dying? As a form of investment, the costs, particularly as measured in terms of human life but in material terms too, were out of all proportion to the likely return.

This was a problem to which Dr M'William in his *Medical History of the Expedition to the Niger* (1843) could provide no solution. The causes of the fever appeared to him as mysterious as ever. He dismissed out of hand 'doctrines of planetary influence, the want of elasticity in the atmosphere, and of animiculae entering the body through various channels'. Quinine, he believed, might usefully be employed as a tonic during recuperation after the usual treatment by bloodletting, blistering, mercury, purgatives and diaphoretics had been applied, although he also noted that if administered earlier it did seem somewhat to reduce the severity of the paroxysms.[10]

In spite of having collected elaborate data on the progress of the fever, one detail to which he failed to give attention was the fact that all three of the doctors aboard the *Wilberforce* remained in good health. They were, indeed, the only identifiable group to do so, although of the remainder, apart from those who had recently lived in Africa, it is notable that all save two were either medical personnel or stewards.[11] How many of these took quinine, to which they presumably had access, we do not know, but one at least did. This was Dr Thomas Thomson, who dosed himself with half a gram or more daily and, in spite of spending a good deal of time on shore, escaped the fever. After leaving the coast he gradually reduced the doses and was surprised to find, on reaching Plymouth, when he stopped taking them entirely, that he came down with a mild attack. He recorded the experience in an article entitled 'On the Value of Quinine in African Remittent Fever' which appeared in the February 1846 number of the *Lancet*.[12] In it he speculated as to 'whether quinine in full doses has the power or not of warding off entirely the remittent fever?'

The idea was promptly taken up by Dr Alexander Bryson, a senior naval physician, who included the regular use of quinine among his recommendations to naval personnel serving on the Coast. He also warned surgeons not to use mercury or emetics, or to bleed patients, all of which treatments he described as worse than useless. In 1848 the Director General of the Medical Department of the Army sent a circular to British officials in West Africa recommending the regular use of quinine by troops stationed there. As for Professor Daniell's ideas about hydrogen sulphide, subsequent tests cast doubt not only on his theory but on his ability to carry out simple laboratory experiments.[13]

What finally demonstrated the effectiveness of quinine as a prophylactic beyond any reasonable doubt was the ascent of the Niger in 1854 by Macgregor Laird's *Pleiad*. In spite of his own unhappy experiences and the prevailing sense of disillusionment, Laird had remained a firm believer in Africa's potentialities. The *Pleiad*, a 250-ton iron steamer built at the family's Birkenhead shipyard, was the first screw-driven vessel to attempt the Niger. John Beecroft had undertaken to lead the expedition, but on its arrival in Fernando Po it turned out that he had died only a few days previously (from what looked like the long-term effects of chronic malaria) so that it fell to Dr William Baikie to assume command. Armed with Dr Bryson's medical instructions, and with a crew made up of twelve Europeans and fifty-four Africans, the *Pleiad* spent sixteen weeks on the river, penetrating some 250 miles further upstream than any previous European vessel, and returned to Clarence Cove with everyone still in excellent health. This was a spectacular achievement which, as Laird lost no time in informing the Foreign Secretary, opened up not only the Niger but the whole of Africa to European penetration.[14]

Other expeditions followed. In 1857 Laird's *Dayspring* went up the river followed in succeeding years by the *Rainbow* and the *Sunbeam*. The site of the model farm was found to be so overgrown with trees and bushes that is was impossible to tell that there had ever been a settlement there. Even the villages on top of Mount Patti were now deserted, their inhabitants having been driven across the river or into the hills by the *mujaddidun*. The only tracks through the bush were those made by elephants.

Among the participants in these expeditions was Samuel Crowther. His superiors in the Church Missionary Society had been impressed by his and Friedrich Schön's reports on their 1841 experiences. Unlike the general public, the CMS had not regarded that expedition as a failure. Half a century's experience of sending missionaries to Africa had made them sufficiently familiar with its problems not to have been swept along in the popular euphoria which preceded the expedition nor greatly cast down by its results. They had, in fact, gleaned a good deal of useful information about the river and its peoples, which was all that they had expected at that stage. In their conclusions Schön and Crowther both pointed out that the only effective way of carrying the Gospel to the Niger would be by employing Africans capable of speaking the language of the region. This had also been Buxton's conclusion. But when he had talked about native agency, it had seemed very much like a second best if, indeed, it represented any sort of option at all. For the CMS, with its African recaptives, mission schools and Fourah Bay College, the prospect looked very different.[15]

One consequence of the Niger expedition, therefore, was that at a crucial time the initiative for developing what later became British Nigeria passed from the British Government to the missionary societies. In the case of the Niger basin this meant principally the CMS. Unlike the Government, or for that matter the traders, the missionaries were entirely dependent on local goodwill and so could not ride roughshod over the beliefs, customs and political arrangements of those whom they were seeking to influence. Resources were limited. If Africa was to be changed by them it would need to be by consent rather than force.[16]

At first CMS efforts were directed principally towards Yorubaland, from where the largest number of recaptives had come. Crowther, who had been summoned to England in 1842 and ordained the following year, spent the next decade working first at Badagri and then at Abeokuta. But after accompanying the *Pleiad* expedition of 1854 and Laird's subsequent *Dayspring* expediton of 1857 the Niger became his principal area of activity. In 1864 he was ordained the Church of England's first black bishop and given responsibility for a diocese covering 'Western Equatorial Africa beyond the Queen's Dominions'. By the 1870s, thanks largely to his efforts, there were mission stations all the way up the Niger from the Delta to Nupe.[17]

The task which Crowther and his colleagues set themselves had much in common with that attempted by Buxton a generation earlier. It meant not merely spreading the word of the Gospel but persuading Africans, or at all events an élite group of them, to adopt European standards of behaviour and even dress. Thus the mission stations, and in particular their schools, were at the spearhead of the Westernizing process, seeking to imbue a new generation with the attitudes necessary to begin transforming their own societies. They became, in fact, the civilizing nuclei of which Buxton had dreamed. Crowther's own preference was for a type of education that emphasized practical skills. He persuaded parents that by sending their children to the school they would be enabling them eventually to earn good pay as clerks or engineers working for the traders. Christianity, in short, was seen as being allied to civilization in ways that rendered one almost indistinguishable from the other.[18]

Encouraged by what they saw happening, some former members of the African Civilization Society, among them Edward Buxton, Thomas

Ackland and Sir Robert Inglis, formed a Native Agency Committee which took upon itself the task of bringing a succession of young Africans to England for training in medicine, horticulture, building technique and other useful pursuits. Most of the training of black teachers, catechists and missionaries, however, continued to be centred on Sierra Leone. The idea of exiles returning to their homelands, carrying with them their newly acquired skills and knowledge was one that would have appealed to Buxton.[19]

Friedrich Schön began training interpreters in the various native languages and set himself the task of mastering Hausa and Ibo. He was later to be awarded an honorary doctorate by Oxford for his studies of the Hausa language. A number of other survivors of the 1841 expedition subsequently returned to Africa. John Duncan became the first British explorer to penetrate into what is now the Republic of Dahomey and in 1847 published a two-volume account of his travels. He was subsequently appointed Vice-Consul at Whydah but died while on the way to take up his post.[20] William Stanger became Surveyor General of Natal. Like several other survivors he suffered recurrent bouts of illness as a result of his 1841 experiences.[21] Because of his ill health Henry Trotter was obliged to turn down offers of several important posts, including command of the Indian Navy and the Governorship of New Zealand. He eventually returned to active service at the time of the Crimean War as Commodore in charge of the Cape of Good Hope. No such offers were made to William Allen, who never returned to active service. However, he appears to have led a busy life, exhibiting paintings at the Royal Academy and engaging in various literary pursuits, including the writing, in collaboration with Dr Thomas Thomson, of what became the standard history of the expedition.[22] William Cook's attempts to gain a government post do not appear to have borne fruit.[23]

The steamers used on the expedition were subsequently assigned to the African Squadron, the last of them, the *Wilberforce*, being withdrawn in 1850. Up to his death in 1854, John Beecroft played an increasingly influential role in West African affairs. In 1843, the Spanish, who eventually decided not to part with Fernando Po, recognized his *de facto* position by appointing him Honorary Governor of the island. Six years later, Palmerston, anxious to promote British interests in that part of Africa, made him British Consul to the Bights of Benin and Biafra, in which capacity he was largely responsible for the British occupation of Lagos in 1851 and the deposition of King Pepple of Bonny in 1854.[24] George Maclean, already under suspicion at the time of the Niger expedition on account of his supposed lack of diligence in combatting the slave trade and slavery, was in 1844 removed by the Colonial Secretary from his position as President of the Council of Government on the Gold

Coast. He accepted the decisions with commendable grace and agreed to stay on at Cape Coast, acting as second-in-command to a governor answerable to the Colonial Office. He died there in 1847, by which time the ruin of the system of alliances he had so painstakingly built up was already apparent.[25]

The ways of the two Asante princes parted after their return to Kumase. William Kwantabisa, having been found guilty of adultery, never fully regained the trust either of his own people or the British. John Ansah, on the other hand, more than fulfilled the hopes of his British mentors by having a long and distinguished career in the service of Asante, becoming, in his later years, effectively its prime minister.[26]

Meanwhile the pattern of trade on the Niger was changing. The number of slaves exported annually from the Gulf of Guinea, averaging around 20000 in the 1830s and 10000 in the 1840s, dropped to a mere 3000 in the 1850s and had ceased entirely by the mid-1860s.[27] Over the same period yearly exports of palm oil from the Delta rose from 11000 to around 30000 tons.[28] Most of it continued to be purchased from the coastal middlemen by Liverpool traders. One result of the *Pleiad*'s successful voyage, however, was to revive the British Government's interest in the potentialities of the hinterland. In 1857 it agreed to provide a yearly subsidy of some £8000 to allow Macgregor Laird to maintain a steamer service on the river.[29]

There remained the problem of overcoming the opposition of Brass and the other city-states of the lower Delta. King Boy had died in 1846, but his people remained bitterly hostile to the steamers which they continued to regard, not without reason, as a threat to their livelihood.[30] In 1859 Laird's *Rainbow* was fired on and two of its crew killed, an episode which provoked him into defining 'moral force in Africa as meaning a 32-pounder with an English sailor standing behind it'.[31]

Palmerston, now Prime Minister, shared Laird's view and responded by ordering the navy to provide armed escorts. But so dangerous had the situation become that in 1860 the Commander-in-Chief of the African Station, Commodore Edmonstone, refused to allow his vessels into the river. As a result, Crowther was unable to visit his mission stations that year and Laird, who had gambled heavily on sending a large amount of trade goods up-river, was obliged to auction them off along the coast at a substantial loss. (When he died the following year it was revealed that since 1859 his Niger efforts had cost him £26000.) Unwilling to be defeated by what it regarded as mere savages the Government renewed its instructions to the commander of the African Station to provide escorts, in consequence of which HMS *Espoir* bombarded three villages in the area where the attack on the *Rainbow* had occurred and trade was resumed.[32]

A pattern of intermittent warfare was thus initiated which was to continue almost to the end of the century. Trading ships passing up and down the river would be fired on. In the dry season installations would also be attacked and burned. In response, gunboats belonging either to the navy or, as was later more often the case, the Niger Company, would duly ascend the river with the first of the floods and shell the villages of those supposedly responsible. The Delta people, in turn, encouraged, many believed, by their Liverpool trading partners who were equally reluctant to see the prevailing patterns of trade disrupted, began acquiring nine-pounders and other heavy weapons with which to retaliate.[33]

The Obi did not live to see his dreams of direct trade with the Europeans realized. On his death in 1844 the town's leaders were unable to agree on a successor and the community found itself divided into two rival factions, one led by the able and energetic Ejeh and the other by Ejeh's half brother Chukuwuh. One bone of contention between the two groups was their attitude towards the traders. Contrary to the Obi's expectations, when trading posts and a mission station were established in the late 1850s, the principal centre of operations was not Aboh but Onitsha, some sixty miles to the north on the border with Igala. This angered Ejeh who claimed that trade was being diverted away from Aboh and publicly regretted that his father had not supported Brass and resisted the invaders. His manner became increasingly arrogant and overbearing and European visitors were subjected to threats and angry diatribes. When the news arrived in 1860 that Laird's steamers were stranded in the estuary Ejeh and his supporters attacked and destroyed the trading posts at Onitsha and at Aboh itself. Following Ejeh's death in 1862 a new Obi was elected and relations with the British temporarily improved, but the pattern of trade had shifted and Aboh was plainly a declining power.[34]

The same was also true of Igala, similarly plagued by factional disputes. The Attah who at the time of the 1841 expedition had only recently assumed office survived until the mid-1850s. But even before his death the revival of a long-standing feud between his family and a rival branch consisting of the descendants of his predecessor's brother had led to a major exodus from the town. At the time of the *Dayspring*'s visit in 1857 whole quarters were quite deserted and the streets overgrown with grass.[35]

By contrast, Nupe, under Masaba's forceful leadership, was by the 1860s emerging from its years of chronic instability and becoming the major power on the river. In spite of religious differences, the Fulani and the British soon found that they had interests in common. In 1871 Masaba undertook to guarantee them protection against interruptions of trade on the Niger in return for an agreement that all commerce with the northern Emirs would pass exclusively through Nupe. As Bishop Crowther shrewdly commented, 'it is better to have to do with one ruler who keeps order and the people in subjection, although with tyranny, whether he be a heathen or a Mohammedan, than to have to do with a people in a state of anarchy.'[36] The British saw Nupe as a stabilizing force in the area while her rulers regarded them as useful allies and, above all, as the principal source of the firearms upon which their authority ultimately depended.[37]

In the trade wars of the later nineteenth century the British became increasingly high-handed. When the Delta and the interior were declared separate protectorates, Brass traders found themselves excluded from the river trade on the grounds that they were foreign nationals. The effect on Brass was much as King Boy had feared. Faced with commercial ruin and incipient starvation the Delta peoples fought back, thereby providing grounds for yet further repressive measures. One consequence was to alienate the missionaries, especially the Sierra Leonians who, not unnaturally, tended to identify with those whose rights were being progressively curtailed, while the traders, in turn, came to regard the missionaries as troublemakers. Nor were relations improved by such incidents as the bombardment of Onitsha in 1879, in the course of which the school and mission house were destroyed. Commerce and Christianity, it seemed, did not always go together.[38]

So routine did such attacks become that the occasions for them are seldom recorded. In 1883 Aboh came under fire from three naval gunboats. Usually before a bombardment began townspeople fled into the bush but on this occasion they swarmed on to the shore to repel the attackers in consequence of which the area was left strewn with the bodies of 'several hundred' dead. Idah was bombarded on the same occasion. It was later reported that three sailors had been killed in the course of the action. Before the century ended Nupe too was destined to feel the effects of British firepower. Life on the Niger, it began to appear, was becoming more hazardous for Africans than for Europeans.[39]

Steamers, quinine and rapid-fire weapons opened up West Africa, first to the traders, then to the colonizers. By weighting the odds in favour of the invaders they also changed British perceptions of the region. Instead of being a white man's grave it became a place where stirring deeds were performed, often at no great risk to the performers. As accounts of these events filtered back to England, and in due course became the stuff of popular fiction, it was easy for the British to persuade themselves that they were superior beings, natural rulers, whose destiny it was to bring order to a land of barbarism.

The mood at the Colonial Office, too, was quite different from what it had been in James Stephen's day. When Africa was mentioned the talk was apt to turn to notions of conquest and imperial destiny. Other powers were crowding in. The French were particularly to be feared but the Germans and the Belgians also had designs on West Africa. At the Congress of Berlin in 1884–5 the treaties negotiated with the Obi and the Attah, dismissed by Lord Stanley as 'so much waste paper', were used as a basis for Britain's claims to have a long-standing sphere of influence in the region.[40] During the 1880s and 1890s the Niger Company, which had bought out its rivals and now effectively controlled the trade of the river, was allowed to play a quasi-governmental role, negotiating treaties and administering justice, until, in 1900, in consequence of deteriorating relations with nearby French colonies, authority passed to the Crown.

In Britain concern over slavery, although more muted, remained a political issue. The British and Foreign Anti-Slavery Society, its aims and methods much altered since Sturge's time, kept a close eye on African developments. One of its duties was seen as being to keep those responsible for administering African affairs, whether in Britain or Africa itself, constantly reminded of Britain's antislavery commitment.[41]

In 1873, as he lay dying at Ilela on the northern Zambesi, the last words recorded by David Livingstone in his journal and inscribed on his grave in Westminster Abbey when he was buried there the following year, was a plea that 'heaven's rich blessing come down on every one, American, English or Turk, who will help to heal this open sore of the world'. As late as 1889 the British public could still be aroused to antislavery fervour, as was shown by its response to the exhortations of the Belgian Cardinal Lavigerie. What principally concerned Livingstone and Lavigerie was the Islamic slave trade rather than domestic slavery, which remained a feature of African societies even after the imposition of European rule.[42]

One of the principal effects of such calls was, in fact, to give an air of moral legitimacy to the European's scramble for colonies. In the case of the Niger basin, slavery persisted long after the ending of the Atlantic slave trade and despite the burgeoning of legitimate commerce. Slaves were still needed to produce the goods that were being exported. There was even evidence that in some areas the demand for them had grown.[43] How else could workers be obtained in such ethnically divided and socially stratified societies? Domestic slavery in Africa was, of course, very different from plantation slavery in the New World, but to the British public the distinction was not always clear. It was thus tempting and easy to manipulate opinion in ways that Buxton would have deplored, as when Joseph Chamberlain, Colonial Secretary from 1895 to 1903, noted in relation to Sokoto, 'sooner or later we shall have to fight some of the slave dealing tribes and we cannot have a better *casus belli* ... [as] public opinion here requires that we shall justify imperial control of these savage countries by some effort to put down slave dealing.' Like the Mogul Empire in Clive's day, the Empire of Sokoto was a plum ready for the picking.[44]

The imperialists of the later nineteenth century often sounded remarkably like the humanitarians of an earlier era. They too believed that Victorian civilization represented the highest point so far reached in mankind's development and that it was Britain's destiny to spread Christianity, commerce and civilization around the globe. Slavery and human sacrifice were acknowledged evils. It was true that imperial designs had not been entirely absent from the minds of those who sponsored the 1841 expedition. All the same, a radical change was evident in the emphasis now placed on the need for colonies and the frank admission of the willingness to employ force in the process of their acquisition. As Chamberlain told the Royal Colonial Institute at its annual dinner in 1897, 'In carrying out this work of civilization we are fulfilling what I believe to be our national mission, and we are finding scope for the exercise of those faculties and qualities which have made us a great governing race.' He went on to speak in approving terms of the recent military expeditions against Asante, Benin and Nupe and to pour scorn on those who believed that the same ends could have been achieved by more conciliatory methods. 'You cannot have omelettes without breaking eggs; you cannot destroy the practices of barbarism, of slavery, of superstitions, which for centuries have desolated the interior of Africa, without using force.' It was, he concluded, a gigantic task Britain had set herself but one that her history and her national character had called upon her to perform.[45]

Whether what was being proposed would help or harm the inhabitants of Africa was now a secondary consideration. It was convenient to claim, as Chamberlain did, that the ultimate effects would be beneficent, but with the growing tide of racialism that was sweeping across Europe it was a proposition that many doubted. As the influence of evangelical religion faded it was the turn of science to cast its baleful light on Africa. Darwin's biological concept of the survival of the fittest was readily adapted to the notion of a struggle between races. Even those who rejected such crude notions of biological determinism were sceptical about Britain's capacity to change African ways. Could Africans be raised up into the higher reaches of civilization? Was it even right, as missionaries apparently believed, to attempt to make them culturally indistinguishable from Europeans? Mary Kingsley, whose highly influential *Travels in West Africa* was published in 1897, doubted it.

Alas for the energetic reformer – the African is not keen on mountaineering in the civilization range. . . . He admires the higher culture very much, and the people who inconvenience themselves by going in for it – but do it himself? No. And if he is dragged up into the higher reaches of self-abnegatory religion, six times in ten he falls back damaged, a morally maimed man, into his old swampy country fashion valley.[46]

But, whatever the eventual outcome, it was generally agreed that it was the task of the more vigorous races, at least for the time being, to rule on their behalf.

Britain's imperial enthusiasm reached its apogee that same year with the celebration of Queen Victoria's Diamond Jubilee. Along the Strand, decked out in red, white and blue buntings, past Exeter Hall, clattered the royal cavalcade. It was a much grander occasion than that sober, frock-coated gathering addressed by the Prince Consort fifty-seven years earlier. Among the 50 000 troops taking part in the parade were contingents from every corner of the Empire including West Africa. According to *The Times*, which had now crossed over into the imperial camp, they were 'the most impressive element in the whole of the magnificent display'. It would take 'a very cold heart and a very stagnant imagination' not to be moved by the splendour of the occasion. The *Graphic* went so far as to call it 'the greatest day in English history. There have been great days before, but they were days of sowing. The Diamond Jubilee is the day of greatest reaping – the harvest festival of the greatest Empire, of the most glorious epoch, of the longest reign.'[47]

New dreams, new illusions. It was left to Rudyard Kipling, who knew more about the travails of empire than most, to provide a prophetic comment on the vainglory of the occasion:

The tumult and the shouting dies;
The Captains and the Kings depart:
Still stands our ancient sacrifice,
An humble and a contrite heart . . .
Far called, our navies melt away;
On dune and headland sinks the fire:
Lo, all our pomp of yesterday
Is one with Nineveh and Tyre!
Judge of the Nations, spare us yet,
Lest we forget – lest we forget.[48]

Notes

CHAPTER ONE

1. Buxton to Hannah Buxton, 2 June 1840, Buxton Papers, Rhodes House, Oxford, 19/290, henceforward referred to as BP. In order to avoid excessive notation I have inserted references to this collection only in those cases where the origins of statements or quotations are not already clear from the text. The bulk of the material in the collection is chronologically arranged. Most references, therefore, come from vols. 16–20A which cover the years 1837–44. For further information about the collection readers should refer to Patricia M. Pugh's superb *Calendar of the Papers of Sir Thomas Fowell Buxton, 1786–1845* (List and Index Society, 1980), which gives synopses of all the correspondence and contains both a name and a topic index.

2. Theodore Martin, *The Life of the Prince Consort*, 6th edn., 4 vols. (London, 1879), i. 87.

3. Society for the Extinction of the Slave Trade and for the Civilization of Africa, *Proceedings of the First Public Meeting of the Society ... Prince Albert ... in the Chair* (London, 1840). Verbatim accounts of the meeting also appeared in *The Times*, 2 June, and the *Watchman*, 3 June 1840. See also, *Morning Advertiser*, 2 June; *Morning Chronicle*, 3, 4, 9 June; the *Globe*, 9 June 1840. Clippings from these and other papers are in BP vols. 40–2.

4. A collection of Buxton's private reflections are in BP 4/353–93. For background material on Buxton see Charles Buxton, *Memoirs of Sir Thomas Fowell Buxton, Bart., with selections from his Correspondence* (London, 1848); Augustus J.C. Hare, *The Gurneys of Earlham*, 2 vols. (London, 1895); R.H. Mottram, *Buxton the Liberator* (London, 1946).

5. Hare, ii, frontispiece. By far the fullest account of Buxton's early career, concern with prison reform and of the many interlocking committees on which he and his relatives served will be found in F.C. Stuart, 'A Critical Edition of the Correspondence of Sir Thomas Fowell Buxton, Bart., with an Account of his Career to 1823', 2 vols. (unpublished MA Thesis, University of London, 1957), i, chapters 2, 3 and 5.

6. See, for example, M.R.D. Foot (ed.), *The Gladstone Diaries*, 11 volumes to date (Oxford, 1968–9), i. 334, 401; also Josiah Forster, *Extracts from my Note Book: From 1831–1854* (Tottenham, 1865).

7. Priscilla Johnston to Buxton, 18 Nov. 1842, BP 20A/293c; Charles Buxton, *Memoirs*, 191.

8. For further details see W.L.

Mathieson, *Great Britain and the Slave Trade, 1839–1865* (London, 1929); Christopher Lloyd, *The Navy and the Slave Trade: The Suppression of the African Slave Trade in the Nineteenth Century* (London, 1949); W.E.F. Ward, *The Royal Navy and the Slavers: The Suppression of the Atlantic Slave Trade* (London, 1969); David Eltis, *Economic Growth and the Ending of the Transatlantic Slave Trade* (New York, 1987).

9. Buxton to J.J. Gurney, 18 Aug.–4 Sept., 1838, BP 17/199 a–h; Hare, ii. 55–6; Pugh, ii–iii; Buxton to Sarah Maria Buxton and Anna Gurney, 17 May 1838, BP 17/147 g–k.

10. These ideas are discussed at length in Philip Curtin, *The Image of Africa: British Ideas and Action, 1780–1850* (Madison, Wisconsin, 1964). See esp. chapters 2, 9, 10 and 11.

11. Douglas A. Lorimer, *Colour, Class and the Victorians: English Attitudes to the Negro in the Mid-Nineteenth Century* (Leicester, 1978). Although notions about the inherent inferiority of blacks had been current in the eighteenth century, by the 1830s the dominant belief, certainly in humanitarian circles, was that all races of men were equal – both in the sight of God and in their potentialities for development and achievement, though not in their existing state of culture. See Philip Curtin, ' "Scientific" Racism and the British Theory of Empire', *Journal of the Historical Society of Nigeria*, ii (December 1960), 40–51. Buxton to Wilson, 9 March 1839, BP 17/374–9. The Lady Mico Trust was established in 1670 when Lady Mico left £1000 'for the redemption of poor Christian slaves in Barbary'. By 1827 the sum had grown to £120 000. Buxton appealed to the Court of Chancery which agreed to release the money so that it could be used to found

colleges and schools in the West Indies. J.H. Parry and P.M. Sherlock, *A Short History of the West Indies* (London, 1963), 248. In the event, Buxton's plans to send Lady Mico graduates to Africa failed to materialize.

12. Betty Fladeland, *Abolitionists and Working-Class Problems in the Age of Industrialization* (London, 1984); Howard Temperley, *British Antislavery, 1833–1870* (London, 1972), 72–5.

13. Howard Temperley, 'Capitalism, Slavery and Ideology', *Past and Present* (1977), 94–118, and 'Anti-Slavery as a Form of Cultural Imperialism' in Bolt, Christine, and Drescher, Seymour (eds.), *Anti-Slavery, Religion and Reform* (Folkstone, 1980), 335–50. See also Eltis, Ch. 1.

14. Temperley, *British Antislavery*, Ch. 2. For Brougham's role see the interview with Glenelg referred to in note 17 below.

15. Buxton's initial views on the subject are set out in a printed letter to Josiah Forster, 3 Nov. 1837, BP 16/159 e–m.

16. J. Gallagher, 'Fowell Buxton and the New African Policy', *Cambridge Historical Journal*, x (1950), 39–47. Gallagher places too much emphasis on the Government's Machiavellian intentions. It is, nevertheless, the best, and indeed virtually the only, account of the political background of the Niger expedition.

17. Buxton to Hannah Buxton, 26 March 1838, BP 17/106–8. Details of Buxton's subsequent interviews with Glenelg and other ministers will be found in BP 17/129–65 April–June 1838.

18. Thomas Fowell Buxton, *(Private) Letter on the Slave Trade to the Lord Viscount Melbourne and the Other Members of Her Majesty's Cabinet Council* (London, 1838).

19. Buxton to Priscilla Johnston, 14 Aug. 1838, BP 17/188–90.
20. Ibid. 90–1.

CHAPTER TWO

1. Elizabeth Jane Whately, *Life and Correspondence of Richard Whately, Late Archbishop of Dublin*, 2 vols. (London, 1866), ii. 452. For a shrewd analysis of Melbourne's conservatism see ibid. 451–2.
2. Melbourne to Russell, 2 Oct. 1838, Melbourne Papers, Windsor Castle, Box 13/77, henceforward referred to as MP.
3. Melbourne to Russell, 3 Sept. 1838, MP Box 13/69; see also his letter to Russell, 5 Sept. 1838: 'I am sure that Buxton must have sent you his pamphlet. He brought it to me with all the air of a Measure. I said he should send it to all other Ministers. . . . We might try to gather information as to the present state and extent of the traffic from some source that can be depended upon, from some quarter not tainted either by interest or altruism. The present position is very embarrassing if there be foundation for Buxton's assertion that our present measures increase the extent and aggravate the cruelty of the traffic.' Ibid., Box 13/71.
4. Viscount Esher, *The Girlhood of Queen Victoria: A Selection from Her Majesty's Diaries, 1832–1840*, 2 vols. (London, 1912), ii. 28.
5. Palmerston to Melbourne, 27 Feb. 1838, MP Box 11/72.
6. Palmerston to Melbourne, 4 Sept. 1838, MP Box 11/82.
7. For an account of Palmerston's views on Africa see R.J. Gavin, 'Palmerston's Policy Towards East and West Africa, 1830–1865' (unpublished Cambridge PhD Thesis, 1958), esp. 12–24, 347–64.

The general thrust of British policy in this period is ably described in Ronald Hyam, *Britain's Imperial Century, 1815–1914: A Study of Empire and Expansion* (London, 1976), chs. 1 and 2; see also Paul Kennedy, 'Continuity and Discontinuity in British Imperialism, 1814–1914' in C.C. Eldridge (ed.), *British Imperialism in the Nineteenth Century* (London, 1984), 20–38.
8. Palmerston to Glenelg, 24 Sept. 1838, Foreign Office Papers, Public Record Office, Kew, 54/2/134, henceforward referred to as FO. For an account of Palmerston's negotiations with Portugal see L.M. Bethell, 'Britain, Portugal and the Suppression of the Brazilian Slave Trade: The Origins of Lord Palmerston's Act of 1839', *English Historical Review*, 80 (1965), 761–84. Palmerston's 'reign of terror' is described in Gavin, 138–43.
9. Palmerston to Minto, 14 April 1838, FO 84/262.
10. Buxton to Hannah Buxton, 4 Oct. 1838, BP 17/213; Buxton to Priscilla Johnston, 7 Oct. 1838, BP 17/217.
11. Spring Rice to Buxton, 16 Nov. 1838, BP 17/245.
12. Buxton to Spring Rice, 12 Nov. 1838, BP 17/244.
13. Buxton to William Allen, 28 Nov. 1838, BP 17/259; William Allen to Buxton, 1 Dec. 1838, BP 17/259 a–d; note by Priscilla Johnston, BP 17/260–1. In fact Brougham had merely glanced at the book while dining at William Allen's.
14. Buxton to Glenelg, 7 Sept. 1838, copy in FO 54/2/110.
15. Captain Cogan to Palmerston, 25 Sept. 1838, FO 54/2/140; Palmerston to Glenelg, 14 Oct. 1838, FO 54/2/181.
16. Buxton to Glenelg, 5 Dec. 1838, BP 17/282–6.
17. Note to Sarah Buxton, n.d., BP 17/266.

18. Buxton to Hannah Buxton, 22 Dec. 1838, BP 17/299.
19. Priscilla Johnston to Anna Gurney and Sarah Buxton, 28 Dec. 1838, BP 17/302–4.
20. Memorandum, 30 Dec. 1838, BP 4/391–3.
21. Lloyd C. Sanders, *Lord Melbourne's Papers* (London, 1889), 402.
22. Brougham to Napier, 28 July 1838, in Macvey Napier, *Selections from the Correspondence of the Late Macvey Napier* (London, 1879), 267–8. For other trenchant comments by Brougham see ibid. 240 and 357.
23. Tavistock to Russell, June 1838, Russell Papers, Public Record Office, Kew, 30/22/3B/157. See also Russell to William Clay, 4 July 1838, ibid. 171, and the Earl of Essex to Russell, June 1838, ibid. 73.
24. Lansdowne to Buxton, 13 Jan. 1839, BP 17/335 a–h.
25. Priscilla Johnston to Anna Gurney, 14 Feb. 1839, BP 17/350; Buxton to J.J. Gurney, 5 March 1839, BP 17/362–5; Minute by Lord Glenelg 18 Feb. 1839, BP 17/358–9.
26. Buxton to Priscilla Johnston and Anna Gurney, 23 April 1839, BP 18/62–7. In fact there were no reliable statistics on mortality rates in the 'lands about Boussa' or on conditions anywhere else in the African interior at that time. Buxton's belief that the interior was healthier than the coast was, as events proved, purely wishful thinking. What the available statistics *did* show was that the annual death rate among troops stationed in Sierra Leone was three times higher than among those stationed in Jamaica (483 as opposed to 130 per 1000). Philip Curtin, *Death by Migration: Europe's Encounter with the Tropical World in the Nineteenth Century* (Cambridge, 1989), 8.
27. Temperley, *British Antislavery*, 1–41.
28. Buxton to Priscilla Johnston, 24 Nov. 1837 in F.C. Stuart, 'A Critical Edition of the Correspondence of Sir Thomas Fowell Buxton', i. 371–3.
29. For Sturge's plans see Temperley, *British Antislavery*, ch. 4. Information on the Buxton–Sturge feud comes from BP 18.
30. Spring Rice to Buxton, 27 April 1839, BP 18/72 a–d; Andrew Johnston to Priscilla Johnston, 8 May 1839, BP 18/87–8.
31. The full correspondence is in the Colonial Office Files, Public Record Office, Kew 2/21/209–56 (20 April–22 Oct. 1838), henceforward referred to as CO.
32. A copy of the list of questions is in BP 18/160–2.
33. Notes by Anna Gurney and Sarah Buxton, 31 July 1839, BP 18/181–4.
34. Buxton to Anna Gurney and Sarah Buxton, 8 and 9 Aug. 1839, BP 18/199, 200 a–h.

CHAPTER THREE

1. Buxton *et al.* to Normanby, 27 Aug. 1839, CO 2/21/242–9.
2. Parry to Buxton, 17 Aug. 1839, BP 18/334 a–d. See also *Dictionary of National Biography*.
3. Allen's original charts are in Admiralty Papers 13/183, Public Record Office, Kew, henceforward referred to as Adm. For Allen's career see *Dictionary of National Biography*. The Bay of Biscay episode is graphically described in Duncan MacGregor, *A Narrative of the Loss of the Kent East Indiaman by Fire in the Bay of Biscay on the 1st of March 1825* (Edinburgh, 1825).
4. Trotter and Allen to James Stephen, 28 Sept. 1839, CO 2/21.
5. See ibid., marginal notes by Stephen and Vernon Smith.

6. Buxton to Trew, 17 Oct. 1839, BP 18/407–11.
7. Parry to Colonial Office, 14 Nov. 1839, CO 2/22/29.
8. Palmerston had failed to brief the Colonial Secretary on the new, aggressive measures he was intending to take against the slave trade. The confusion this caused within the Colonial Office is reflected in its responses to the Gold Coast Committee's request for additional funds. See memoranda by James Stephen and Sir George Grey, April–May 1838, CO 267/150/ 494–506, 553, 573–4.
9. Russell to Admiralty, 20 Nov. 1839, CO 2/22/8–11; Treasury to Colonial Office, 20 Dec. 1839, CO 2/22/40.
10. Buxton to Anna Gurney, 25 Sept. 1839, BP 18/392 a–d; Russell to Treasury, 26 Dec. 1839, CO 2/ 22/34–9.
11. Russell to Buxton, 13 Nov. 1839, BP 18/434 e–h. Lairds were well qualified to carry out the work required. They were the acknowledged leaders in the field, having already built some two dozen iron steamships, among them a number of flat-bottomed vessels for the East India Company. The East India Company had been quicker than the Admiralty to recognize the usefulness of iron steamers in opening up inland waterways to trade, also as gunboats in time of war. Early models had been shipped to the East in sections and were already in use on the Tigris, Euphrates and Indus. More recently Lairds had begun work in a new line of vessels, slightly larger than those specified by Trotter and Allen but otherwise almost identical, capable of reaching the East under their own steam. The first of these, the *Nemesis*, was destined shortly to play a crucial role in the Opium War. For a brief account of gunboat technology and its significance, see Daniel R. Headrick, *The Tools of Empire: Technology and European Imperialism in the Nineteenth Century* (New York, 1981), 26–57.
12. Buxton to Priscilla Johnston, 18 Nov. 1839, BP 18/247–50.
13. See Colonial Office memoranda, 3–31 Jan. 1840, CO 2/22/235–8.
14. Reported in Sir Thomas Fowell Buxton, *The African Slave Trade and its Remedy* (London, 1840), 555–60.
15. Trotter to Colonial Office, 25 Feb. 1840, CO 2/22/136–41.
16. Stephen to Vernon Smith, 27 Feb. 1840, CO 2/22/130–1.
17. Parry to Russell, 31 March 1840, CO 2/21/339–60.
18. For an over-view of tropical epidemiology and mortality rates in the nineteenth century see Curtin, *Death by Migration, passim.* The experiences of Europeans who went to West Africa are described in somewhat more detail in his *Image of Africa*, 483–7. For early exploration of the Niger see Christopher Lloyd, *The Search for the Niger* (London, 1973); Howard J. Pedraza, *Borrioboola-Gha: The Story of Lokoja, the First British Settlement in Nigeria* (Oxford, 1960); Sanche de Gramont, *The Strong Brown God: The Story of the Niger River* (London, 1975); also C.C. Ifemesia, 'British Enterprise on the Niger, 1830–1869' (unpublished PhD Thesis, University of London, 1959). A brief description of earlier exploits and of the hopes entertained that a well-equipped naval expedition would avoid many of the dangers previously encountered will be found in William Allen and T.R.H. Thomson, *A Narrative of the Expedition to the River Niger in 1841*, 2 vols. (London, 1848), i. 7–21.
19. According to K. Onwuka Dike, Laird lost his entire fortune as a result of the 1832 venture and was

ruined a second time on account of his investment in Niger enterprise in 1860. See K. Onwuka Dike, *Trade and Politics in the Niger Delta, 1830–1885* (Oxford, 1956), 62, 174, 213. The unfortunate fate of the Rhode Island expedition is described in Macgregor Laird and R.A.K. Oldfield, *Narrative of an Expedition into the Interior of Africa*, 2 vols. (London, 1837), i. 344–8.

20. See Laird's review of *The African Slave Trade and its Remedy* in *London and Westminster Review*, 34 (June, 1840), 125–65. The quotation, slightly adapted, is from Jonathan Swift, 'Cadenus and Vanessa'.

21. David Boswell Reid, 'Ventilation of the Niger Steam Ships', *Friend of Africa* (24 March 1841), 66; Allen and Thomson, ii. 165.

22. Ifemesia, 147. The problems of African epidemiology and nineteenth-century theories concerning them are admirably described in Curtin, *Image of Africa*; see esp. 71–87.

23. The malarial parasite was first seen under the microscope by Alphonse Laveran in 1880, but it was only in 1897 that Major Ronald Ross made the epochal discovery that the female anopheles mosquito was the vector. See P.F. Russell, *Man's Mastery of Malaria* (London, 1955).

24. Inspector General of Naval Hospitals to Secretary of the Admiralty, 31 March 1841, Adm. 13/182. For the folk wisdom on the subject see Gary Puckrein, 'Climate, Health and Black Labor in the English Americas', *Journal of American Studies* 13 (1979), 179–93; also Thomas Morgan to Russell, 27 Dec. 1839, CO 2/22/337.

25. Printed letter from M.J.K. to Colonial Office, 19 Feb. 1841, CO 2/22/268.

26. A full account of Professor Daniell's experiments and copies of his reports and correspondence are reprinted in *Friend of Africa* (15 Jan.,

15 and 25 Feb. 1841), 18–23, 40–1, 53. For Daniell's career see *Dictionary of National Biography*. Contemporary views on the relationship between odour and disease are described in Alain Corbin, *The Foul and the Fragrant: Odor and the French Social Imagination* (Leamington Spa, 1986), 1–8.

27. 'Dr Reid on the Ventilation of the Niger Steam Vessels', *Friend of Africa* (1 Feb., 24 March 1841), 43–7, 65–73. See also James Ormiston M'William, *Medical History of the Expedition to the Niger* (London, 1843), 253–68. For Reid's career see *Dictionary of National Biography*.

28. Lushington to Buxton, 29 Oct. 1840, BP 19/455 r–s.

29. BP 17/194–5, 223–4, 254–6; 18/329–31, 365–6, 439–41, 445–6; 19/261, 281a–c, 413–14, 437, 456, 470; 20/275. There is a brief account of Jeremie's career in the *Dictionary of National Biography*.

30. Thomas Wemyss Reid, *The Life of W.E. Forster*, 2 vols. (London, 1888), i. 123–6.

31. For Buxton's views on sovereignty, see BP 33/1–108.

32. Memorandum, 21 Sept. 1839, CO 2/22/427–33. The quotation regarding the uselessness of establishing British dominion in Africa is taken from Christopher Fyfe, *A History of Sierra Leone* (Oxford, 1962), 217. For Stephen's general views on African matters see T.J. Barron, 'James Stephen, the "Black Race" and British Colonial Administration, 1813–1847', *Journal of Imperial and Commonwealth History* 5 (1977), 131–50; also Paul Knaplund, *James Stephen and the British Colonial System, 1813–1847* (Madison, Wisconsin, 1953).

33. Buxton to Russell, 7 Aug. 1840, CO 2/21/265–70.

34. Russell to Commissioners, n.d. CO 2/21/275.

35. British and Foreign Anti-Slavery

Society, *Proceedings of the General Anti-Slavery Convention . . . Held in London from Friday, June 12 to Tuesday June 23, 1840* (London, 1841), 242–6, 490–8.

36. Catherine Buxton to Priscilla Johnston, 28 May 1840, BP 19/284; Buxton to Lushington, 31 Oct. 1840, BP 19/457–60; Buxton to James Houghton, 27 Oct. 1840, BP 19/453.

37. Katherine Fry to Louisa Perry, 19 Nov. 1840, BP 20/37–43. A full account of the meeting will be found in *The Times*, 21 Nov. 1840.

38. Sir George Stephen, *A Second Letter to . . . Lord John Russell on the Plans of the Society for the Civilization of Africa* (London, 1840); Buxton to James Stephen, 25 June 1840, BP 19/302–3; Buxton to Trotter, 30 Sept. 1840, BP 19/420–1.

39. Jamieson to Russell, 11 Jan. 1840, CO 2/22/298; Russell to Jamieson, 21 Jan. 1840, ibid. 299.

40. This was also the view of Macgregor Laird, *London and Westminster Review*, 34 (June 1840), 125–65. Laird believed that the only practicable way to reduce the slave trade was by making free-labour sugar cheaper than the slave-grown variety. This could be achieved, he argued, by encouraging a free migration of blacks from Africa to Trinidad and Guiana. Although not entirely hostile to the Niger expedition he feared that the only effect of sending so many Europeans to Africa 'must be the moral effect of a succession of funerals', ibid. 156–9, 164. For an up-to-date modern assessment of the scale of the Atlantic slave trade at that time see Eltis, *Economic Growth*, 251.

41. Robert Jamieson, *A Further Appeal to the Government and People of Great Britain Against the Proposed Niger Expedition* (London, 1841). Jamieson's observations concerning Sierra Leone's poor economic per-

formance were amply justified. Producing goods for export, or, indeed, work of any kind, was not high in the settlers' list of priorities. See Fyfe, 256–9. And maintaining the colony was expensive. In 1840 Parliamentary grants-in-aid to Sierra Leone totalled £53 404 (in aid of the civil government – £13 684; military, including naval, expenditure – £39 730). J.F.A. Ajayi and Michael Crowder, *A History of West Africa*, vol. 2, second edn. (Harlow, Essex, 1987), 327.

42. Herman Merivale, *Lectures on Colonization and Colonies Delivered Before the University of Oxford in 1839 and 1841*, 2 vols. (London, 1841), i. 302–3.

43. For a full account of the meeting see *The Times*, 14 Nov. 1840.

44. *The Times*, 14–30 Nov. 1840. The policies and political attitudes of *The Times* at this time are described in *The History of the Times*, vol. i 'The Thunderer in the Making', 1785–1841 (London, 1935). Its hostility to African settlements was of long standing: see Christopher Fyfe, *A History of Sierra Leone* (London, 1962), 165.

45. Buxton to Rear-Admiral John Washington, 31 Oct. 1840, BP 19/460–2; Sir George Stephen to Buxton, 12 Nov. 1840, BP 20/31 e–f; Andrew Johnston to Buxton, 23 Nov. 1840, BP 20/47 a–d; Priscilla Johnston to Buxton, 25 Nov. 1840, BP 20/49 a–d; Buxton to Andrew Johnston, 2 Dec. 1840, BP 20/57.

46. *The Times*, 25, 28 Dec. 1840.

47. Buxton to Anna Gurney, 6 Dec. 1840, BP 20/65–9.

48. *Hansard*, 3rd series, 56 (11, 16 Feb. 1841), cols. 510, 692–703.

49. *The Times*, 4 Feb., 30 March, 3 May 1841.

50. Paul Read, *Lord John Russell, Sir T.F. Buxton and the Niger Expedition* (London, 1840); Carson to Russell, 22 Feb. 1841, CO 2/22/272–84.

51. David Eltis puts the figure for 1840

at 53 600. Eltis, *Economic Growth*, 251.

52. Stirling to Russell, 20 March 1841, with marginal comments by Stephen, Vernon Smith and Russell, CO 2/22/365–9.

CHAPTER FOUR

1. Jamieson to Russell, 21 Jan., 13 Feb. 1841, CO 2/22/310–11.
2. Trotter to Admiralty, 3 Feb. 1841, copy in CO 2/22/98 with marginal notes by Stephen, Vernon Smith and Russell.
3. For information on early paddle steamers see Bernard Cox, *Paddle Steamers* (Poole, Dorset, 1979); also Bernard Dumpleton, *The Story of the Paddle Steamer* (Melksham, Wiltshire, 1973), and Headrick, *Tools of Empire*, 17–57.
4. 'Papers Relative to the Expedition to the River Niger', *Parliamentary Papers*, 1843 (472), xlviii. 3–5, henceforward referred to simply as *Parliamentary Papers*; James Ormiston M'William, *Medical History of the Expedition to the Niger During the Years 1841–42* (London, 1843), 3, 6; Office of Ordinance memorandum, 5 Jan. 1841, Adm. 13/180; Allen and Thomson, *Narrative*, i. 31.
5. *The Times*, 31 March 5 April, *Morning Chronicle*, 9 April 1841; Allen and Thomson, i. 29–32, 35–6.
6. Various accounts of these festivities will be found in the Buxton Papers for March 1841 in BP 20/181–210; see also *Memoir of the Life of Elizabeth Fry . . . Edited by Two of Her Daughters*, 2 vols. (London, 1847), ii. 385.
7. Quoted in T.J. Barron, 'James Stephen', 139.
8. Catherine Buxton to Anna Gurney, 23 March 1841, BP 20/192–3.

There are many references to the Asante Princes in the Buxton Papers, including accounts of their presentation to the Queen and Lord Melbourne. See BP 20/207 a–d. For an account of their career in England and subsequently see G.E. Metcalfe, *Maclean of the Gold Cost: The Life and Times of George Maclean, 1801–1847* (London, 1962), 270–4, and Ivor Wilks, *Asante in the Nineteenth Century* (Cambridge, 1975), 596–665.

9. Catherine Buxton to Anna Gurney, 29 March 1841, BP 20/199–201; John Duncan, 'Some Account of the Last Expedition to the Niger', *Bentley's Miscellany*, 22 (1847), 412; William Simpson, *A Private Journal Kept During the Niger Expedition* (London, 1843), 2.
10. M'William, 7–8, 16–17.
11. Ibid. 18, 23.
12. Simpson, ii–x, 1–5, 129–31.
13. See note 9 above. There is a brief, but so far as the expedition is concerned not entirely accurate, account of Duncan's career in the *Dictionary of National Biography*.
14. J.R.T. Vogel, 'Journal of the Voyage to the Niger' (trans. F. Sheer), in Sir W.J. Hooker (ed.), *Niger Flora* (London, 1849), 23–5. The personnel of the expedition, including the civilians, are listed in *Parliamentary Papers*, 108–11.
15. Allen and Thomson, i. viii–x, 57.
16. Simpson, 15–16.
17. Vogel, 5.
18. Duncan, 412; Allen and Thomson, i. 56–7.
19. Allen and Thomson, i. 72, 382–3; Simpson, 21.
20. Allen and Thomson, i. 73–5.
21. Ibid. 76; Vogel, 30; Christopher Fyfe, *A History of Sierra Leone*, 144–5, 190–1.
22. Fyfe, 168–72, 182–3, 203–5.
23. Fyfe, 218–19; Jeremie to Russell (February ?), 1841, Adm. 13/181; Allen and Thomson, 75–6, 81.

24. Allen and Thomson, i. 79; M'William, 30. For a full listing of model farm personnel see Carr's report of 1 Oct. 1841, in Adm. 13/180.

25. Allen and Thomson, i. 76–8, 122–4; Christopher Lloyd, *The Navy and the Slave Trade*, 18; Simpson, 22.

26. J.F.A. Ajayi, 'A New Introduction' to J.F. Schön and S.A. Crowther, *Journals of the Rev. James Frederick Schön and Mr Samuel Crowther, Who ... Acompanied the Expedition up the Niger in 1841* (London, 1842, reprinted Frank Cass, 1970), and 'Introduction to the Second Edition' to Samuel Crowther, *Journal of an Expedition up the Niger and Tshadda Rivers in 1855* (London, 1855; reprinted by Frank Cass, 1970). See also Crowther's 1837 report on his captivity which appears on pages 371–83 of the 1841 Schön – Crowther *Journal*. The Church Missionary Society's instructions to Schön, dated 3 Dec. 1840, are in Adm. 13/180.

27. Duncan, 413; Society for the Extinction of the Slave Trade and for the Civilization of Africa, *Friend of Africa* (Oct. 1841), 178; Simpson, 19–21.

28. Elizabeth Helen Melville, *A Residence at Sierra Leone* (London, 1849), 71–2, 96; Fyfe, 221; Allen and Thomson, i. 83.

29. Allen and Thomson, i. 87, 90; M'William, 31.

30. Duncan, 413; Allen and Thomson, i. 87–9; Tom W. Shick, *Behold the Promised Land: A History of Afro-American Settler Society in Nineteenth Century Liberia* (Baltimore, 1980), 38–40.

31. Allen and Thomson, i. 89.

32. Ibid. 93–7; Vogel, 6–8.

33. Simpson, 25–6; Allen and Thomson, i. 103–4.

34. Allen and Thomson, i. 105.

35. Ibid. 106–9; Penelope Campbell, *Maryland in Africa: The Maryland State Colonization Society, 1831–1857* (Urbana, Illinois, 1971), 88, 132–43. See also Peter Duignan and L.H. Gann, *The United States and Africa: A History* (Cambridge, 1984), 93–5. After further quarrels with the Maryland settlers the Wilsons removed their mission to the Gabon. In 1852 they returned to New York where John became Secretary of the Board of Foreign Missions. There is an account of his career in the *Dictionary of American Biography*.

36. Schön and Crowther, *Journal*, 10–13.

37. John Ansah to the Reverend Thomas Pyne, 22 July 1841, *Friend of Africa* (Nov. 1841), 202.

38. Allen and Thomson, i. 121, 235–6; Simpson, 24; M'William, 37.

39. For a detailed and sympathetic anthropological account of West African religions see P.A. Talbot, *The Peoples of Southern Nigeria*, 4 vols. (London, 1926), ii. 14–28.

40. Admiralty to Trotter, 22 Sept., 2 Nov. 1840, in Adm. 13.182; Allen and Thomson, i. 132, 139; Vogel, 10. The actual value of 6.5 million cowries, in terms of sterling, was about £450. See *Parliamentary Papers*, 75.

41. Metcalfe, *Maclean of the Gold Coast*, 102–4, 232–3; John Leighton Wilson, *Western Africa* (New York and London, 1856), 147–8.

42. The history of the Gold Coast immediately before and during Maclean's time is ably dealt with in Metcalfe, chapters 3–9. The quotation is from page 287.

43. Ibid. 88–9.

44. Allen and Thomson, i. 145–6; M'William, 41.

45. Henry Reeve to Amelia Opie, 7 March 1839, BP 17/314–18; Fyfe, *Sierra Leone*, 147, 165, 187, 189; Metcalfe, 240.

46. Cook to Stanley, 11 March 1843, CO 2/24/184–6. This section

of Cook's account was deleted when the Commissioners' reports were presented to Parliament. See Chapter 9 below.
47. Metcalfe, 216–21, 260–3, 277–8.
48. Ibid. 270–1.
49. Ibid. 272; Schön, 22–5; Simpson, 28.
50. M'William, 31, 42, 44–5.
51. Duncan, 414; Vogel, 8–9, 42–3.
52. Allen and Thomson, i. 157–8; Simpson, 32.

CHAPTER FIVE

1. Allen and Thomson, *Narrative*, i. 159–61, 166–7; Vogel, 'Journal', 45–7; Simpson, *Private Journal*, 35–6. A day-to-day account of meteorological conditions is given in *Parliamentary Papers*, 122–3.
2. M'William, *Medical History*, 47; Allen and Thomson, i. 161.
3. Allen and Thomson, i. 168–70. Schön's subsequent enquiries upriver strengthened his conviction that the woman had been sacrificed. Schön, *Journal*, 49.
4. M'William, 48–50; Allen and Thomson, i. 168–72, 339, ii. 298.
5. Eltis, *Economic Growth and the Ending of the Transatlantic Slave Trade*, 181; E.J. Alagoa, *The Small Brave City State: A History of Brass-Nambe in the Niger Delta* (Ibadan and Wisconsin, 1964), 57–8.
6. Laird and Oldfield, *Narrative*, i. 70, 75, 78–80, 82, 342. According to Oldfield, the crime for which Louis was executed was adultery. Ibid. 335. Allen and Thomson, i. 176.
7. Laird and Oldfield, i. 314, 327.
8. *Parliamentary Papers*, 89.
9. Dike, *Trade and Politics in the Niger Delta*, 19–36. Ajayi and Crowder, *History of West Africa*, 48–9, 64; Paul E. Lovejoy, *Transformations in Slavery: A History of Slavery in Africa* (Cambridge, 1983), 88–107.

10. Allen and Thomson, i. 171–2.
11. Laird and Oldfield, i. 75–6, 79–80, 82, 91–2, 95, 97, 327; Alagoa, 57–8; C.C. Ifemesia, 'The "Civilizing" Mission of 1841: Aspects of an Episode in Anglo-Nigerian Relations', *Journal of the Historical Society of Nigeria*, 2 (1962), 306.
12. Commissioners to Russell, 18 Aug. 1841, in *Parliamentary Papers*, 31.
13. Here, as elsewhere, my description of the voyage is based on the accounts given by Allen and Thomson, Duncan, M'William, Schön and Crowther, Simpson and Vogel. The quotation is from Allen and Thomson, 173.
14. Mungo Park, *Travels in the Interior Districts of Africa* (London, 1799) chapter 24; Schön, 42–4; Allen and Thomson, i. 184–91.
15. C.C. Ifemesia, 'British Enterprise on the Niger, 1830–1869' (unpublished PhD Thesis, University of London, 1959), 21–2.
16. Allen and Thomson, i. 196–7, 202; Schön, 37, 44–5; Vogel, 55.
17. Crowther, *Journal*, 281–2.
18. Allen and Thomson, i. 236.
19. Laird and Oldfield, i. 103; Dike, 26–7.
20. Allen and Thomson, i. 207; Simpson, 41. Allen's account is supported by John Duncan, who describes the Obi as 'about forty-five or fifty years of age, rather interesting in appearance than otherwise, and bears a very good character among his subjects'. Duncan, 'Account', 469.
21. Allen and Thomson, i. 204–9.
22. A largely verbatim account of these will be found in *Parliamentary Papers*, 141–5. A printed copy of African Civilization Society's 'Address to the Chiefs of Africa' can be found in BP 20/169a.
23. *Parliamentary Papers*, 92.
24. Allen and Thomson, i. 231; M'William, 61.
25. Schön, 56–7; Allen and Thomson, i. 231–2.

26. Simpson, 44; Allen and Thomson, i. 244–9.
27. List of ethnographic queries prepared by Dr J.C. Prichard, n.d. [April 1841?], Adm. 13/182. For information on craniometry and craniology at the time see Stephen Jay Gould's superb *The Mismeasure of Man* (New York, 1961).
28. Schön, 58–9.
29. *Parliamentary Papers*, 145; Allen and Thomson, i. 258–61; Schön, 65–7; Duncan, 416.
30. The full text of the treaty is in *Parliamentary Papers*, 33–5. For information regarding the gifts see ibid. 145 and CO 2/23/29 and 129.
31. M'William, 265–8.
32. The expedition's visit to Idah is described in all the narratives. The most detailed descriptions, on which the following account is largely based, will be found in Allen and Thomson, i. 278–331 and Schön 77–108.
33. For Allen's views on domestic slavery in Africa, see Allen and Thomson, ii. 430–2.
34. CMS to Schön, 3 Dec. 1840, Adm. 13/180.
35. Schön, 96, 99–100.
36. CO 2/23/50 and 129.
37. A copy of the treaty itself and of the commissioners' notes on their negotiations with the Attah can be found in *Parliamentary Papers*, 38–40,145–9.
38. Simpson, 50.

CHAPTER SIX

1. In particular, ulceration is not among the normal symptoms of malaria but would be quite consistent with a diagnosis of mercury poisoning. The relative shortness of Peglar's illness – only four days – is also indicative. A detailed description of the case will be found in M'William, *Medical History*, 203–5.

For M'William's views on the fever and reports on others who died see ibid. 131–244; also Allen and Thomson, *Narrative*, ii. 159–67. The history of medical thinking and practice with respect to the treatment of West African fevers is surveyed in Curtin, *Image of Africa*, 343–62, and Headrick, *Tools of Empire*, 58–79. For information on the pathology of malaria I have relied principally on R. Stephen Phillips's, *Malaria* (London, 1983), esp. 17–18.

2. Allen and Thomson, i. 330–2.
3. Schön, *Journal*, 111.
4. Crowther, *Journal*, 294–5; Vogel, 'Journal', 64.
5. Crowther, 296–7; M'William 77; Duncan, 'Account', 473.
6. Allen and Thomson, i. 341; Schön, 113; Duncan, 474.
7. Allen and Thomson, i. 342–3.
8. Vogel, 17.
9. Allen and Thomson, i. 349–52; *Parliamentary Papers*, 41–2, 150.
10. Simpson, *Private Journal*, 53; Vogel, 16; Schön, 129.
11. *Parliamentary Papers*, 151–2.
12. M'William, 80–81. An account of the *Soudan*'s descent of the river will be found in Allen and Thomson, ii. 20–5.
13. The official minutes of the meeting are in *Parliamentary Papers*, 152–3. For Allen's own account, see Allen and Thomson, i. 364–8.
14. This account of the *Wilberforce*'s descent is taken from Allen and Thomson, ii. 1–19.
15. The *Albert*'s ascent from the confluence to Egga and its subsequent return to the sea is described by M'William in Allen and Thomson, ii. 79–141, and *Medical History*, 81–105. See also Schön, 108–237; Crowther, 301–38, and Duncan, 475–80.
16. Crowther, 324.
17. Allen and Thomson, ii. 118.
18. Schön, 145; Crowther, 306; Allen and Thomson, ii. 115–7.

19. Dixon Denham and Hugh Clapperton, *Narrative and Discoveries in Northern and Coastal Africa in the Years 1822, 1823 and 1824*, 2 vols. (London, 1828), i. 330–79; Hugh Clapperton, *Journal of a Second Expedition into the Interior of Africa from the Bight of Benin to Soccatoo by the late Commander Clapperton* (London, 1829), 203–24; Richard Lander, *Records of Captain Clapperton's Last Expedition to Africa*, 2 vols. (London, 1830), 24–55.
20. H.A.S. Johnston, *The Fulani Empire of Sokoto* (London, 1967), 26–60; Ajayi and Crowder, *History of West Africa*, ii. 5–47, 98–100. The theological and intellectual origins of the jihad are ably described in John E. Flint (ed.), *The Cambridge History of Africa*, vol. 5, *c.1790 to c.1870* (Cambridge, 1976), 125–65.
21. By far the best account of these struggles is to be found in Michael Mason's 'The Nupe Kingdom in the Nineteenth Century: A Political History' (unpublished PhD Thesis, University of Birmingham, 1970). See also S.F. Nadel, *A Black Byzantium: The Kingdom of Nupe in Nigeria* (London, 1942), 77–80; Laird and Oldfield, *Narrative*, ii. 38, 53, 76; Schön, 191.
22. Schön, 160, 190–1; Allen and Thomson, ii. 107–8.
23. Schön, 190–1.
24. Mason, 94–5; Nadel, 78–80.
25. Crowther, 317–18, 324–5; Schön, 198.
26. Schön, 139, 153–90.
27. Schön, 170.
28. Allen and Thomson, ii. 85–8; Schön, 147–8.
29. Crowther, 319–24.
30. Denham and Clapperton, ii. 334.
31. Schön, 180–3; Mason 1–14; Marion Johnson, 'Cloth on the Banks of the Niger', *Journal of the Historical Society of Nigeria* 6 (June 1973), 353–64. One of the expedition's discoveries was that, contrary

to Buxton's belief concerning the suitability of the coastal plains for growing commercial cotton, cotton production was – as it still remains – a northern speciality.
32. Schön, 167–71. See also Crowther, 316.
33. These artefacts are now in the collection of the Ethnography Department of the British Museum. A number of other articles, including several exceptionally fine ceremonial robes, collected by Dr William Stanger during the expedition, are held by the Fenland Museum, Wisbech, Cambridgeshire. For a description of these, see Colleen Kriger, 'Robes of the Sokoto Caliphate', *African Arts*, vol. 21, no. 3 (Los Angeles, May 1988), 52–7, 78–9, 85–6.
34. Duncan, 476.
35. Crowther, 325.
36. Allen and Thomson, ii. 112–13; Schön, 196–8.
37. Report of Ralph Moore, 9 Oct, 1841, Adm. 13/180; Allen and Thomson, ii. 128; report of Alfred Carr, *Friend of Africa* (Feb. 1842), 22–4.
38. Instructions given by M'William to King, 9 Oct. 1841, Adm. 13/180.
39. Allen and Thomson, ii. 130.
40. Crowther, 335–6; Allen and Thomson, ii. 133–6. For Stanger's account of the visit to Aboh see Hannah Buxton to Anna Gurney, 5 Feb. 1842, BP 20A/9 c.
41. Crowther, 337; Allen and Thomson, ii. 137.
42. Duncan, 488.

CHAPTER SEVEN

1. For details of the sugar duty question, see Temperley, *British Antislavery*, 137–52.
2. See the account of Edward Buxton's speech in Exeter Hall on 14 May

1841 in *The Times*, 15 May 1841; also Buxton's letter in the *Record*, 24 May 1841 and Richenda Buxton to Andrew Johnston, 18 May 1841, BP 20/252.

3. Buxton to Anna Gurney, 20 March – 2 April 1841, BP 20/209; Buxton to Fowell and Charles Buxton, 6 Sept. 1841, BP 20/313.

4. Buxton to Trew, 10 Nov. 1841, BP 20/328–9.

5. Stanley to Peel, 25 Oct. 1841, and Peel to Stanley 26 Oct. 1841 (with enclosures to be found on pages 132 ff.), Peel Correspondence, British Library Add. MSS. 40467. See also Gallagher, 'Fowell Buxton and the New African Policy', 52, 57.

6. Stanley to Niger Commissioners, 11 Nov. 1841, *Parliamentary Papers*, 57.

7. Quantamissa to Pyne, 20 May 1841, BP 20/253.

8. Quoted in Buxton to Washington, 10 Nov. 1841, BP 20/330.

9. Buxton to Dr Philip, 16 June 1841, BP 20/264; Buxton to Trotter, 12 Nov. 1841, BP 20/332.

10. These are in CO 2/25/110–23.

11. Hannah Buxton to Anna Gurney, 12 Dec. 1841, BP 20/353.

12. Buxton to Trew, 4 Dec. 1841, BP 20/346.

13. Ibid.

14. Minute by Stephen, 28 Dec. 1841, CO 2/25/127.

15. See letters from William Allen and others, CO 2/25/129–47; also minute by Stanley, 11 Jan. 1842, ibid. 130.

16. Buxton to Anson, 11 Jan. 1842, BP 20/409.

17. Buxton to Bird Allen, 10 Jan. 1842, BP 20/407.

18. Priscilla Johnston to Anna Gurney, 20 Jan. 1842, BP 20/430.

19. Buxton to Trew, 21 Jan. 1842, BP 20/434.

20. *The Times*, 22 Jan. 1842.

21. *Morning Herald*, 20 Jan. 1842.

22. J.J. Gurney to Buxton, 21 Jan. 1842, Robert Hanbury to Buxton, 22 Jan. 1842, Lushington to Buxton, 19 Jan. 1842, BP 20/437; Elizabeth Fry to Hannah Buxton, 22 March 1862, *Memoir of the Life of Elizabeth Fry*, ii. 424; Daniel Wilson to Buxton, 9 April 1842, BP 20A/67.

23. Trotter to Colonial Office and Admiralty, 25 Oct. 1841, *Parliamentary Papers*, 44–8.

24. Minute by Stanley, 24 Jan. 1842. CO 2/25/160.

25. Lady Parry to Richenda Buxton, n.d. [29 Jan. 1842?], BP 20/454. See also Simpson, 59. The autopsy on Vogel revealed that he was also suffering from tuberculosis. M'William, 242.

26. Hannah Buxton to Anna Gurney, 5 Feb. 1842, BP 20A/9.

27. Buxton to Anna Gurney, 29 Jan. 1842, BP 20A/3; Edward Buxton to Priscilla Johnston, 1 Feb. 1842, BP 20A/6; Richenda Buxton to Priscilla Johnston, 29 Jan. 1842, BP 20/452.

28. Buxton to Anna Gurney, 29 Jan. 1842, BP 20/446–51; W.J. Nixon to Priscilla Johnston, 1 Feb. 1842, BP 20A/5; Priscilla Johnston to Dr Philip, 11 Feb. 1842, BP 20A/16–17. For Moore and Carr's reports, see Adm. 13/180 and *Friend of Africa* (Feb. 1842), 22–4.

29. Trotter to King, 6 Nov. 1841, Adm. 13/180; Trotter to Buxton, 25 Jan. 1842, BP 20/445; Buxton to Anna Gurney, 29 Jan. 1842, BP 20/446–51.

30. W.J. Nixon to Priscilla Johnston, 8 Feb. 1842, BP 20A/13.

31. Buxton to Priscilla Johnston, 12 Feb. 1842, BP 20A/17.

32. Ibid.

33. Buxton to Lushington, 18 Feb. 1842, enclosing a draft copy of a letter to Stanley, BP 20A/22–3.

34. Buxton to Rev. C.W. Bingham, 21 Feb. 1842, BP 20A/25–6.

35. Buxton to Lushington, 7 March 1842, BP 20A/36; Stokes to Stanley, 29 March 1842, CO 2/25/13–20;

Edward Buxton to Stanley, 4 April 1842, CO 2/25/35–6.

36. Trotter to Admiralty, 15 March 1842, Trotter to Colonial Office, 1 April 1842, *Parliamentary Papers*, 53–9.

37. Lord Stanley's minute, 13 April 1842, ibid. 59–60. The first clear statement of Government policy is a draft memorandum to the Admiralty, written in Stanley's own hand, of 26 March 1842, CO 2/25/179–81.

38. Memorandum from Stephen to Hope, 13 April 1842, CO 2/25/3–7.

39. Allen to Captain Beaufort, 1 Feb. 1842, CO 2/25/29–33.

40. For a full breakdown of the vital statistics see M'William, 126–30.

41. *Parliamentary Papers*, 132.

42. Ibid., 49.

43. Allen and Thomson, *Narrative*, ii. 70–1.

44. See Allen to Lee, 3 March, and Allen to Tucker, 10 March 1842, Adm. 13/183; also the correspondence in Adm. 13/180.

45. Trotter to Commissioners, 19 Nov. 1841, Adm. 13/183.

46. Allen and Thomson, ii. 74–5.

47. Brown's deposition, dated 3 Feb. 1842, is in Adm. 13/180.

48. Laird and Oldfield, *Narrative*, i. 344–8.

49. Cook's account of the matter is set out in his report to Lord Stanley, CO 2/24/192–4.

50. Allen's views are fully set out in CO 2/25/284–337.

51. Commissioners' Report, 3 Feb. 1842, *Parliamentary Papers*, 155.

52. Metcalfe, *Maclean of the Gold Coast*, 274–5; Allen and Thomson, ii. 181; Ivor Wilks, *Asante in the Nineteenth Century: The Structure and Evolution of a Political Order* (Cambridge, 1975), 596.

53. See 'Trifling and vacillating conduct of Capt. Allen and culpable neglect of the Public Service', CO 2/24/191–7.

54. Allen and Thomson, ii. 187, 323; Simpson *Journal*, 94; *Parliamentary Papers*, 61–2, 153–5.

55. Minutes of Commissioners' Meeting, 11 April 1842, quoted in Allen's response to Cook's charges, CO 2/25/284–337.

56. What the Government was proposing to do instead Stanley did not explain. *Hansard*, 61 (4 March 1842), Cols. 99–101.

57. Minutes of Commissioners' Meeting, 16 April 1842, quoted in Allen's response to Cook's charges, CO 2/25/284–337.

58. Allen to Cook, 20 April 1842, CO 2/24/199.

59. See ibid. 199–227.

60. Allen to Stanley, 19 May 1842, *Parliamentary Papers*, 61–2, 133; Allen and Thomson, ii. 245–72.

61. Allen and Thomson, ii. 324–5; Simpson, 117–18.

62. The full correspondence, which Cook sent to the Colonial Secretary, is in CO 2/24/216–28; Allen's justification of his conduct will be found in CO 2/25/284–337.

63. Simpson, 120–5.

64. Allen and Thomson, ii. 328–9.

CHAPTER EIGHT

1. Allen and Thomson, *Narrative*, ii. 327; *Parliamentary Papers* 69, 108–11.

2. Allen to Webb, 29 June 1842, *Parliamentary Papers*, 64–5.

3. Except where otherwise noted this account of the *Wilberforce*'s ascent is taken from Webb's official report to the Admiralty dated 2 January 1843, in *Parliamentary Papers*, 69–80.

4. Ward, *The Royal Navy and the Slavers*, 167–78; Lloyd, *The Navy and the Slave Trade*, 94–5; Fyfe, *Sierra Leone*, 220; Mathieson, *Great Britain and the Slave Trade*, 60–2.

5. Thomas King's journal, quoted in

Allen and Thomson, ii. 361.

6. For what happened on the model farm see the accounts by Webb and King above; also *Friend of Africa* (Dec. 1842), 173–8, and *St James's Chronicle*, 22 Dec. 1842.
7. Trew to Buxton, 29 Nov. 1842, BP 20A/313 a – h.
8. Webb to Usman Zaki, 2 July 1842, *Parliamentary Papers*, 80.
9. Webb to Secretary of the Admiralty, 8 Dec. 1842, ibid. 66–7.
10. Allen and Thomson, i. 506.
11. *The Times*, 22, 26, Nov. 1842.
12. Trew to Buxton, 29 Nov. 1842, BP 20A/313 a – h; *Friend of Africa* (Dec. 1842), 173–8; *St James's Chronicle*, 22 Dec. 1842.
13. Memorandum by Stephen, 21 Feb. 1843, CO 2/23/192.
14. Notations on Webb to Secretary of the Admiralty, CO 2/23/217 ff.
15. Memorandum by Hope, 12 Dec. 1842, CO 2/25/260.
16. Memorandum by Stephen, 12 July 1843, and Treasury to Colonial Office, 3 Aug. 1843, CO 2/25/275, 365.
17. Treasury to Colonial Office, 20 June 1842, CO 2/25/245.
18. Allen to Stanley, 10 Nov. 1842, and Stanley to Allen, 18 Nov. 1842, CO 2/23/183–5.
19. Cook's full report, with sections crossed out by Stanley, is in CO 2/24/175–228. See also Stephen's and Stanley's memoranda of March 1843, in CO 2/23/260, and Stanley to Cook, 31 March 1843, CO 2/23/262.
20. Allen's response to Cook's charges, including the suppressed minutes of the commissioners' meetings of 11 and 16 April 1842, are in CO 2/25/284–337.
21. Buxton to Andrew Johnston, 24 Dec. 1842, in Stuart, Correspondence, ii. 471–2. Priscilla Johnston to Miss Clowes, 5 April 1842, E. MacInnes (ed.) *Extracts from Priscilla Johnston's Journal and Letters* (privately printed, Carlisle, 1862), 160; Buxton to Lushington, 30 Dec. 1842, BP 20A/327–8; Buxton to Gurney, 8 Dec. 1842, BP 20A/319; Hannah Buxton to Priscilla Johnston, 1 Feb. 1843, BP 20A/331 p–q.
22. Charles Buxton, *Memoirs of Sir Thomas Fowell Buxton*, chapter 30.
23. *British and Foreign Anti-Slavery Reporter*, 5 March 1845.
24. *The Times*, 22 Feb. 1845.

EPILOGUE

1. A copy of the printed advertisement for the 'Testimonial' is in the Peel Papers, British Library, Add. MSS. 40 574/f.9.
2. The circumstances surrounding the commissioning of the memorial are described in the final chapter of Charles Buxton's *Memoirs of Sir Thomas Fowell Buxton*, chapter 30.
3. Thomas Carlyle, 'Occasional discourse on the Nigger Question', *Fraser's Magazine* 40 (Dec. 1849), 670–9. The point about the racism of the 1840s and 1850s being a reassertion of older beliefs is made in Seymour Drescher, 'The Ending of the Slave Trade and the Evolution of European Scientific Racism', *Social Science History*, vol. 14, no. 3 (Durham, North Carolina, 1990).
4. The *Examiner* (19 Aug. 1848), 531–3.
5. Charles Dickens, *Bleak House* (1853), chapter 4.
6. The *Examiner* (19 Aug. 1848), 533.
7. Dr Livingstone to Dr Tidman, 17 Oct. 1851, in David Chamberlain (ed.), *Some Letters from Livingstone, 1840–1872* (Oxford, 1940), 156.
8. William Gordon Blaikie, *The Personal Life of David Livingstone* (London, 1880), 227.
9. Reginald Coupland, *The British Anti-Slavery Movement* (London, 1933), 206–11.

10. M'William, *Medical History*, 159, 198.
11. Ibid. 126–30.
12. The *Lancet* (28 Feb. 1846), 244–5.
13. Curtin, *Image of Africa*, 345 and *Death by Migration*, 64–5; Headrick, *Tools of Empire*, 68–71. Comments on Professor Daniell's work and details of Bryson's views on mercury and other traditional remedies are given in T.J. Hutchinson, *Narrative of the Niger, Tchadda and Benue Exploration* (London, 1855), 194–200, 225–31.
14. Macgregor Laird to the Earl of Clarendon, 5 March 1855, in Samuel Crowther, *Journal of an Expedition up the Niger and Tshadda Rivers . . . in 1854* (London, 1855), x. For an account of the expedition and the use of quinine, see also W.B. Baikie, *Narrative of an Exploring Voyage up the Rivers Quorra and Binue* (London, 1856), 34; also Hutchinson, 194–200, 225–31.
15. Schön and Crowther, *Journals . . . of the Expedition up the Niger in 1841*, 349, 358–66.
16. J.F.A. Ajayi, *Christian Missions in Nigeria, 1841–1891: The Making of a New Elite* (London, 1965), xv – xvi, 13.
17. Ibid. 206–32; see also Ajayi's introduction to the 1970 edition of Crowther's 1854 journal of the *Pleiad* expedition cited above. For Crowther's own account of his efforts see Samuel Crowther and John Christopher Taylor, *The Gospel on the Banks of the Niger*, 2 vols. (London, 1859, 1863).
18. Ajayi, *Christian Missions*, 13–16, 162, 216–22.
19. Ibid. 127–30, 144–5, 164, 210.
20. *Dictionary of National Biography*.
21. Obituary, *Gentleman's Magazine* (July 1854); *Dictionary of South African Biography*, vol. 2 (Capetown and Johannesburg, 1972).
22. See the references to Trotter and Allen in the *Dictionary of National Biography*, W.R. O'Byrne's *Naval Biographical Dictionary* (London, 1849) and Frederic Boase's *Modern English Biography* (London, 1892).
23. See Cook to Stanley, 22 March 1843, CO 2/23/264 and Stephen's reply, CO 2/23/267.
24. K.O. Dike, 'John Beecroft', *Journal of the Historical Society of Nigeria*, vol. i, pt. i (1956), 5–14.
25. Metcalfe, *Maclean of the Gold Coast*, 276–335.
26. Ivor Wilks, *Asante in the Nineteenth Century*, 596–665.
27. Eltis, *Economic Growth*, 251–2.
28. Dike, *Trade and Politics*, 98–100, 198.
29. William N.M. Geary, *Nigeria Under British Rule* (London, 1927), 158.
30. Alagoa, *Small Brave City State*, 57–8.
31. Quoted in Baikie to Russell, 29 Feb. 1860, in FO 2/34. There is a facsimile of the letter in Pedraza, *Borrioboola-Gha*, 57.
32. Dike, *Trade and Politics*, 174, 213; Geary, 162–4.
33. Malcolm Crowder, *The Story of Nigeria*, 4th edition (London, 1978), 147–8; John E. Flint, *Sir George Goldie and the Making of Nigeria* (London, 1960), 28–9.
34. K.O. Ogedengbe, 'The Aboh Kingdom of the Lower Niger, c.1150–1900' (unpublished PhD Thesis, University of Wisconsin, 1971), 87, 340–92.
35. Crowther, *Journal . . . 1854*, 34, and *Gospel on the Banks of the Niger*, i. 47–8; Baikie, 54–77; Hutchinson, 52–8; A.C.G. Hastings, *The Voyage of the Dayspring, being the Journal of . . Sir John Hawley Glover* (London, 1926), 35. The feud between Abokko and the former Attah is described in Laird and Oldfield, i. 402–3.
36. Quoted in Ajayi, *Christian Missions*, 214.
37. Mason, 'The Nupe Kingdom', 158–62; Ajayi and Crowder, *History of West Africa*, 116, 120, 123.

38. Flint, 28–9, 101, 146–7; Ajayi, 221.
39. Geary, 158; Flint 243–55; Headrick, 58–79, 115–241.
40. Ifemesia, 'British Enterprise', 109; minute by Stanley of 2 Feb. 1842, quoted in Gallagher, 'Fowell Buxton', 57.
41. Temperley, *British Antislavery*, 263–9.
42. Coupland, 203–31.
43. Paul E. Lovejoy, *Transformations in Slavery: A History of Slavery in Africa* (Cambridge, 1983), 159–83; Flint, *Cambridge History of Africa*, 210–14; Ajayi and Crowder, 511–13.
44. Suzanne Miers, *Britain and the Ending of the Slave Trade* (London, 1975), 118–19, 121–34, 146–9, 201–6. The quotation from Chamberlain is taken from page 294.
45. Charles W. Boyd (ed.), *Mr Chamberlain's Speeches*, 2 vols. (London, 1914), ii. 1–6.
46. Mary Kingsley, *Travels in West Africa* (London, 1897), 680.
47. Edward Grierson, *The Imperial Dream: The British Commonwealth and Empire, 1775–1969* (London, 1972), 113–25. The quotations are taken from pages 113, 114, and 119.
48. Rudyard Kipling, 'Recessional' (1897).

Bibliography

I MANUSCRIPT SOURCES

The Papers of Sir Thomas Fowell Buxton, 1786–1845, Rhodes House, Oxford (microfilm edition by Harvester Microform, 17 reels, 1983). The collection consists of 46 volumes and covers the whole of Buxton's career. Of particular interest, so far as the Niger expedition is concerned, are:

> Vol. 4. Private reflections and memoranda.
> Vols. 16–20A. General correspondence for the years 1837–44.
> Vols. 28–33. A selection of letters concerning Africa, sovereignty, the slave trade, etc.
> Vols. 40 and 42–4. Newspaper clippings, 1837–44.
> An invaluable guide to the collection is Patricia M. Pugh's *Calendar of the Papers of Sir Thomas Fowell Buxton 1786–1845* (List and Index Society, London, 1980).

Colonial Office Records, Public Record Office, Kew.

> Volumes CO 2/21–5 contain all the official correspondence and many private memoranda by James Stephen and successive Secretaries of State. Some of the official correspondence was later published in *Parliamentary Papers* but the manuscript of William Cook's report, which was thought too inflammatory for publication, is in CO 2/24/175–228.

Admiralty Records, Public Record Office, Kew.

> Volumes Adm. 13/180–3 cover the outfitting of the expedition and the various naval aspects of the operation up to the time of its collapse.

Foreign Office Records, Public Record Office, Kew.

> FO 54/2 contains correspondence with Buxton, Glenelg and Captain Cogan relating to Fernando Po, Mombasa and African settlements generally.

Melbourne Papers, Windsor Castle (microfilm edition by E.P. Microform, 51 reels, 1975).

> The Palmerston correspondence (Box 11) contains useful material on African and slave trade policy and the Russell correspondence (Boxes 13 and 14) on Buxton's plans and the role of Prince Albert.

Peel Papers, British Library, London.

> Add. MSS. 40467, contains correspondence with Lord Stanley relating to changes in African policy.

Russell Papers, Public Record Office, Kew.

> Useful comments on the general political background but otherwise containing little of note. The principal sources for Russell's views are the Colonial Office files and the Buxton and Melbourne Papers.

II PRINTED SOURCES

(a) *Books and pamphlets published prior to the expedition's departure*

(Note: some additional printed materials and a substantial collection of newspaper clippings are to be found in the Buxton Papers; there are also some printed materials in Colonial Office papers)

Buxton, Sir Thomas Fowell, *(Private) Letter on the Slave Trade to the Lord Viscount Melbourne and the Other Members of Her Majesty's Cabinet Council*, London, 1838.
—— *The African Slave Trade*, London, 1839.
—— *The Remedy, Being a Sequel to the African Slave Trade*, London, 1840.
—— *The African Slave Trade and its Remedy*, London, 1840.
—— *Abridgment of Sir T. Fowell Buxton's Work on the African Slave Trade and its Remedy*, London, 1840.
Jamieson, Robert, *An Appeal to the Government and People of Great Britain Against the Proposed Niger Expedition*, London, 1840.
—— *A Further Appeal to the Government and People of Great Britain Against the proposed Niger Expedition*, London, 1841.
Read, Paul, *Lord John Russell, Sir T.F. Buxton and the Niger Expedition*, London, 1840.
Society for the Extinction of the Slave Trade and for the Civilization of Africa, *Proceedings of the First Public Meeting of the Society . . . Prince Albert . . . in the Chair*, London, 1840.
—— *Friend of Africa*, London, 1841–3.
Stephen, Sir George, *A Letter to the Rt. Hon. Lord John Russell in Reply to Mr Jamieson on the Niger Expedition*, London, 1840.
—— *A Second Letter to the Rt. Hon. Lord John Russell on the Plans of the Society for the Civilization of Africa*, London, 1840.
—— *A Third Letter to the Rt. Hon. Lord John Russell on the Plans of the Society for the Civilization of Africa*, London, 1840.

(b) *Reports, books and articles by participants*

Allen, William and Thomson, T.R.H., *A Narrative of the Expedition to the River Niger in 1841*, 2 vols., London, 1848.
Duncan, John, 'Some Account of the Last Expedition to the Niger', *Bentley's Miscellany*, 22 (1847), 412–16, 469–80.
House of Commons, 'Papers Relative to the Expedition to the River Niger,' *Parliamentary Papers*, 1843 [472], xlviii. 39–207. (Contains official correspondence with the Commissioners and narratives by Trotter, Allen and Webb.)
M'William, J.O., *Medical History of the Expedition to the River Niger During the Years 1841–42*, London, 1843.
Schön, J.F., and Crowther, Samuel A., *Journals of the Rev. James Frederick Schön and Mr Samuel Crowther, Who . . . Accompanied the Expedition up the Niger in 1841*, London, 1842.
Simpson, William, *A Private Journal Kept During the Niger Expedition*, London, 1843.
Vogel, J.R.T., 'Journal of the Voyage to the Niger' (trans. F. Sheer), in Hooker, Sir W.J. (ed.), *Niger Flora*, London, 1849.

III GENERAL BIBLIOGRAPHY

Ajayi, J.F.A., *Christian Missions in Nigeria, 1841–1891: The Making of a New Elite*, London, 1965.
—— and Crowder, Michael, *History of West Africa*, vol. 2, second edn., Harlow, Essex, 1987.
Alagoa, E.J., *The Small Brave City State: A History of Brass-Nembe in the Niger Delta*, Ibadan and Wisconsin, 1964.
Allen, William, *Picturesque Views on the River Niger, Sketched during Lander's Last Visit in 1832–33*, London, 1840.
Baikie, W.B., *Narrative of an Exploring Voyage up the Rivers Quorra and Binue*, London, 1856.
Barron, T.J., 'James Stephen, the "Black Race" and British Colonial Admin-

istration, 1813–1847', *Journal of Imperial and Commonwealth History*, 5 (1977).

Bethell, L.M., 'Britain, Portugal and the Suppression of the Brazilian Slave Trade: The Origins of Lord Palmerston's Act of 1839', *English Historical Review*, 80 (1965), 761–84.,

Bovill, E.W., *The Golden Trade of the Moors*, London, 1958.

British and Foreign Anti-Slavery Society, *Proceeding of the General Anti-Slavery Convention... Held in London from Friday, June 12 to Tuesday June 23, 1840*, London, 1841.

Buxton, Charles, *Memoirs of Sir Thomas Fowell Buxton, Bart., with selections from his Correspondence*, London, 1848.

Buxton, Hannah, *Memorials of Hannah, Lady Buxton*, privately printed, London, 1883.

Cambell, Penelope, *Maryland in Africa: The Maryland State Colonization Society, 1831–1857*, Urbana, Illinois, 1971.

Clapperton, Hugh, *Journal of a Second Expedition into the Interior of Africa from the Bight of Benin to Soccatoo by the Late Commander Clapperton*, London, 1829.

Coupland, Reginald, *The British Anti-Slavery Movement*, London, 1933.

Cox, Bernard, *Paddle Steamers*, Poole, Dorset, 1979.

Crowder, Michael, *The Story of Nigeria*, 4th edn., London, 1978.

Crowther, Samuel, *Journal of an Expedition up the Niger and Tshadda Rivers... in 1854*, London, 1855.

—— *The Gospel on the Banks of the Niger*, 2 vols., London, 1859, 1863.

Curtin, Philip, ' "Scientific" Racism and the British Theory of Empire', *Journal of the Historical Society of Nigeria*, ii (Dec. 1960), 40–51.

—— *The Image of Africa: British Ideas and Action, 1780–1850*, Madison, Wisconsin, 1964.

—— *The Atlantic Slave Trade: A Census*, Madison, Wisconsin, 1969.

—— *Death by Migration: Europe's Encounter with the Tropical World in the Nineteenth Century*, Cambridge, 1989.

Denham, Dixon, and Clapperton, Hugh, *Narrative and Discoveries in Northern and Central Africa in the Years 1822, 1823 and 1824*, 2 vols., London, 1828.

Dickens, Charles, Review of *Narrative of the Expedition... to the River Niger in 1841* in the *Examiner*, 19 Aug. 1841, 531–3.

Dike, K. Onwuka, 'John Beecroft, 1790–1854', *Journal of the Historial Society of Nigeria*, i (Dec. 1956), 5–14.

—— *Trade and Politics in the Niger Delta, 1830–1885*, Oxford, 1956.

Drescher, Seymour, 'The Ending of the Slave Trade and the Evolution of European Scientific Racism', *Social Science History*, vol. 14, no. 3, Durham, North Carolina, 1990.

Dumpleton, Bernard, *The Story of the Paddle Steamer*, Melksham, Wiltshire, 1973.

Eldridge, C.C. (ed.), *British Imperialism in the Nineteenth Century*, London, 1984.

Eltis, David, *Economic Growth and the Ending of the Transatlantic Slave Trade*, New York, 1987.

Esher, Viscount, *The Girlhood of Queen Victoria: A Selection from Her Majesty's Diaries, 1832–40*, 2 vols., London, 1912.

Ferryman, A.F.M., *British Nigeria*, London, 1902.

Fladeland, Betty, *Abolitionists and Working-Class Problems in the Age of Industrialization*, London, 1984.

Flint, John E. (ed.), *Sir George Goldie and the Making of Nigeria*, London, 1960.

—— *The Cambridge History of Africa*, vol. 5. *c.1790 to c.1870*, Cambridge, 1976.

Fyfe, Christopher, *A History of Sierra Leone*, London, 1962.

Gallagher, J., 'Fowell Buxton and the New African Policy', *Cambridge Historical Journal*, x (1950), 36–58.

Geary, William N.M., *Nigeria under British Rule*, London, 1927.

Gavin, R.J., 'Palmerston's Policy towards East and West Africa, 1830–1865', unpublished PhD Thesis, University of Cambridge, 1958.

Gramont, Sanche de, *The Strong Brown*

God: The Story of the Niger River, London, 1975.

Hare, Augustus J.C., *The Gurneys of Earlham*, 2 vols., London, 1895.

Hastings, A.C.G., *The Voyage of the Dayspring, being the Journal of . . . Sir John Hawley Glover*, London, 1926.

Headrick, Daniel R., *The Tools of Empire: Technology and European Imperialism in the Nineteenth Century*, New York, 1981.

Hogben, S.J., and Kirk-Greene, A.H.M., *The Emirates of Northern Nigeria*, London, 1966.

Hutchinson, T.J., *Narrative of the Niger, Tchadda and Benue Exploration*, London, 1855.

Hyam, Ronald, *Britain's Imperial Century, 1815–1914: A Study of Empire and Expansion*, London, 1976.

Ifemesia, C.C., 'British Enterprise on the Niger, 1830–1869', unpublished PhD Thesis, University of London, 1959.

—— 'The "Civilizing" Mission of 1841: Aspects of an Episode in Anglo-Nigerian Relations', *Journal of the Historical Society of Nigeria*, 2 (1962), 291–310.

Johnson, Marion, 'Cloth on the Banks of the Niger', *Journal of the Historical Society of Nigeria*, 6 (June 1973), 353–64.

Johnston, H.A.S., *The Fulani Empire of Sokoto*, London, 1967.

Knaplund, Paul, *James Stephen and the British Colonial System, 1813–1847*, Madison, Wisconsin, 1953.

Kriger, Colleen, 'Robes of the Sokoto Caliphate', *African Arts*, vol. 21, no. 3 (Los Angeles, May 1988), 52–7, 78–9, 85–6.

Laird, M., and Oldfield, R.A.K. *Narrative of an Expedition into the Interior of Africa by the River Niger in 1832–34*, 2 vols., London, 1837.

Lander, R. and J., *Journal of an Expedition to Explore the Course and Termination of the Niger . . .* 3 vols., London, 1832.

Lander, Richard, *Records of Captain Clapperton's Last Expedition to Africa*, 2 vols., London, 1830.

Lloyd, Christopher, *The Navy and the Slave Trade: The Suppression of the African Slave Trade in the Nineteenth Century*, London, 1949.

—— *The Search for the Niger*, London, 1973.

Lorimer, Douglas A., *Colour, Class and the Victorians: English Attitudes to the Negro in the Mid-Nineteenth Century*, Leicester, 1978.

Lovejoy, Paul E., *Transformations in Slavery: A History of Slavery in Africa*, Cambridge, 1983.

Low, Sidney, and Sanders, L.C., *The History of England during the Reign of Victoria, 1837–1901*, London, 1911.

MacQueen, James, *A Geographical and Commerical View of Northern Central Africa*, Edinburgh, 1821.

Mason, Michael, 'The Nupe Kingdom in the Nineteenth Century: A Political History', unpublished PhD Thesis, University of Birmingham, 1970.

Mathieson, William Law, *Great Britain and the Slave Trade, 1839–1865*, London, 1929.

Melville, Elizabeth Helen, *A Residence at Sierra Leone*, London, 1849.

Metcalfe, G.E., *Maclean of the Gold Coast: The Life and Times of George Maclean, 1801–1847*, London, 1962.

Miers, Suzanne, *Britain and the Ending of the Slave Trade*, London, 1975.

Mottram, R.H., *Buxton the Liberator*, London, 1946.

Nadel, S.F., *A Black Byzantium: The Kingdom of Nupe in Nigeria*, London, 1942.

Napier, Macvey, *Selections from the Correspondence of the Late Macvey Napier*, London, 1879.

Newbury, C.W., *The Western Slave Coast and its Rulers*, Oxford, 1961.

Ogedengbe, K.O., 'The Aboh Kingdom of the Lower Niger, *c.*1150–1900', unpublished PhD Thesis, University of Wisconsin, 1971.

Park, Mungo, *Travels in the Interior Districts of Africa*, London, 1799.

Pedraza, Howard J., *Borrioboola-Gha: The Story of Lokoja, the First British Settlement in Nigeria*, Oxford, 1960.

Phillips, R. Stephen, *Malaria*, London, 1983.

Prest, John, *Lord John Russell*, London, 1972.

—— *Politics in the Age of Cobden*, London, 1977.

Prothero, R. Mansell, *Migrants and Malaria*, London, 1965.

Reid, Thomas Wemyss, *The Life of W. E. Forster*, London, 1888.

Reynolds, Edward, *Stand in the Storm: A History of the Atlantic Slave Trade*, London, 1985.

Robinson, R., Gallagher, J., Denny, A., *Africa and the Victorians: The Official Mind of Imperialism*, London, 1961.

Russell, P.F., *Man's Mastery of Malaria*, London, 1955.

Shick, Tom W., *Behold the Promised Land: A History of Afro-American Settler Society in Nineteenth-Century Liberia*, Baltimore, 1980.

Snelling, R.C., and Barron, T.J., 'The Colonial Office and its Permanent Officials, 1801–1914', in Sutherland, Gillian (ed.), *Studies in the Growth of Nineteenth-Century Government*, London, 1972.

Stuart, F.C., 'A Critical Edition of the Correspondence of Sir Thomas Fowell Buxton, Bart., with an Account of his Career to 1823', 2 vols., unpublished MA Thesis, University of London, 1957.

Talbot, P.A., *The Peoples of Southern Nigeria*, 4 vols., London, 1926.

Temperley, Howard, *British Antislavery, 1833–1870*, London, 1972.

—— 'Antislavery' in Hollis, Patricia (ed.), *Pressure from Without in Early Victorian England*, London, 1974.

—— 'Capitalism, Slavery and Ideology', *Past and Present* (1977), 94–118.

—— 'Anti-Slavery as a Form of Cultural Imperialism' in Bolt, Christine, and Drescher, Seymour (eds.), *Anti-Slavery, Religion and Reform*, Folkstone, 1980, 335–50.

Thomson, T.R.H., 'On the Value of Quinine in African Remittent Fever', the *Lancet* (28 Feb. 1846), 244–5.

Times, The, The History of the Times, vol. i 'The Thunderer' in the Making, 1785–1841, London, 1935.

Ward, W.E.F., *The Royal Navy and the Slavers: The Suppression of the Atlantic Slave Trade*, London, 1969.

Whately, Elizabeth Jane, *Life and Correspondence of Richard Whately, Late Archbishop of Dublin*, 2 vols., London, 1866.

Wilks, Ivor, *Asante in the Nineteenth Century: The Structure and Evolution of a Political Order*, Cambridge, 1975.

Wilson, John Leighton, *Western Africa*, New York and London, 1856.

Ziegler, Philip, *Melbourne*, London, 1976.

Index

Aboh 93, 98–106, 123–4, 133, 153–4, 159, 174, 175
Accra 86–7
Adda Kudu 118–9, 121, 131
Africa: British attitudes towards 11–4 and n.11, 80–2, 166, 168, 175, 177–8; problem of assuming sovereignty over settlements in 53–5, 136, 141; European mortality in 45–6, 170, 175; Islamic influences on 12, 112, 125–31; religious and tribal warfare in 77, 79, 84, 126–8, 156, 158
African: beliefs about Europeans xii, 76, 96, 109; artifacts 107–8, 112, 129, 130 and n.33; customs 80–2, 90–1, 103–5, 109, 111–2; recaptives (i.e. liberated by the British navy) 75–6, 97, 165
African Civilization Society 1–5, 55, 57, 69, 73, 102, 140–1, 163
African Institution 9
African squadron 10, 15, 20, 27, 154, 172, 173
African traders 58–60, 83, 85, 173–4, 176
Agency Anti-Slavery Society 18, 33
Airy, Professor George 68
Albert, Prince 2, 5, 67, 68, 137, 163
Algeria 24, 25
Akassa 89, 91
Allen, Commander Bird 42, 69, 122, 129, 133, 138, 139, 160
Allen, Commander William 42, 43, 76, 78, 80–1, 87, 99, 100, 121–4, 142, 143–51, 152, 163, 172
American abolitionists at World Anti-Slavery Convention 55–6

American Colonization Society 55 (*see also* Liberia)
Ansah, John 69, 77, 81, 86, 148, 173
Anti-Slavery Society 33
Apprentices, *see* West Indian freedmen
Asante 83, 86, 173, 177
Asante princes 69, 77, 81, 86, 136, 148, 173
Ascension 122, 143–4
Attah of Igala, the 102, 108–9, 111, 113, 125, 158–9, 167, 174

Bandinel, James, Chief Clerk at the Foreign Office 38, 45
Beecroft, John 18, 66, 133, 150, 160, 170, 172
Benue river 118, 119–20, 132
Birney, James G. 55
Board of Trade 23, 31
Boy, King 91–4, 99, 124, 146, 154, 159, 160, 173
Brass 91–4, 160, 175
British and Foreign Anti-Slavery Society 36, 55
Brougham, Lord 16–7, 27, 29, 30, 37
Brown, coloured clerk 98, 133, 146–6
Bue, Amanda 107, 108, 110, 112, 156, 158
Buxton, Hannah 11, 53, 163
Buxton, Sarah Maria 10, 11, 18
Buxton, Thomas Fowell: Exeter Hall speech 3–4; early career 6–9; hopes of cutting off slave trade at source 9; collects information 10, 14–5; lobbies ministers 15–9, 27–8, 30–1, 37–9; *Letter to Lord Melbourne* 20–2; discounts dangers of climate 32; attitude to use of